The Reader
and the
Detective Story

The Reader
and the
Detective Story

George N. Dove

Bowling Green State University Popular Press
Bowling Green, OH 43403

Other books by George N. Dove

The Boys from Grover Avenue
Cops and Constables
(coedited with Earl Bargainnier)
The Police Procedural
Suspense in the Formula Story

Copyright © 1997 Bowling Green State University Popular Press

Library of Congress Cataloging-in-Publication Data
Dove, George N.
   The reader and the detective story / George N. Dove.
     p.   cm.
   Includes bibliographical references.
   ISBN 0-87972-731-4 (cloth : alk. paper). -- ISBN 0-87972-732-2
(pbk. : alk. paper)
   1. Detective and mystery stories--History and criticism.
   2. Reader-response criticism.   I. Title.
PN3448.D4D68   1996
809.3'872--dc21   96-47340
                                                               CIP

Cover design by Dumm Art

Contents

1

The Different Story

What is a detective story? Publishers' advertising usually lists it simply as "mystery," and many critics treat detective fiction and crime fiction as the same thing. For practical purposes the differences are negligible, because most detective stories involve crime, and in the mind of the reading public the detective story often merges with spy fiction and science fiction, because all are mysteries. For purposes of this study, however, it will be necessary to make some distinctions, because much of what we will say about the tale of detection does not apply to any of the others. There is a "differentness," arising from the fact that the detective story is essentially play transformed into art, and this condition has a critical effect on the basic purpose of the genre. True, detective fiction shares many of the themes common to all popular fiction, but it has a unique structure in which, as we will see shortly, the reader is directly involved, and which can not be adequately described without taking the reader into consideration.

So, instead of What is a detective story? it might be more fruitful to ask, What are we talking about in speaking of the detective story? and examine some specific cases. For example, how about Wilkie Collins's novel *The Woman in White*. Is it a detective story? Howard Haycraft refuses to call it detection, classing it as "a mystery but not a detective story."[1] Julian Symons, on the other hand, admits Collins's novel to the class of detective fiction because it is a crime story.[2] Crime, however, cannot be a considered a criterion for classifying a book as a detective story, because of such examples as the Sherlock Holmes story "A Case of Identity," or, more recently, Amanda Cross's *No Word from Winifred*, in which there is no crime at all. Haycraft rejects Poe's "The Gold Bug," on the grounds that the reader is not given an opportunity to examine the evidence before the solution (9). This is a matter of considerable interest to the present study, because here is an early recognition of the fact that the reader cannot be excluded from the definition of the tale of detection.[3]

1

2 The Reader and the Detective Story

Untroubled by niceties of definition, the early writers continued to write detective stories and friendly critics to justify them as both a legitimate and a unique type of popular fiction. The feeling of the "differentness" of the genre, especially in the work of the pioneer apologists, has persisted into the discussions of our own time. Four qualities of the tale of literary detection set it apart, in the opinion of critics past and present, from other popular fiction: the detective story is transitory, without long-range goals or purposes; it is fundamentally an intellectual undertaking; it is recreational, intended primarily to relax; and it is a disciplined, delimited literary form.

W.H. Auden offers the reader's view of the transitoriness of detective fiction when he says that he forgets a story as soon as he has read it, and has no wish to read it again.[4] For David Grossvogel, the tale of detection is "optimistic and self-destructing," and its mode is to "create a mystery for the sole purpose of its effortless dissipation."[5] It "offers confirmation and continuity at the price of a minor and spurious disruption" (41). The point of reference of both Auden and Grossvogel is the classical formal-problem story, not the hard-boiled novel, but most of these principles apply to the private-eye story to the same degree as they do to the classic.

The argument for the intellectuality of the detective story is especially strong in the early author/apologists, as part of their attempt to establish the legitimacy and respectability of the genre, which was widely regarded as trash, on a level with the sensational crime story, and therefore a waste of time. The case is stated without apology by R. Austin Freeman, author of the Dr. Thorndyke stories, who argues for the detective novel as a work of both imagination and ratiocination, as an exhibition of mental gymnastics, in which the reader is invited to take part,[6] and an argument conducted under the guise of fiction (12-13). A generation later, S.S. Van Dine, author of the Philo Vance series, represents the detective novel as an intellectual game, or a sporting event ("Twenty Rules for Writing Detective stories," AMS 189), and in a separate article, under his real name of Willard Huntington Wright, as a "complicated and extended puzzle cast in fictional form" ("The Great Detective Stories," AMS 35).

The recreational value of detective fiction has always been recognized by the reading public, and a veteran reader can testify to the pleasure of curling up with a good "whodunit" in the evening as the best means of blanking out the problems of the external world. Auden compares the addiction to detective stories with any other, like smoking or drinking (*DF* 15), and John Cawelti describes the genre as a transformation of crime into game or puzzle, "the aestheticizing of crime."[7] Not surprisingly, a number of critics have commented on the play—or game-quality in detective fiction, as in Grossvogel's characterization of the "metaphysical mode replaced by the mode of play" (*MIF* 16), and Roger Caillois, in a specific treatment of the play element, suggests that the pleasure a reader gets from the detective novel is not that of listening to a story but of watching a magic trick, which the magician immediately explains.[8] Harrison R. Steeves offers a key to the idea of the detective story as recreation when he describes the mood in which he reads them as one of "conditioned irresponsibility" ("A Sober Word on the Detective Story," *AMS* 515). The phrase is especially apt: his irresponsibility is *conditioned*, that is, delimited and disciplined, as it characteristically is in detective stories.

Thus there was built into the detective story from the beginning an apparent contradiction: people read detective fiction for recreation, but they also read it for intellectual stimulation. Most critics agree that the apparent paradox is resolved by the limited structure of the genre, which adds interest to the play activity by imposing some rules upon it; as Wright proposes, the detective story is not fiction in the normal sense, but is rather a complicated and extended puzzle. "Indeed," he says, "the structure and mechanism of the cross-word puzzle and of the detective novel are very similar" (*AMS* 35). The figure is particularly insightful, because the structure of the crossword puzzle imposes its own game-type intellectuality. The parallel should become clearer when we turn to a discussion of the Gadamerian concept of play transformed into art: both the crossword puzzle and the detective novel are free of stress, each offers the reader a task or set of related tasks, both are shaped by convention, and neither has any goal beyond itself. John Dickson Carr, in an essay entitled "The Grandest Game in the World," asks, "What, after all, is the game itself?" and answers that it is a hoodwinking contest, a duel between author and reader, in which the reader challenges the author to produce a new solution, and the author responds with a "legitimate dirty trick," whereupon author and reader have at it, with the reader alert for every casual clue, every self-betrayal, every contradiction that may mean guilt.[9] Carr's vision of the reader as active combatant rather than concerned observer is open to question, because the relationship between reader and author is that of parties to a compact, not contenders for a title. That compact underlies the detection formula, governing the whole area of what the reader may expect from the narrative. The role of the reader is both recreational and intellectual; the reader voluntarily accepts the limits (agrees to the rules), in order to permit the game to be played.

A better resolution is the one proposed by Jacques Barzun, who says of detective fiction, "It is an art of symmetry, it seeks the appearance of logical necessity, like classical tragedy, and like tragedy it cherishes the unity of place—the locked room, the ship or train in motion" ("Detection and the Literary Art," *DF* 148). Especially in a conventionalized literary form like detective fiction, there is a genuine correspondence between the rules of a game and the restraints upon the author's selection and handling of his or her narrative material.[10] A writer writes (and a reader reads) with an understanding of what is acceptable within the limits of the literary form, of what inventions and experiments are permissible, and what traditions must be observed. A baseball game in which one side is allowed four strikes while the other is limited to three is unacceptable in the same way as a fifteen-line sonnet would be, or a detective story in which the solution is achieved accidentally.

Barzun's comments introduce the fourth quality of detective fiction that has attracted the attention of critics, its limited purpose. Primarily, the tale of detection is limited by what Frank Kermode calls its "hermeneutic specialization," a mode that forces the reader to interpret the text in terms of the anticipated outcome of the story (*PM* 188, 181). These limits are imposed by tradition, as Auden notes when he says that the story must conform to certain formulas (*DF* 15), and George Grella, that the detective story commits its vision to a set of conventions and attempts only to meet the requirements of those conventions ("The Hard-Boiled Detective Novel," *DF* 101). Most of the writers I have cited limit their judgments to the classical formal-problem detective story, in the tradition of Edgar Allan Poe and Arthur Conan Doyle, without reference to the hard-boiled private-eye pattern set by Dashiell Hammett and Raymond Chandler. Although the private-eye story is not as tightly limited as the classical, and its effect is less transitory, it is none the less unique among popular genres. As we will see, the private-eye formula shares most of the conventions of the classical, and it has also developed, during its history, a whole set of its own.

As a rule, these four marks of differentness are still accepted by critics of detective fiction, though the "intellectuality" of the story must be treated with considerable reservation. Some interpreters question both the primacy of recreational value and the delimited scope of the tale of detection; they would reject the idea of "conditioned irresponsibility" and especially the conception of the detective story as a "hoodwinking contest," arguing a higher seriousness of purpose. There are also a considerable number of critics like Julian Symons who insist upon the definition of the detective story as crime story, not "aestheticized crime."

This book will share the assumption of the uniqueness of the detection formula, with the reservation that the sense of "differentness" of the detective story is to be found to a greater degree in the manner in which it is read and only secondarily in the text. Undeniably the detection text offers a different set of signals from those of the western or the science fiction story, but the significant difference lies in the special interpretation of those signals by a reader who is experienced in the traditions of literary detection. In a crime story, for example, an early confession by a suspect is an almost certain sign of guilt; in the detective story, it is almost as sure a sign of innocence. In the perspective of the special reading mode of detective fiction, I will offer two proposals regarding the uniqueness of the genre.

The first of these is that play transformed into art becomes the conditioner or regulative context of detective fiction, which sets the ground rules for the reading of the story. I will use the term *mode* instead of *code*, because codes are text based, while *mode* designates the sense in which the story is read, arising from the whole set of expectations the reader brings to the act of reading: the "detective-story sense" has a special application that will not apply in other types of fiction. I will not undertake further development now, because we will turn shortly to a detailed consideration of Hans-Georg Gadamer's theory of the transformation of play into art.

As a result of the dominance of the play mode, detective fiction is structurally, though not thematically, a conservative genre; its conservatism is that of the organized game, preserving custom and convention as essential to its own continuation. Detective fiction adapts easily to thematic, but not to structural, invention. As any reader of contemporary private-eye fiction knows, this kind of story has introduced all sorts of new themes but is structurally detective fiction still.

6 The Reader and the Detective Story

The world of V.I. Warshawski is not that of C. Auguste Dupin, but her stories follow the plot-pattern and share many of the other conventions of "The Murders in the Rue Morgue." The conservatism of transformed play is the determinant of the really constitutive differences between the reading of detective fiction and that of other popular genres, as in the fact that the reader's past experience with the detective story proves a much more demanding guide for present reading. One of the most useful recurrent conventions of the tale of detection, for example, is the one we will call the death warrant, in which anybody who makes an appointment with a detective for the purpose of delivering vital information will probably be murdered before the appointment can be kept. A reader inexperienced in the genre will walk right into the development without a hint of what is to come, but the very appearance of a cooperative informant in the story signals the veteran reader that a familiar complication is about to take place. What we retain from these repetitions, of course, is a structure for future thematic developments. Thus, for the reader experienced in the genre, no reading is completely "new," and in this sense, every reading is a rereading.

Most of these principles are present in any detective story, but I will illustrate them by reference to a recent novel, *Amateur Night* by K.K. Beck (1993). The protagonist is Jane da Silva, an amateur detective who is trapped into the investigation by the terms of her eccentric uncle's will, which make it impossible for her to inherit his money until she solves some hopeless case and so rights a wrong done to an innocent person. Here is a reflection of one of the regulatory qualities of detective fiction, its persistent conventionality. The convention of the trapped detective is among the oldest in the genre: we remember how Dupin was drawn into the investigation of the murders in the Rue Morgue because of an obligation to Adolphe Le Bon, who was unjustly accused. The same thing has happened to countless detectives since, including Nick Charles, who was trapped into the case in *The Thin Man* by his friendship for the Wynants.

The remarkable theme of *Amateur Night* is worth mentioning at the outset, because it provides the setting for one of the two points of essential "differentness" in the novel. Throughout the book Jane reminds herself that the bizarre demands of her uncle's will are her chief motivation, and she is frequently moved to consider the whole thing outlandish, as when she thinks of herself as "running around doing Uncle Harold's work" (181).[11] The effect is the substantial elimination of stress from the story; the reader may find the mystery intensely challenging but is not likely to experience any deep emotional involvement with a problem that Jane thinks of as "some sort of sorority girl pledge initiation stunt" (177). The other factor in the mitigation of stress is the overriding presence of one of the "givens" of the detection genre, its assurance of solution. Even when Jane has been trapped by the murderer and is in imminent danger of death, the reader can proceed with the assurance that she will emerge safely and that she will solve the case.

The tale of detection has yet another method of de-stressing itself, namely its curious habit of frequent reference to other detectives in other books, thus reminding the reader that this is only a detective story. Moreover, the general tone of the books referred to usually reflects the mode of the present work. On this basis, we cannot expect a high stress-level in a story that makes one reference to Inspector Clouseau, one to detectives in books and on TV generally, one to Graham Greene, and two to Nancy Drew.

The other point of generic differentness in *Amateur Night* is that in this story, as in detective fiction generally, the blanks are *programmed*. All fiction is characterized by "blanks," those gaps that raise questions but do not answer them; in nondetectional fiction, the blanks are "structured," that is, they are given form or statement, but nothing else. Detective fiction is rich in blanks, but in this case the blanks are not only stated but are, as a result of conventionalization, supplied with suggestions regarding later developments. Early in the story Jane calls a woman with information she urgently needs and gets an unexpectedly strong emotional reaction (62). The blank gives the question its proper structure by posing a question, Is this episode relevant? In a tale of detection, however, the convention of the Death Warrant also suggests a program: when some important information is temporarily unavailable to the detective, the chances are that the custodian of that information will be found murdered, as proves the case here (71). There are several other ways in which an understanding of programming can help to make clear the difference between the detective story and the crime story. At one point Jane discovers that a young man important to the case is missing. In a crime story, the blank would again be structured: Is this fact important? In the detective story it is also programmed: it must be important because ordinarily detective fiction does not waste time; anything receiving this much attention must have at least some special significance. Besides, one of the axioms of the detective story is its basic purpose (what I will call its "hermeneutic specialization"), which gives precedence to the reader's need to find out what happens next.

The theoretical basis of this study is the interpretation theory of Hans-Georg Gadamer, summarized by him in *Truth and Method*, plus those portions of the Gadamerian concept that were subsequently modified by two of his students, Wolfgang Iser (*The Act of Reading*) and Hans Robert Jauss (*The Aesthetics of Reception*). For present purposes I am making two further adaptations: the first is to draw upon Gadamer's theory of transformed play for the structure of the detective story, and the second, to modify the theoretical concepts of Iser and Jauss to fit the reading of detective fiction, which I will treat as a special case of interpretation.

Gadamer's approach to interpretation, widely accepted in comtemporary literary theory, is philosophical rather than analytical; it raises questions regarding the value systems and the procedures of the interpreter as well as the thing being interpreted. The Gadamerian quest for meaning is an activity of mind in which subject, object, and mental processes meet and act upon one another, with the result that the object of interpretation is affected by the subject and is never the same for two interpreters.[12] Gadamer is concerned with the "situated" nature of interpretation, and he uses the term *horizon* to describe our situatedness in the world. Gadamer's horizon is not fixed or closed; we move into it and it moves with us. Thus, our prejudices represent a horizon beyond which we cannot see, and prejudice becomes not a hindrance to but a condition of understanding.[13]

Both Iser and Jauss bear the mark of Gadamer's teachings, especially his insistence upon the prestructured nature of understanding. There is, however, nothing in either of them to reflect the influence of the theory of play transformed into art. Consequently, I will summarize those aspects of their theories of reception and response related to Gadamer, and leave play-theory for fuller development further along in this chapter.

In the reception aesthetics of Iser and Jauss, the generation of meaning is the work of both reader and text. They are unwilling to go all the way with "straight" reader-response theory, especially the proposition that readers "make" meaning or that the text "disappears" during the process of reading. In Iser especially, the generation of meaning is the result of an interchange between reader and text, but the text tends to become the dominant partner and to function independently of the reader's role.[14]

Two of Iser's basic ideas are especially relevant to any consideration of the reading of fiction: first, the nature of reading as an act of communication between text and reader, and second, the presence of "areas of indeterminacy" in the text, which point the direction of the reading process. Like Gadamer, Iser frequently compares the act of reading to a conversation, but he argues in addition that communication in reading differs from normal dyadic conversation, because in reading there exists no point of reference or "regulative context" to assist the reader's understanding. Areas of indeterminacy are the result of incomplete instructions in the text; they are passages that can be interpreted in several different ways. The most familiar kind of indeterminacy encountered in reading is a *blank*. Blanks are not vacancies, but are what Iser calls the "propellants" of the text, indicators of pattern and direction.[15]

Jauss uses the term *horizon of expectations* to designate the system of reference or mind-set that an individual reader brings to a text. These "horizons" include knowledge of literary conventions or norms, and they explain the perspective from which the reader views the text. A book, although it may be new to a given reader, does not really present itself as something absolutely new but predisposes its audience to a specific kind of reception; it awakens memories of that which was already read and so enters the reader's horizon of expectations.[16]

My departure from Iser's description of the reading process arises from a specialized quality of the detective story, the existence of a regulative context or common ground of reference, which, according to Iser, is present in face-to-face conversation but missing from reading, leaving the reader no alternative but to accept the guidance of the text. I would add, in the special case of the detective story, "the guidance of the text on terms set by a special agreement between writers and readers, which is understood by both and which in turn sets the special reading mode for detective fiction."

The reader's understanding of this agreement, which I will be calling the *individual genre*, shares a great deal with Jauss's horizon of expectations, with one important difference: unlike any other genre, the detection formula is based upon a single literary prototype: in a sense, every detective story is a retelling of Poe's "The Murders in the Rue Morgue." It is this high degree of conventionalization, as we will see, that separates the tale of detection from other fiction and makes necessary some modification of Jauss's view of the predisposition of its audience by a new work of fiction.

Before undertaking any further discussion of theoretical perspectives, I will clarify some of the terms I will be using in a special sense in the following pages.

Unless otherwise indicated, reader refers to the veteran reader of detective fiction, who has sufficient experience in literary detection to be guided by the special qualities of the genre, such as its conventionality or its absolute dependence upon solution. Such a definition does not of course overlook the possibility of the atypical reader, like the one who reads the solution first in order not to be unduly concerned over the mystery, or the one who carefully analyzes every clue in order to reach the solution before the detective does. I mention this latter projection especially because some critics treat the reader of detective fiction as an armchair sleuth. Even so perceptive a commentator as Richard Beach is capable of the remark, "Having read hundreds of mystery stories, [readers] intuitively know, along with the detective, how to sort out clues and to spot red herrings" (*TIRT* 18). Beach's picture will not fit most readers, who know how to sort out clues and spot red herrings but prefer to get on with the story and leave the role of active participant to one of the characters.

The term *detective story* in this study refers to the kind of narrative originated by Poe in the Dupin stories, further developed and enriched by Doyle in the Sherlock Holmes series, and later modified in the novels of Hammett and Chandler. The detective story has four identifiable qualities. First, the main character is a detective; this person may be male or female, professional or amateur, public or private, single or multiple, but there is an identifiable detection role. Second, the main plot of the story is the account of the investigation and resolution; there may be love themes, ghost themes, social themes, or others, but the detection retains precedence. Third, the mystery is no ordinary problem but a complex secret that appears impossible of solution. Finally, the mystery is solved; the solution may be unknown to the detective-protagonist, the official police, or anybody else in the story, but it must be known to the reader.

The term *rules* will be used in a descriptive sense only, to apply to the special qualities of detective fiction, such as the four basics just mentioned, the other conventions incorporated into the genre at its inception, and those it has picked up during its subsequent history. As we will see, the rules of the tale of detection are the rules of organized play; they exist only to make possible the playing of the game.

Formula and *genre* will be used almost interchangeably, for reasons that will be developed more fully in chapter 3. The identification seems especially appropriate in respect to so formulaic a genre as detective fiction.

In the selection of illustrations from the vast literature of detection, I have tried to achieve at least a justifiable cross-section of the genre, involving a reasonable distribution with respect to chronological period and theme ("hard-boiled" vs "soft-boiled"). I have tried to avoid special priority for the best or greatest: some of my examples are recognized masterpieces, but some, although popular in their time and hence representative of the formula, are obviously short on literary quality. In the selection of examples and illustrations, I have purposely favored books published since 1990, for two reasons: in concentrating on currently popular books I hope to draw upon material already generally familiar to my readers, and in following such a plan of selection I have sought to demonstrate the continuity of the formula right on up to the present year.

One point that seems impossible to make too often: this is *not* a historical survey, and many writers are hence necessarily omitted as a result of the sheer weight of numbers.

The bulk of commentary on detective fiction is enormous, most of it biography, literary history, and discussion of the themes of the detective story, such as social conditions, the uses of humor and irony, and the treatment of reality. Relatively few studies have actually applied contemporary literary theory to the interpretation of the detection genre, though two recent anthologies have undertaken to do so, *The Poetics of Murder* (1983), edited by Glenn Most and William Stowe, and a somewhat more modest undertaking, *The Cunning Craft* (1990), edited by Ronald Walker and June Frazer.

Most of the essays and shorter articles, including those to be found in these collections and elsewhere, fall into two classes. First, there are those which employ the detective story as model for some application of critical theory, like O'Toole's analysis of "The Sussex Vampire," in which he uses the Holmes story to illustrate the difference between analytic and synthetic methodologies in criticism. Studies like O'Toole's do not contribute much to the interpretation of the genre, except as reminders of the infinite variety of methodology available to the critic in the field.[17] The other is the application of specific theory to the interpretation of detective fiction, as in several of the essays in *The Poetics of Murder*: Porter's reading of Chandler's *The Big Sleep* in "Backward Construction and the Art of Suspense," Kermode's of Bentley's *Trent's Last Case* in "Novel and Narrative," and Stowe's interpretation of Doyle's "A Case of Identity" and Chandler's *Farewell My Lovely*, in "From Semiotics to Hermeneutics: Modes of Detection in Doyle and Chandler." Porter's study is a morphological analysis, but the other two are of more special interest to us, in that Kermode demonstrates the application of *hermeneutic* criticism in the detective story sense, and Stowe of *philosophical hermeneutics* as applied to literary interpretation.

Book-length studies of detective fiction are also abundant, most of them concerned with a single author or school of writers, and several dealing with the ideologies of detective fiction, but very few touching upon its unique structure. One standard work in the field is Cawelti's *Adventure, Mystery, and Romance*, which is the definitive statement regarding formula in popular fiction, valued by scholars and fans for its detailed treatment of both the classic and hard-boiled schools of literary detection. Among Cawelti's most significant contributions is his recognition of the conventionality of the genre, which I will discuss at greater length later in this study. My own major difference with Cawelti arises from his tendency to treat the formula as text-bound, to the neglect of the function of reader-expectations in formula-building. For much the same reason, I depart from his treatment of the formula as a cultural object, which, as we will see later, applies only in a minor degree in the case of the detection formula.

I should also mention two other book-length studies to be discussed later, Champigny's *What Will Have Happened* (1977) and Grossvogel's *Mystery and Its Fictions* (1979). The Champigny volume, though somewhat limited in scope, is valuable chiefly because of its special view of the temporality of the detective story as more complex and meaningful than the simple past-time-mystery present-time-investigation formula assigned to it by many interpreters. It is to Champigny's credit that he recognizes the basic nature of the ludic element in detective fiction, which too many critics ignore.

Grossvogel is almost unique among critics in his recognition of the structural permanence of the detection formula, which remains essentially unchanged in spite of thematic innovation. He is also one of the very few critics to recognize the primacy of the play mode in detective fiction, along with its transitory nature, and its limited purpose and scope.

There has been no full-length study of the *reading* of detective fiction.

The most significant book to date dealing with the reading of popular fiction is Janice Radway's *Reading the Romance* (1984), which is founded on the assumption that "if we wish to explain why romances are selling so well, we must first know what a romance is for the woman who buys and reads it. To know that we must know what romance readers make of the words they find on the page.[18]

In her introduction, Radway rejects two extreme approaches to the study of the reading process. The first is the elitist text-centered study, which holds that the real meaning embedded in the romance is available only to trained literary scholars who are alone capable of peeling away layers of complexity in order to reveal the true significance of the text (3). At the same time, she rejects those mass-culture studies that represent the reader as only a passive consumer of meaning embedded within cultural texts; the analogy can be dangerous, she says, especially when it is carried too far, in its being used to explain the comprehension of a text, for example (5-6). Her own approach to criticism accepts the fundamental assumptions of reader-response theory, especially those of Stanley Fish and his associates, including the premise that linguistic and textual facts are products, not objects, of interpretation, and that meaning is consequently not something to be found in the text: the process of production is itself controlled by interpretive strategies and conventions that the reader has learned to apply as a member of a particular "interpretive community" (11).

The most significant aspect of Radway's study is her analysis of "the actual construction of texts by real women who inhabit a particular social world." These are her "Smithton women," a population that was in a sense ready-made, a group varying in number between fifty and seventy-five customers of a single salesperson who had gained a considerable reputation as knowledgeable in the field of the women's popular romance (12). Through semiotic analysis of information gained from such devices as the interview and the questionnaire, Radway sought to formulate what she calls her informants' "covert agenda": working first from their conscious beliefs about their own behavior, she posited such additional desires as seemed to complement those beliefs. Her account consequently, as she puts it, "oscillates back and forth between the readers' perceptions of themselves and their activities and more distant view of them that makes an effort to include the unseen cultural ground or set of assumptions upon which they stand" (10).

It is not my purpose to undertake a companion-piece to Radway's study; the two are hardly comparable, since her method is empirical, mine hermeneutic. I have undertaken to follow the reception aesthetic of Iser and Jauss rather than the reader-response theory of Fish and others, and I consequently rely upon Iser's regulative context (the reciprocal effect of reading and genre) and Jauss's horizons of expectations as the controlling influence in reading, instead of Fish's interpretive strategies or interpretive communities. In place of an actual population, I have posited a reader experienced in the detection formula, whose interpretation of a text is guided in part by that reader's own perception of the genre.

Finally, I postulate the deep structure of Gadamer's transformed play as identical to that of detective fiction. The substance of the detection formula is a compact, composed of a set of conventions or rules, between authors and readers. Some of these conventions are simply regulatory, in the sense that they set the standards of behavior for the narrative.

One such regulatory convention would be that of the most likely suspect; if the author changes the usual direction of this convention and makes the most likely suspect guilty, no harm is done. Some, on the other hand, are constitutive conventions: they define the genre. An example would be the one that makes detection the main plot. An author who allows some other element to take precedence over the detection plot might write a highly suspenseful tale, but it would not be a detective story.

Some critics resent any reference to the "rules" of the tale of detection, but the constitutive conventions I have been discussing are very much like the rules of a game like baseball or football. The *regulatory* conventions serve the same purpose as regulatory rules: they are the "etiquette" of the game or story. *Constitutive* conventions are like the constitutive rules of a game, which are not designed to inhibit the game but make it possible to play it.[19]

When I call the detective story a play-experience, I do not mean that everything in it is a source of fun, or that it is not to be taken seriously. Instead, I use the term *play* in the sense in which Hans-Georg Gadamer uses it, to designate a "mode of being," an identity independent of the state of mind of both creator and player, an aesthetic concept that has its own proper spirit and imposes its own special attitude. Gadamer calls it a structure that finds its measure in itself and measures itself by nothing outside it.[20]

Gadamer uses "play" almost interchangeably with "game," with the exception that he gives the game special definition: play becomes a game when the player faces some kind of opponent. "In order for there to be a game, there always has to be, not necessarily literally another player, but something else with which the player plays and which automatically responds to his moves with a countermove" (105-06). In reading, this opponent may take many forms: paradox, challenge, problem, or perhaps nothing more than the demands of context. In the tale of detection, convention exerts an unusually heavy influence upon the playing of the game, as does the special drive of the plot toward the unveiling of the secret. During the reading of a detective story especially, the traditions of the genre place upon the reader the obligation not only to accomplish certain objectives but to accomplish them in to a certain way; one does not, for example, sneak a premature look at the solution.

The development by which human play achieves its consummation in becoming art Gadamer calls "transformation into structure and total mediation" (110). Transformation in this sense means more than alteration or transportation; what previously existed no longer exists but has become something completely different. Thus, the thing transformed assumes a structure: a new shape, a new set of intrinsic internal relationships. The word Gadamer uses here is *Gibilde*, which appears in translation as *structure*; it means, in a general sense, "shape" or "form." He calls it the "character of a work," and elsewhere he quotes Dilthey's statement that structure is "distinguished by its referring to a totality of relationships that do not depend on a temporal, causal succession but on intrinsic connections" (223). Human play, thus transformed, is no longer mere play but the framework for future creation.

Champigny notes the tendency toward transformation in all fiction, and most especially in detective fiction: when a story is read for the first time, he says, "the interest is broadly ludic. . . . If it is reread, and if the reader has retained a notion of the whole, the interest becomes more narrowly 'esthetic.'"[21] The effect can be illustrated by a quality of the detective story that seems paradoxical to the noninitiated, what Cawelti calls the "aestheticizing of crime": the transformation of violent death, deceit, concealment, and disgrace, into a stress-free experience (*AMR* 99). As a result, the title of Haycraft's history of the genre, *Murder for Pleasure*, is descriptive rather than shocking.

Total mediation means that the medium as such is superseded; the process of mediation serves as a go-between, a selective carry-over between former (the ludic sense) and newer (the aesthetic sense), preserving certain basic qualities but not others. In the detective story, plot is mediated into pattern when, for example, the experienced reader is able to see beyond the apparent purpose of a given segment and to sense its real design. A familiar example is the challenge to the reader that became a trademark of the early Ellery Queen novels. At a point fairly late in the story, the author informs the reader that all the evidence has now been presented and that the reader should be able to solve the mystery. Queen's fans soon learned not to take the challenge seriously; most of the highly involved puzzles could never be resolved under any circumstances, unless the reader was willing to spend more time sorting over the evidence than to read the entire novel, and also happened to have access to a huge storehouse of the arcane knowledge most of the solutions required. Here, as the reader sees, the avowed purpose of the challenge is superseded by the real design, which is the forward impetus toward solution and explanation. The effect of the new pattern is a balanced relationship between foreground and background, with both the literal intent of the passage and the perception of the author's real purpose simultaneously claiming the reader's attention. We do not want to miss the point that the ultimate test of the transformation of play into art is its effect upon the behavior of the reader: "The work of art has its true being," says Gadamer, "in the fact that it becomes an experience that changes the person who experiences it" (*TM* 102).

Gadamer approaches the meaning of the word *play* through an examination of its metaphorical uses and finds that what is intended is to-and-fro movement that would not produce a conclusion (103). Play is, moreover, free of stress; it may involve considerable effort, but it is what would in the 1990s be called a no-sweat experience (105). The third quality, says Gadamer, is that the player voluntarily assumes special tasks with make-believe goals that give meaning to the play (107).

Characterizing the action of play as to-and-fro does not imply that the movement is random, but rather that it does not go anywhere. It is movement that has no goal beyond itself (unless the player voluntarily assumes one of those special tasks that make the game more interesting); it does not reach a point of termination, but renews itself through constant repetition (*TM* 103). The motion of a child bouncing a ball, or of two people playing catch stops only when the players have had enough of it. Transformed, the pattern fits the motion of detective fiction, where most of the action is an end in itself, and where, according to Champigny, the text functions as both teammate and opponent (*WWHH* 4). Grossvogel characterizes the detection genre as "optimistic and self-destructing": if literature is an attempt to come to terms with mystery beyond consciousness, then "the mode of the detective story is to create a mystery for the sole purpose of effecting its effortless dissipation" (*MIF* 15). If Grossvogel is right, this feature should explain why most detective stories will not bear a second reading; because of the heavy influence of context, *every* reading is a rereading. Auden agrees in principle: "I forget the story as soon as I have finished it, and have no wish to read it again. If, as sometimes happens, I start reading one and find after a few pages that I have read it before, I cannot go on" (*DF* 15).

"The ease of play," says Gadamer, "does not refer to any real absence of effort but rather to the absence of strain" (105). For the remainder of this discussion we will use the word *stress* to designate that kind of destructive pressure that the activity of play is intended to avoid, and reserve the term *strain* for the stress-free exertion rendered by Gadamer's translator as *effort*. Two people playing catch may wear themselves to a state of physical exhaustion and enjoy every moment of the activity because it relaxes and restores them; this is the kind of effort we would normally call strain. *Stress* seems the better designation for the exhaustion these same two people might experience as business competitors, resulting in anxiety and inability to relax. Popular and critical opinions agree regarding the nature of the detective story as a medium of relaxation. For Auden, the reading of a detective story is "an addiction, like tobacco or alcohol" (*DF* 15). Regardless of theme, the detection genre shares the deep structure of transformed play. In his discussion of the current ironic phase of literature, Frye makes the provocative point that the detective story "might be considered advanced propaganda for the police state if it were possible to take it seriously." But it seems not to be possible. The "protecting wall of play is still there."[22] One of the strongest evidences of the absence of strain in the tale of detection is the assurance of resolution; the reader proceeds with confidence that the mystery will be solved, presumably by the detective, and the reading is consequently relieved of the normal stresses of problem-solving.

It may be, however, that our catch-players decide to inject some purpose into their activity in order to break the monotony, and they start keeping score. Now their effort has become a *game*, and the players may also agree upon some kind of limit that will bring it to an end. Is it still play? Is the motion to-and-fro, and is it still stress-free? The difference, says Gadamer, is a matter of goals; what these players have done is voluntarily to impose a task upon themselves, in order to add meaning to their activity. A child gives itself tasks in playing with a ball, but they are playful ones "because the purpose of the game is not really solving the task, but ordering and shaping the movement of the game itself" (107). Or a fly-fisherman will see how close to a leaf he can come with each cast, in order to alleviate the monotony of repetition. Thus, the play is tied to make-believe goals, but "the meaning of these goals does not in fact depend on their being achieved. Rather, in spending oneself on the tasks of the game, one is in fact playing oneself out" (108). The player cannot experience the freedom of play without transforming the purposes of the behavior into assumed tasks of the game.

To speak of the detective story as a game is not to equate the term with *puzzle*, *problem*, or *intellectual exercise*, but rather to assert that the narrative is built on a set of expectations that correspond to the mode of play or game. This integrative frame underlies all kinds of detective fiction, including the hard-boiled, the "inverted," and the police novel, as well as the classic formal-problem story. Does it not underlie all formula fiction, all popular fiction, *all* fiction? To a degree it does, except that the reading of detective fiction is governed by the hermeneutic structure to a greater degree than are the other genres; in the reading of a detective story, the compulsion to see how the story turns out is much stronger than in other fiction. The difference, in the detective story, is based upon the degree and intensity of the hermeneutic impulse. The reader may want to know how any fiction is going to end, but in most fiction that need is not dominant. A novel like *The Bridges of Madison County* could be read without much loss if the present conclusion were missing, but the same omission in a story like *Death of an Expert Witness* would be fatal.

If the detective story is a game, it can be defined in terms of two components or functions. First, there must be definitional rules that do not simply regulate the playing of the game but make it possible for the game to be played. Such rules would provide limits or frames within which innovation could take place, plus pre-understandings and defined tasks. Second, there must be a definition of the game in terms of foreground-background, space, and its identity in terms of its own history and its place among other games, its "mystique."

We need to discuss briefly the word *hermeneutic*, which will be used extensively throughout this study. The term is employed in a philosophical sense in reference to the interpretation of texts, with special emphasis upon perception of the relationships between the parts and the whole of a work, and among the parts themselves.[23] Most of the critics I will cite, however, make the term interchangeable with *mystery, suspense,* or *detective.* Champigny, for example, says, "A mystery story is a hermeneutic tale" (*WWHH* 13). Kermode conveniently summarizes the idea when he writes that it is possible to tell a story in such a way that the "principal object of the reader is to discover, by an interpretation of clues, the answer to a problem proposed at the outset. All other considerations may be subordinated to this interpretative, or . . . hermeneutic activity." Most stories have hermeneutic aspects, but in the detective story the reader asks of any information "how it 'fits in'" and "how it will all 'come out'" (*PM* 179). This need to know the truth acts as a structuring force, exercising control over the reading of detective fiction, because the desire to know the outcome of the story leads the reader to pay special attention to those features that can be organized as answers to questions raised by the reading process.[24]

Many commentators have used the word *game* in a different context from the one in which I am using it here, making the tale of detection a "game" between author and reader, to determine whether the reader can reach the solution ahead of the detective. Some commentators use the term to designate the contest between detective and culprit. Here, I am speaking of a game in which the reader assumes the role of interested spectator, who is free to accept or decline the challenges of the story, a contest in which the fun of the game is in the playing. The detective story abounds in small tasks tied to make-believe goals. Sometimes they are obvious, as in Ellery Queen's challenges, or in the Philo Vance stories of Van Dine, which lay out an array of awesome clues with the implied invitation to sort them out and reach the only logical conclusion. Usually, though, they are more subtle, as when a woman of mystery enters the scene and the reader is invited to tie her in, or in which the detective suddenly murmurs, "So that's the way it was," and leaves the reader to decide what he or she is talking about.

The important thing to remember here is that these invitations may be accepted or declined without the least damage to the satisfaction of the reading. It is more useful to think of the reader as an involved spectator who watches the game in anticipation of solution (Grossvogel *PM* 254) rather than as participating player, because, as Gadamer says, the purpose is not really to solve the task but to give order and shape to the game. The reader retains the role of observer rather than participant, however, as is evident in the fact that however—it is not through the reader's efforts that the game is brought to an end. The tale of detection is a game that is neither "won" nor "lost." Most readers enjoy a story in which the outcome is a complete surprise as much as if they had been able to solve it themselves in advance. Actually, I doubt if we should take seriously the idea of the reader's "solving" the case at all; what most readers want is not the ability to reach the solution early (and thus spoil the fun) but a means of *interpreting* the problem in the special sense in which detective-fiction problems must be interpreted. This special sense is what John Dickson Carr's Dr. Gideon Fell calls the "detective story sense," which I will discuss more fully in chapter 7.

The critic must take care not to confuse the *playfulness* of some detective fiction with the transformed play (the "mode of being") that underlies the whole genre.[25] Many writers reduce the stress element of a story with such gratuitous devices as the name of the village of Long Piddleton in Grimes's *The Man with a Load of Mischief* or the law firm of Darwin, Darwin, Erasmus and Mendel in Cross's *No Word from Winfred*. Such usages are results rather than manifestations of the play element in literary detection. If we seek evidence of what Gadamer calls "transformation into structure," we can turn to a different kind of example from *The Man with a Load of Mischief*, the convention of the Missing Person. Fairly early in that story we learn that a woman named Ruby

Judd has not returned from a visit (57). A few pages later we come across another casual mention of Ruby (72), and another considerably later (157).

The experienced reader will soon catch on that Ruby is dead, which indeed she proves to be before many more pages have passed (178). The device is conventional in detective fiction, and it is essentially transformed play, in that it achieves the double purpose of offering a task (What has happened to Ruby?) and also relaxes stress with the assurance that this is, after all, a detective story, and that all this mystery will be cleared up before the conclusion. Here again the hermeneutic impulse acts as the structuring force: the reader pushes to know, first, what has happened to Ruby, and second, what the relationship is between Ruby's death and the other murders.

A few writers of detective stories have achieved reputations for sheer playfulness, as for example Agatha Christie in her depiction of Mrs. Oliver, who is an easily recognizable parody of the literary detective, or the whimsies of Christie's Tuppence and Tommy. The evidences of genuine transformed play, however, are not limited to instances of persiflage but are to be found in all detective fiction. They are easy enough to discover in Christie: when the party host, early in *Cards on the Table*, sets up the bridge tables with all the murder suspects at one and all the detectives at another (28), the reader knows very well that he has something special in mind and may elect to accept the task of deciding what it is. One convention especially familiar to readers of stories of the formal-problem type is the one in which the author carefully identifies and locates each of the people who may later become subjects of the investigation. The device has become conventional to the extent that the experienced reader knows murder is upcoming within the next few pages; the sense of assurance generated serves both to eliminate stress from the reading (the problem will be solved before the end of the story) and at the same time to present the reader with a task of detection (which of those suspects has motive, means, and opportunity?).

The difference between the two levels will probably not even be noticed by the inexperienced reader, who will recognize the playful purpose of Christie's parodic characters, but not the convention of the contrived situation (placement of the bridge-players as suspects or detectives), where play is transformed into hermeneutic structure. The veteran reader of literary detection, however, should have no trouble with either of these or with the other familiar device, the placement of potential murderers (placement with respect to access to the victim), because this is one of those conventions that have been structured into detective fiction through almost endless repetition. In his discussion of the transformation of play, Gadamer speaks of the kind of play that is "in principle repeatable and hence permanent" (110). Transformed play, then, shares two qualities with the conventionality of the detective story: it serves to relieve the stresses of the narrative, and it is endlessly repeatable. The immanence of the play element accounts for that peculiar capacity of detective fiction for tolerating subsequent repetitions by other writers that would soon become outworn in another genre.

Thus, when we refer to the deep structure of transformed play as identical with that of detective fiction, we do not imply that play is *part of* the structure, or that it is a major theme of the genre, or that it is even reflected in the text. I will for the occasion borrow de Beaugrande's term "integrative frame" to designate a stabilizing influence that manages the complexities of writing and reading.[26] Throughout the following pages, the idea of play as integrative frame will be discussed in the Gadamerian sense, in which human play assumes the character of a work of art; it is "transformed into structure," that is, into a mode of being marked by absence of stress, by movement that renews itself in constant repetition, and by voluntary acceptance of tasks that are bound to make-believe goals (*TM* 103-08).

The role of the reader in the tale of detection may become clearer with some discussion of the manner in which reading takes place. Proceeding through the story, the reader will encounter open spaces or blanks, those areas of perception that raise more questions than they answer and impel the reader to bridge the space and push ahead to the outcome. Such spaces occur in all kinds of reading, but they have particular force in the mystery, in the sense that the drive to discover the resolution will override every other aim in reading. The special quality of the detective story, one that distinguishes it from all other fiction, is the fact that the blanks in the story are *programmed* by the genre; that is, the blanks themselves suggest methods of discovery. When, for example, a strongly "sympathetic" character appears to be the guilty party early in the narrative, the reader of any other kind of story may wonder if this is indeed the culprit and be driven to read on and find out, but in detective fiction the very presence of this particular blank space (which is recognizable as one of the oldest and most familiar conventions of detective fiction) also assures the reader that this suspect is quite probably innocent and that the reader need not feel any anxiety on his behalf. Here is one of the instances so abundant in the tale of detection, in which the "protecting wall of play" serves to de-stress the reader's expectations.[27]

Three novels will illustrate the effect of transformed play as the integrative frame of detective fiction. The first is *The Red Thumb-Mark* (1907) by R. Austin Freeman, who characterized the detective story as "an exhibition of mental gymnastics in which [the reader] is invited to take part" and as "an argument conducted under the guise of fiction" (in *AMS* 11, 13-14). The second is Robert Parker's *The Judas Goat* (1978), featuring his series private investigator Spenser. The third example, by Trevanian (Rodney Whitaker), is *The Main* (1976), a police novel whose detective-protagonist is Lieutenant Claude LaPointe of the Montreal police. On the basis of the themes they develop, *The Red Thumb-Mark* is usually categorized as a representative of the "classic" or "formal-problem" school, while *The Judas Goat* and *The Main* are considered "hard-boiled."

One of the elements that make the reading of the detective story different from that of any other fiction is that the reader approaches the narrative at the outset with much of the context already supplied; before turning to the first page, for example, the reader is already assured that this story will deal with a mystery that is not only deeply but doubly wrapped and veiled and that it will be solved by the detective-protagonist before the story ends. For this context, *The Red Thumb-Mark* is indebted, as is all the rest of detective fiction, to Poe's "The Murders in the Rue Morgue" in four respects. First, there is the detective-protagonist, who is the prime mover of the action of the narrative. Second, there is the detection plot, which supplies the major theme of the story; there may be minor themes, but the detection is always basic. Third, there is the problem to be solved, invariably represented as insoluble. And finally, there is the solution, which is always reached before the story ends.

The Red Thumb-Mark features Dr. John Thorndyke, one of the first of the great scientific detectives, a stern practitioner of the strict logic advocated by his creator, who was among the ablest early defenders of the integrity of detective fiction. The main plot is the account of Dr. Thorndyke's efforts to exonerate his client, Reuben Hornby, who is accused of stealing a bag of diamonds from a safe, and whose guilt appears to be sealed by the presence, on the bottom of the safe, of Hornby's bloody thumb-print. He is assisted in the story by Dr. Jervis, who is also the narrator, and the minor plot is the account of Dr. Jervis's falling in love with Juliet Gibson, one of the young women in the case. To the experienced reader of detective fiction, the strength of tradition in the genre is clear in the pattern, which is a variation upon the theme of *The Sign of the Four*, with Dr. Thorndyke in the role of Holmes, Dr. Jervis as Dr. Watson, and Juliet Gibson as Violet Strange. The reader's awareness of the familiar (and comfortable) pattern is of special importance, because it has a marked influence upon the reading of the tale of detection.

For the experienced reader, the recognition of the pattern is reassuring and free of stress. Because of the ready-made context, we know that the problem, presented as unbreakable paradox in chapter 2, will be solved, and that it will be solved by Dr. Thorndyke. What we are calling the "context" of detective fiction is the generalization of the reader's earlier experience of the formula, which supplies the framework for interpretation of the signals of the text. As was pointed out earlier, the experienced reader receives the signal of the almost certain guilt of Reuben Hornby with a contextual frame different from that of any other genre. As a result of the presence of the convention of the most likely suspect, the reader's expectation is that Hornby is probably innocent; for that reader, the blank space is programmed. Thus, the textual signals of the detective story carry with them a set of heuristics [methods of discovery see example on page #] for their interpretation. The reader's expectations are shaped by the traditions and conventions of the genre, to the degree that the reader, relieved of anxiety, is free to enjoy the playing out of the game.

Even though it develops themes different from those of *The Red Thumb-Mark*, *The Judas Goat* belongs in the detection genre, because it also follows the conventions of the "Murders in the Rue Morgue" formula. Parker's private investigator Spenser, although his methods are different from those of Dr. Thorndyke, is the prime mover; it is his story. The work of detection is the main plot; the mystery is a tightly veiled secret, but the reader proceeds through the novel with the assurance that it will be resolved.

Novels like *The Judas Goat* are customarily called hard-boiled because the detective tends to solve problems by means of pursuit and conflict rather than reason. They are also known as "private eye" novels because the detective protagonist is a professional private detective instead of a gifted amateur or a policeman. In addition to the Poe traditions, these novels follow the pattern established in the works of Dashiell Hammett and Raymond Chandler. In the first place, Spenser tells his own story, as did the Continental Op, Philip Marlowe, and most of the others of the private-eye school. Secondly, although the original commission is completed long before the end of the story, Spenser continues pursuit in order to solve a secondary problem in which he has become personally interested. And finally, the book contains a considerable amount of narrative material not directly related to the detection plot.

At the beginning of the novel, Spenser is commissioned by a wealthy Bostonian named Dixon to hunt down a group of terrorists who had set off a bomb in London the previous year, permanently crippling him and killing his wife and two daughters. Dixon makes it clear that Spenser's mission is that of bounty hunter: he wants the terrorists brought in dead or alive. Following some rough and dangerous preliminary contacts with his quarry in London, Spenser decides that he needs some help and calls in his associate, Hawk, a skilled and highly intelligent operator with some effective homicidal capabilities. The two pursue the terrorist gang to Copenhagen, then to Amsterdam, and finally to Montreal. During the running battle they pick up a woman terrorist, Kathie, who, abandoned by the leader of the gang, decides to work with Spenser and Hawk.

Like *The Red Thumb-Mark*, *The Judas Goat* carries a love-interest, the continuing serial affair between Spenser and Susan Silverman. While he and Hawk are in Montreal, Spenser finds it necessary to make an overnight trip to Boston, and during the course of that visit he spends a diversionary night with Susan (157-69).

Trevanian's *The Main* is in the tradition of the American police novel; its protagonist, Detective Lieutenant Claude LaPointe of the Montreal police, is unlike Dr. Thorndyke in that he employs police techniques instead of scientific method to solve his problems, and unlike Spenser in his professional status, which is that of public servant rather than independent private detective. Thematically, *The Main* is considerably closer to the tradition of *The Judas Goat* than to that of *The Red Thumb-Mark*: LaPointe's methods of crime solving are sometimes rough and physical, and sometimes border on the illegal. In terms of narrative technique, however, the novel comes closer to the classic formula, as do most police novels. Unlike Spenser and his colleagues, LaPointe does not tell his own story, and because of the sheer demands of his profession, he has no time or opportunity to follow up problems that have attracted his interest, as do Spenser and Marlowe.

Like Thorndyke and Spenser, LaPointe is in the tradition of the great detective: the story is his from beginning to end. *The Main* is LaPointe's territory; it is a district that formerly marked the boundary between French and English Montreal, now populated by waves of immigrants entering the city, who are "clustered together for protection against suspicion and prejudice, concentrating in cultural ghettos of a few blocks' extent" (10). Within its limits, LaPointe is the law; he will not go home at night until he has put "his" Main to bed, and the residents of the area have come to look upon him as both intercessor and arbiter, a man with a stern sense of justice tempered by fairness and sympathy. His police skills are impressive, as is his power of observation. During the thirty years of his assignment to the Main he has fired his weapon only seven times (15), and when playing cards he looks at his hand only once briefly before bidding, then remembers what he has (29). Especially in the catalogue of his virtues, LaPointe reminds the reader of Emile Gaboriau's M. Lecoq, and his reference to the Main as "my patch" (123) is more than a little suggestive of "Gideon's mile" in London, in the George Gideon stories of J.J. Marric.

The Main shares the plot structure of the other two novels, with the hermeneutic as the primary plot and a love story as secondary. The detection is concentrated upon a murder committed within LaPointe's territory, and the problem he must solve is the customary Veiled Secret. LaPointe has never seen anything like it: the victim, who has been knifed, has assumed the posture of a priest serving High Mass, kneeling with his face pressed downward into the gravel, and his arms outstretched with the palms down (63). The love story begins with LaPointe's picking up a young prostitute off the street and taking her to his apartment, where he keeps her for several days. It provides the justification of distraction for lengthy delay (199-214), as did the corresponding developments in both *The Red Thumb-Mark* and *The Judas Goat*.

One theme to be developed at some length in this study is that the difference between the detective story and any other type of fiction can be explained almost entirely in terms of a reading mode that is exclusive with the tale of detection. The unique reading strategy of detective fiction arises from two basic structural qualities of the genre, its persistent conventionality and its hermeneutic specialization. The conventionality of the genre is manifested in the mass of traditions the tale of detection has accumulated, including the set of plot conventions inherited from Poe (and, on occasion, Hammett and Chandler) and those dozens of incidental conventions, such as the most likely suspect, of which authors and readers of literary detection seem never to tire. The term *hermeneutic specialization,* as used here, designates that tendency of a story to push the reader on toward the solution, which is the dominant drive of the detective story. Thus, any interpretation of transformed play as the integrative frame of detective fiction must take those two systems into account. In referring to conventionality and hermeneutic specialization as the basics of the *structure* of the detective story, I use the term in the Gadamerian sense, to designate those qualities that give the genre its character, its shape and form.

Of the three manifestations of play discussed by Gadamer, the absence of stress and the voluntary assumption of tasks can be illustrated fairly easily by direct citation. The other one, the to-and-fro motion characteristic of play, requires broader treatment, because it is the quintessence of transformation and mediation of the play mode into hermeneutic structure. *Transformation,* in the Gadamerian sense, goes far beyond mere alteration; it is the change by which human play becomes art (*TM* 110). *Mediation* equates more precisely with the idea of the selective conversion into patterns that are purely aesthetic. When something is mediated, it is not simply transformed; mediation is a selective process, effecting the carry-over of certain qualities but not others into the new state of being. The former medium (play) "cancels itself out"; performance does not become thematic, "but the work presents itself through it and in it" (120). This is the reason why the mediated play mode, now become hermeneutic structure, does not convert the story into a playful experience. The integrative frame of play, although it shapes and directs the structure of the narrative, is not part of that structure; it is not the theme of the detective story and is not reflected in the text (101).

Earlier I defined the to-and-fro motion of play in the Gadamerian sense as motion not bound to any special goal that would bring it to an end. The (transformed) to-and-fro motion of the detective story, for example, is motion that is not intended for any other objective than the resolution of the mystery. *The Red Thumb-Mark* contains no universals, advances no message, poses no great questions; it is not built around the theme of science vs. ignorance, because the genre had already stacked the deck in favor of science. This tendency was already part of the context, as witness Doyle's refusal five years earlier to develop the theme of science vs. superstition in *The Hound of the Baskervilles*. The stories are serious but they are not ideological battlegrounds.

Because of that guiding framework, the detective story is to be "experienced subjectively as relaxation" (*TM* 105), and the reader must remember not to take the book with the wrong kind of seriousness. Like *The Red Thumb-Mark*, which refuses to go beyond the bounds of mediated play, *The Judas Goat* declines the development of socially significant themes, particularly in respect to the potentially stressful subject of race. Hawk, who is black, jokes repeatedly about his own race; when he calls Spenser he leaves the name "Mr. Stepinfetchit" (86), and he seems to enjoy mimicking the artificial speech attributed to black people (93), though his tolerance does not extend to the ideology of the terrorist group (whose motto is "Keep Africa white" 133), and whose neo-Nazi leader refers to him as "the *schwartze.*" The social code in *The Judas Goat* is overridden by the honor code of the fictional private detective: Hawk is not much bothered by the ideology of the situation, but at the end of the story he refuses to split the bonus with Spenser, accepting only the agreed-upon fee and expenses (201).

The Main is a police story, differing from both the formal-problem story like *The Red Thumb-Mark* and the private-eye like *The Judas Goat*. As in those two books, however, the strong hand of convention supersedes every other intention, and this novel stays within the bounds of the detection formula. Most of the early American writers of stories featuring police detectives were determined to make the policemen in their stories act like policemen, avoiding at once the artificialities of the classic detective novel and the sensationalism of the private eye story. There are, they repeatedly said, no heroes on the detective squad; police detectives usually work in teams, with the result that their successes grow out of group effort instead of the achievements of one gifted individual. Most real-life policemen carry heavy caseloads, unable to give their whole time and attention to a single crime, no matter how much it interests them. As a result of persistent overwork, moreover, they are never able to continue with a case that is officially closed, as the fictional private detectives do. Actually, very few writers have succeeded even moderately in the accomplishment of any of these goals; the police story is still a tale of detection, shaped by hermeneutic structure and demanding heroes.

Thus, like most other detective stories, *The Main* follows the conventions of literary detection instead of those of external reality. In the real world, far more cases go unsolved than are solved, but there are never any doubts about the outcome of the police novel: LaPointe will solve it. He is not only LaPointe Invictus but Lecoq and Gideon Redivivi, in charge from start to finish. Not long before the resolution his young assistant expresses a feeling of helplessness over the apparently contradictory nature of the evidence, only to be assured by LaPointe that it will soon be over, because "the leads are starting to thin out" (240). Context dictates that LaPointe is right. As usual in the police novel, there is very little evidence of teamwork in this story, and all LaPointe's normally heavy load is put aside in order for him to give his full attention to the investigation of the murder.

The conventionality of the detection genre is the chief source of that absence of stress which, according to Gadamer, characterizes the play experience (115). The reader begins a detective story with certain assurances and expectations, some of which I have already discussed, the invincibility of the detective and the assurance of solution. Relieved of anxiety regarding the outcome, the reader can enter into the purposes provided by the hermeneutic specialization of the genre, becoming an involved spectator in the playing out of the game of investigation and pursuit.

Thus, the rules of detective fiction (the story must end with a solution, the Most Likely Suspect is almost never guilty, and the like) are the surest source of the elimination of stress from the act of reading. An inexperienced reader, unfamiliar with the influence of transformed play, may feel some anxiety over the statement halfway through *The Main* that "most murders go unsolved, you know" (175). To the reader experienced in the conventionality of detective fiction, the signal allows only one interpretation: this one will be solved.

Reading is relieved of stress in several ways, some of which are supplied by the structure of the genre, such as the comfortable reminder that this story is in the tradition of all those well-remembered stories of the same formula. Determined individualist that he is, Spenser still fits the mold of some of his predecessors, as Dr. Thorndyke did. Intentionally or not, the first chapter of *The Judas Goat* closely parallels the opening scene of Chandler's *The Big*

Sleep, offering the reader the expectation that where Marlowe, after considerable struggle, completed the commission General Sternwood had given him, Spenser will not fail in his mission for Hugh Dixon. The level of stress is also lowered in those parodies of the conventions of literary detection, especially in the passage where Hawk has just returned empty-handed from the deserted apartment of the terrorist leader. Spenser asks if he has found any clues: "You know, like an airplane schedule with a flight to Beirut underlined. A hotel confirmation from the Paris Hilton. Some tourist brochures from Orange County California. A tinkling piano in the next apartment" (137). The bantering allusions to some of the chestnuts of detective fiction remind the reader that this is, after all, a detective story. Parker further relieves the stress element by application of his own sense of humor, which manifests itself in Spenser's tangy repartee, most notably in his exchanges with Hawk, tending rather to persiflage than to substance, like their discussion of unshaved armpits (114) and their trivializations of racial differences (124-27).

One dependable source of freedom from strain is the presence of a strong secondary plot, like the love story in *The Red Thumb-Mark,* to which I have already referred. One of the constitutive conventions of the detective story is that the hermeneutic must be the main plot, but an interesting love story can serve the dual purpose of distraction and delay. Except for the presence of transformed play as the de-stressing element, the love story would become only an irksome interruption of the main business of the novel, but in the tale of detection it serves to legitimize the delay by providing a temporary distraction. The ability of the detective story to tolerate interruption is demonstrated in chapter 12, which is given over almost entirely to the flirtation between Dr. Jervis and Miss Gibson, complicated by Dr. Jervis's battle with his own conscience over trying to steal the affections of Reuben Hornby's beloved, when he should be bending every effort to protect Hornby's interests. The veteran reader, however, should not be irritated by the interruption of the mystery plot, for two reasons: in the first place, such delays are part of the detection formula, and second, the reader's expectations are bolstered by the assurance that the problem will be solved and all loose ends tied up. Annoyance is counterbalanced by assurance, and the two forces that might be in conflict substantially cancel each other out.

The third characteristic of the transformed play-experience is the voluntary acceptance by the participant of tasks that are tied only to make-believe goals. These tasks, says Gadamer, are play-ful ones, because they do not determine the outcome of the game but rather give meaning to the experience of the play itself (*TM* 107). Detective fiction abounds in such offerings, which really serve the purpose of allowing reader to "play themselves out" without actually affecting the outcome of the story. In the "scien-tific" story these invitations are often clothed in impressive terms like *syllogism* and *hypothesis*. Thorndyke is actually inviting the reader to find the fallacy in the syllogism on which the police are acting ("The crime was committed by the person who made this finger-print," "John Smith is the person who made this finger-print," "Therefore, the crime was committed by John Smith" 111), and even more pointedly on the following page when he states the four hypotheses on which he is working: the crime was com-mitted by Reuben Hornby, or by either of two other members of the family, or by somebody else. The unspoken challenge to the reader is to examine the plausibility of these four, not overlooking the possibility that there may be a fifth, which proves to be the right answer. As Gadamer says, these tasks give meaning to the game but are essentially playful, both because they are optional and because the outcome in no way depends upon the reader's successfully resolving them.

As usual in the private eye story, the method of detection in *The Judas Goat* is considerably different from that of novels like *The Red Thumb-Mark*. Spenser is not strong on syllogisms and hypotheses, but his approach to problem solving can be quite effective, as it is where he and Hawk (and, by invitation, the read-er) need to find out where the leader of the terrorist gang has gone from Amsterdam. Questioning Kathie, who knows little more than they do, they eliminate one possibility after another until Spenser happens to use the word *game* and Kathie remem-bers the leader had bought tickets to the Olympics: two pages later, the three of them are on a plane to Montreal (130-42).

The detective story abounds in tasks offered to the reader dur-ing the course of the narrative, but as a rule the offer is not as explicitly stated as it is in the opening pages of *The Judas Goat*. When Spenser meets Hugh Dixon he notices something unusual about his eyes, which "snarled with life and purpose, or some-thing like that. I didn't know exactly what then. Now I do" (6). The challenge in those last three words is clear enough, but the accep-tance is optional as usual; regardless of the decision, the reader will sooner or later know whatever it was that Spenser knew.

As a rule, the tasks offered to the reader in detective fiction are limited by the conventionality of detection and directed by the hermeneutic specialization of the genre. In many instances, the very pattern of the task suggests the technique the author will follow in its development. A typical example is the use of the Recurrent Structure, which is casually dropped in the reader's presence, reinforced a few pages later as a reminder of its importance, and finally, after a longer interval, reintroduced as a major clue. When one of the witnesses in *The Main*, trying to remember the name of a suspect, tells LaPointe that it has "something to do with chocolate" (170), the experienced reader should sense a clue, and the feeling will be confirmed when, after the conventional interval, LaPointe asks another witness, "By the way, does chocolate mean anything to you?" (183). The pattern is completed when LaPointe learns the name of the man he is seeking: Alfredo (Candy Al) Canducci (220).

There is an important point here which should not be overlooked. When the detective story is defined as transformed play, the nature of detective fiction itself is defined at the same time. Literary detection is a stress free experience, whose primary purpose is recreation and relaxation. Moreover, that the resolution of a detective story is ensured by the formula means that much of the motion generated in the act of reading is "not tied to any special goal that would bring it to an end"; the reader does not solve the problem. It is this quality that makes the reader of detective fiction an involved observer rather than a player. Finally, the detective story can be read at more than one level; the reader, half asleep, can simply drift passively with the story, or, alert and intense, accept the tasks that feature such stories. Thus, to define transformed play is at the same time substantially to define the detective story.

By the same token, the differences between classic and hardboiled may be easier to see when both are defined in terms of mediated play as integrative frame. The first of these involves the amount of goal-free nonhermeneutic material: both employ love stories as secondary plots, but not much else is extraneous in *The Red Thumb-Mark*; besides the love story, *The Judas Goat* also abounds in clothes-consciousness (designer labels are an obsession with Spenser), a sense of affluence, and food-consciousness. The second concerns the challenges that "transform the aims of purposive behavior into mere tasks of the game" (*TM* 107). It is not surprising that *The Judas Goat* offers fewer tasks than *The Red*

Thumb-Mark; traditionally, the private-detective approach is considerably less analytical than the classic. As a result of the first-person point of view in the private-eye story, the reader is inside the problem, experiencing it instead of viewing it objectively. Secrecy is the dynamic of the classic story, with the result that the reader is carefully excluded from the purposes of great minds like Sherlock Holmes and Dr. Thorndyke but is very close to the aims and the misgivings of Spenser.

It is possible to summarize the manifestations of transformed play in the detective story in terms of reader expectations, because the fundamental difference between the reading of a detective story and that of any other fiction is a difference in the anticipations with which the reader undertakes the story. At this point I can identify with some confidence three effects of transformed play upon the expectations of the reader.

The first of these is the one previously discussed, the refusal of the detective story to go beyond the bounds of play: *The Red Thumb-Mark* declines a philosophical motif, *The Judas Goat* does not develop the racial theme, and *The Main* refuses to become a parallel of the nonfiction police world. Other commentators have noted this tendency, especially Grossvogel, who writes that "the mode of the detective story is to create a mystery for the sole purpose of effecting its effortless dissipation" (*MIF* 15).

The second effect is that the reader's expectations are directed (that is, *programmed*) by convention, with the result that traditional situations come to be interpreted in terms of the formula. Much of the art of the detective story consists of the author's ability to suggest approaches to the solution of the mystery without giving away the solution itself, and one of the strongest manifestations of the unique liaison between writers and readers in the genre lies in the recognition of familiar conventions that call up certain associated ideas to the reader's consciousness. One of these has just been discreased, the recurrent structure, which is easily recognizable because it follows the standard pattern: the idea is almost casually suggested, then after a few pages it is strengthened by another brief mention, and later, sometimes after several reintroductions, becomes important as a major clue. The device has been used so frequently that it has become part of the genre. Literary detection abounds in other instances, including the convention of the expanded commission, which is familiar to the reader of private-eye stories; almost all stories featuring private investigators open with the detective's acceptance of a job involving some noncapital crime, such as theft, disappearance, or blackmail. The convention is no sooner recognized than it is programmed: the reader knows at once that there will be at least one murder before many pages have passed. Here the effect of detective structure is twofold: it relieves the reader of stress with respect to outcome, and it offers a task that may be accepted or not without affecting the resolution of the mystery.

The play mode affects expectations in one other way: the reader of the detective story tolerates situations that would be rejected in another genre. Especially in the formal-problem story, the cavalier treatment accorded to the reader would seem outrageous in another genre, but to the detection fan it is part of the game. I refer particularly to those instances in which the reader is without apology excluded from the business of detection, as when the detective outlines to his associates an ingenious plan for the solution to the mystery; the reader is invited to guess but not permitted to know what the plan is, and what might be considered a literary flaw in another genre becomes part of the conventional structure.

It is not difficult to demonstrate the theoretical basis of play as the integrative frame of detective fiction by matching these two systems. There is, first, the Gadamerian concept of play, based upon his three attributes of freedom from stress, presence of elective tasks, and movement that is essentially repetition and renewal. Play thus conceived is subject to transformation into the structure of art. The other system is the hermeneutic process of the detective story, with its traditionally limited purposes, its mandatory resolution, its standardized structure, and its access to a stockpile of almost endlessly repeatable conventions.

To-and-fro movement is central to the idea of play, says Gadamer, to the extent that "play is the occurrence of movement as such"; it is not bound to any goal that would bring it to an end, but "renews itself in constant repetition" (*TM* 103). Transformed into structure, the to-and-fro movement of play becomes the source of the two constitutive elements of detective fiction, its hermeneutic specialization and its conventionality.

By definition, the movement of play is always repeatable. The conclusion of one period produces later play: the child bouncing a ball will quit when he has had enough, but will return to it later. The outcome of a single game is never final: there is another one tomorrow, which always begins with a clean slate as if there had been none before. The effect is the same in the tale of detection, where Lieutenant Tragg scorns Perry Mason's methods as if he had learned nothing from their last encounter, and where John Putnam Thatcher is welcome in any company, regardless of the fact that each of his previous appearances has been the prelude to murder. According to the idea of structure as transformed play, the reason for this phenomenon is that the movement of the narrative produces a succession of temporary endings without a goal, since most of the action is *an end in itself*. In the detective story, the hermeneutic impulse, the desire to know how the story will turn out, becomes a drive toward an end that is always only temporary.

Transformed play is not merely *transported* play; it comes to be something new, which Gadamer calls a "mode of being" (101). Transformed into art, it becomes structure, the shape, form, or character of a work. In the case of the detective story, play is transformed into hermeneutic structure, taking the form of the seven-step basic plot of all detective fiction (problem, first solution, complication, priod of gloom, dawning light, solution, explanation); the order may vary within limits, and some of the steps may be eliminated, but every real tale of detection has the shape of this hermeneutic pattern. It also manifests itself as those structural qualities discussed earlier, the four classic elements in "The Murders in the Rue Morgue," plus the special ones from Hammett and Chandler that are the mark of the private-eye story. The "character" of the work, to use Gadamer's own term (110), is a narrative that renews itself through constant repetition (103). The reader's response to this transformation is the expectation of more play, first to achieve a solution of the enigma that effortlessly dissipates itself, then to read another book in the same genre, but never to reread the one just finished.

Thus, the transformation of play into hermeneutic structure results in what I am calling the two "givens" of detective fiction, its hermeneutic specialization and its conventionality. The transformed structure of literary detection results in a story that achieves only temporary closure, with all loose ends tied up but no substantial goals achieved. As a result the detective story declines the opportunity to be anything other than itself, *The Red Thumb-Mark* to adopt a philosophical or *The Judas Goat* a racial theme, or *The Main* to conform to the practices of real-life police work. There are, as any veteran reader knows, detective novels that undertake themes related to race, gender, and other social questions, but they are usually secondary to the business of detection; the formula still favors the low-stress story not tied to any goal beyond hermeneutic preoccupation (Kermode *PM* 185).

The movement of play "renews itself in constant repetition" (Gadamer *TM* 103). In detective fiction, this repetition generates the conventionalization that is part of the formula and that consequently demands a reading that is unlike that of other genres. The reader adapted to the transformed play-pattern will have a considerably different reaction to the appearance of a familiar convention than will one to whom renewal is unfamiliar. A veteran reader is quite comfortable with the reappearance of the familiar Sherlock Holmes formula (as in the case cited earlier, the revival of the *Sign of the Four* plot in *The Red Thumb-Mark*), while a neophyte may be bored by the apparent borrowing.[28] As the reader will see later in this study, one of the most striking qualities of a detective story convention is its persistence: occasionally one will wear out (like the justice thwarted theme that was so popular during the Golden Age but has substantially disappeared today), but most have a capacity for reusability that makes them recyclable (the death warrant, for example, or the dying message).

Because of its capacity for renewal in repetition and its subsequent conventionalization, transformed play itself does not conclude but expresses itself rather in a set of conventions that are almost "endlessly repeatable" (Hall and Whannel *PA* 57). The dissipation and self-destruction that is part of the mode of detective fiction (Grossvogel *MIF* 15) is part of the process of renewal, which in the case of a formulaic genre like detective fiction continues through a process of variation upon a practically inexhaustible store of familiar themes (Cawelti *AMR* 10). As a result, the repeatability of the conventions of the tale of detection do not, for the experienced reader, become outmoded but are met and celebrated at each recurrence like the return of a familiar festival (Gadamer *TM* 121-22).

At several points in the preceding pages I have referred to the problem of the seriousness of the detective story as transformed play, including the question of whether various narrative elements (the challenge to the reader, for example) can be taken seriously. Mere play, says Gadamer, meaning untransformed play, is not serious, but it has a special relation to what is serious. The "serious" side of existence gives play its purpose, as when we play for recreation. More important, "play itself contains its own, even sacred seriousness. Yet, in playing, all those purposive relations that determine active and caring existence have not simply disappeared but are curiously suspended." Play is most effective when the player "loses himself in play," or shifts into the spirit of the game. "Someone who doesn't take the game seriously is a spoilsport," because seriousness is necessary in order to make play wholly play (101-02). The seriousness of the tale of detection is the seriousness of play, and it is assumed as part of the reading mode. A reader who fails to make this adjustment might be alarmed by the fact that any case taken to Philip Marlowe, whether blackmail, disappearance, theft, or whatever, is sure to involve a murder before many pages have passed. Such a reader would ruin the story by taking it too seriously; at the opposite extreme is Gadamer's "spoilsport," who refuses to get into the spirit of the game and becomes annoyed by the fact that the most likely suspect is almost never guilty or that a dying victim can leave behind a message so complex that the best efforts of the detective are required, over a hundred or so pages, to work it out.

The reading of a detective story, then, proceeds with a twofold assurance. On the one hand, it is relieved of the stresses of reality, by the genre's refusal to go beyond the bounds of transformed play, and by the freedom of acceptance or rejection of tasks offered in the process of narration.

On the other hand, the reading is disciplined in much the same sense as an organized game is disciplined, by a formula that has remained basically unchanged since its inception and by the special demands of the hermeneutic mode. The natural parallel is a game of solitaire, in which a player enjoys the greatest relaxation by voluntarily submitting to a set of conventions which are optional but which offer the greatest freedom when they are followed most conscientiously.

Most of the remainder of this book will be predicated on a conception of conventionality and hermeneutic specialization as the structure of detective fiction, its shape, form, and the totality of its relationships. This is the structure that overrides every other influence on the writing and reading of the detective story. The basic member of the equation is the reader: because of the economics of the popular market, it is the reader who determines success or failure and who therefore exerts a decisive influence on the evolution of the genre itself. Reader preferences naturally influence the development of any popular fiction but, as a result of the guidance of the play structure, it has resulted in what amounts to a covenant between readers and writers of detective fiction. In chapter 4 I will develop the notion of the detection genre as essentially conservative, much more ready to retrieve old conventions than to adopt new ones.

This conservatism results from the fact that the protecting wall of transformed play was built into "The Murders in the Rue Morgue," and it has directed the development of detective fiction for more than a century and a half. Gadamer's three elements are there in abundance. Poe opens his story with a straight-faced discourse on the faculty of analysis, then asks his reader to accept the absurd proposition that the Paris police had in their investigation overlooked all the vital clues in the case, thus overlaying the stresses of reality with a liberal application of fantasy. Tasks there are in abundance, most of them centered around the problem of the locked room. Finally, "The Murders in the Rue Morgue" is not tied to any special goal that would bring it to an end; its intention is "to create a mystery for the sole purpose of its effortless dissipation" (Grossvogel 15). And of course the pervasive influence of this story is evident in the number of conventions it established that are likely to be found in the most recent tale of detection on the market: the most likely suspect, the locked room, the assurance of resolution, and several others. Such repetition could soon become deadly elsewhere, but the hereditary structure of transformed play in the tale of detection protects it against banality. Like the players of any game, the readers of detective fiction welcome the old traditions as sources of security instead of resenting them as clichés.

In brief, the to-and-fro motion of play is transformed into the hermeneutic structure and conventionality of detective fiction, the optional tasks are transformed into the blanks of the text, and the absence of stress into the programming of the blanks. For purposes of illustration, we can turn to one of the best-known conventions of detective fiction, the locked room, which dates from "The Murders in the Rue Morgue."

The locked room is a conventional usage that has renewed itself in constant repetition until it has become a subgenre on its own, supplying the theme for a considerable number of detective stories, including such masterpieces as Doyle's "The Speckled Band," Leroux's *The Yellow Room,* and Zangwill's *The Big Bow Mystery.* Its repeatability is evident in that although it was developed and stylized in the classic tradition, it has proved quite successful in both the private-eye story and the police procedural. To a greater degree than in any other convention of detective fiction, the structure of the locked room is nonmimetic and contrived. It has no goals beyond pleasurable mystification; it is doubtful if many tears have been shed over the fate of Madame L'Espanaye and her daughter, because the concern of the reader is with the identity of the murderer and his means of escape from that well-locked apartment. The locked room has even developed a set of conventions of its own, some of them involving such ceremonies as the painstaking examination of the physical setting and the careful establishment of time limits.

Since the movement of play is not tied to any goal that would bring it to a conclusion, the game presents the player with tasks that add meaning to the activity. In the detective story, the availability of these tasks is transformed into the blanks of the text, a matter of some importance because of the hermeneutic specialization of the genre: the reader tries to tie each thing in, as Kermode says, asking how it "fits in" or how it will "turn out." In chapter 2 we will give some special attention to the significance of textual blanks, which in the detective story are not just spaces between segments but invitations to the reader to fill them. In the locked-room convention the blank takes the form of paradox: it is impossible for the murderer to have escaped the scene after the murders were committed, but that is exactly what has happened, and the invitation to the reader is to break the paradox and resolve the mystery. The problem is defined with a great deal of care and quite often with considerable ceremony. Traditionally, the author takes the reader on a tour of the physical premises, to confirm the absence of hidden staircases, "priests' holes," or other means by which the murderer might have effected an escape. Equally thorough is the validation of the time limits: all evidence is that the victim was alive and well when the area was sealed and mystifyingly dead when it was opened. The locked room is an especially good illustration of the transformed task, because the blanks in the story are not only mystifying but may be programmed at more than one level. A part of the programming of the ceremonial validation in the locked-room story is that the author can lead the reader to look in the wrong direction. It may develop that the room was not really "locked" (as it was not in "The Murders in the Rue Morgue"), or that the victim was already murdered when the room was sealed (as in Van Dine's *The Canary Murder Case*), or not dead when it was opened (*The Big Bow Mystery*). The reader is usually surprised at the ending of Poe's story, having been diverted by the heavy bar on the door and the height of the window from the courtyard, overlooking the fact that whereas the room

was indeed "locked" to a human being it was not so to the orangutan. The extra layer of programming also applies to the stories in
which the time limits are breached: the blanks of the text are
loaded with distractions intended to confuse the reader's perceptions of cause and effect.

In the locked-room story, as elsewhere in the detection genre,
the absence of stress is transformed into the programmed blanks
of the text. The programming itself is not textual, but its structure
is easily recognizable to the reader who has had some experience
with the convention. The reader can begin with the generic
expectation that the absolute paradox is false, and that it will be
broken. The experienced reader moves through the story with a
sense of assurance: he or she can decline the invitation to fill in
the blank, with the expectation that it will be filled regardless.
One who accepts, however, has access to a store of context that
adds meaning to the interpretation. The experience of "The
Speckled Band," for example, would undoubtedly be affected by
an earlier reading of "The Murders in the Rue Morgue," another
story involving a nonhuman agent. Most readers, however, prefer the opportunity for full hermeneutic participation, staying
with the story to find how it will turn out, instead of solving it
themselves.

The movement of play, says Gadamer, is "repeatable and
hence permanent" (110). Transformed into the structure of fiction,
this repetition tends to become a guide to the anticipations the
reader brings to the story; in detective fiction, much more persistently than in any other type of novel, that structure not only
guides but governs the anticipations of the reader (Kermode *PM*
181). During the remaining chapters of this book, reader expectations and their effect upon meaning, a topic of supreme importance in the reading of a strongly formulaic genre like detective
fiction, because of the influence of context (the memory of what
has been read) upon future reading. We have just witnessed, in
the locked-room formula, the strength of the reciprocal effect of
experience and context: experience generates context, which in
turn becomes a guide to future experience.

Because the perspective of this study is somewhat atypical, I
will offer a set of statements, some of which have been partially
developed, as a "platform" for the theses explored in this book.

One concept basic to almost every aspect of this study is the
idea of *context*, which will have a broader application here than in
most books. The context of a detective story includes not only the

text in the reader's hand but all previous reading, especially in the detection genre, together with the reader's preconceptions of structure, conventions, and rules. The reader approaches the detective story with much of the context already supplied, including certain expectations that are effective before the book is opened. Anyone about to read a private-eye story, for example, can expect the detective protagonist to be the narrator, especially if the book was written after 1950.

What a reader expects of a detective story is guided by his or her previous experience with detective fiction, and these expectations very largely determine what the reader "gets out of" the story. One of these expectations is that literary detection shares the structure of transformed play. Its intention, like that of play, is the elimination of potential stress elements during the reading of the story. It invites, but does not require, the reader to perform certain tasks associated with the narrative; it tends to avoid social and philosophical themes; and it is dominated by conventions, which renew themselves through continual repetition. This concept explains why people read stories involving violence and other threats to the social order in order to relax.

Detective fiction is structurally a conservative genre, and its conservatism is that of the game. Its rules are not mere constraints but are necessary to permit the game to be played. One such rule is that the story must include a resolution, and any writer undertaking a tale of detection in which there is no resolution, even an implied one, would soon lose an audience composed of detection fans.

The "differentness" of detective fiction is structural, and its deep structure, like that of organized play, is shaped by convention. As a result, the detection genre is generous toward the introduction of new themes but conservative with respect to the conventions of structure. The themes of contemporary detective stories are considerably different from those of a century ago, but the structure has remained unchanged. Today the detective is likely to be a woman, and she feels more at home in the downtown of a large city than in an English country garden. The structure of the story, however, is unchanged: it mandates that it is still *her* story, and no one else in the novel can fill her role.

The detection formula is the product of reciprocal transformation at the generic level. It is dynamic and self-regenerating, as a result of the genetic "code" that was built into it by Poe in the Dupin stories. In addition, the genre is shaped by the preferences of readers; that is, the detection formula is the total of all readers' horizons of expectations. Thus, there is mutual feedback between reader and genre; the individual reader's perception of the genre affects the personal horizon of expectations, which in turn affects future development of the formula. The convention of the expanded commission, which will be discussed in chapter 5, is an example of the relative influence of the "real" sense and the "detective story" sense: the perception of the real world is that a private detective is never called in to investigate a murder, but the expectation of the detection fan is that murder is essential to a tale of detection. Mutual feedback produces the generic convention, which is that the private detective is called in to find a missing person or recover a lost article, but a murder is sure to occur before long.

The reading of a detective story is mediated by a set of norms shared by reader and author. The aggregate of these norms becomes a point of reference or "regulative context," which is common to dyadic conversation but absent from most other fiction. One of these norms is the standard of fair play: the author will avoid such devices as the twin brother from Australia, for example, or the spectral solution.

The detection genre supplies its own intentionality: for the most part, the purpose of a given detective story is not exclusively the author's purpose, nor is it imposed upon the story by the reader alone. Primary intention in detective fiction can be stated in terms of hermeneutic expectation: it is prospective rather than retrospective, and the reader's fundamental aim is to reach the outcome of the story, not to assemble and organize plot elements or to interpret symbolic meanings. The experienced reader develops an almost unconscious feel for the standard plot of a detective novel, sensing intuitively, for example, the transition from the period of despair to the dawning light.

In all fiction, the blanks and gaps are *structured:* they stimulate the reader's thought processes. In the special case of the detective story, they are also *programmed:* they carry a set of heuristics, familiar to the reader, for the filling of a blank or gap. The concept of programming is intrinsic in the detection formula as one quality that differentiates the reading of the detective story from that of any other fiction. In a crime story, for example, the calling in of a private detective to locate a missing person should stimulate the reader to speculate on the detective's course of action and chances of success, but in a detective story the reader can be reasonably assured that the missing-person case will later evolve into a murder case.

Since the critical viewpoint of this study is based on the interpretation theories of Gadamer, Iser, and Jauss, I will devote chapter 2 to a brief summary and review of reception theory/ reader-response criticism, with special attention to the influence of Gadamerian hermeneutics upon contemporary criticism. Chapter 3 will deal with the general idea of formula or genre, especially the detection formula. I will discuss the standard concept of genre as form, then move to a consideration of the special case of the detection formula, as play transformed into structure. Chapter 4 will address the dynamics of the evolution of popular formulas and the special conservatism of the detection genre. In chapter 5 I will examine the one really significant instance of evolution of the detection formula, the hard-boiled (private-eye) novel. Chapter 6 will focus on the programming of the blanks in a detective story, in addition to the normal structuring common to the blanks of all fiction. In the final chapter I will undertake the application of these theoretical concepts to the special process of reading a tale of detection.

2

Reception Theory and the Hermeneutics
of Detection

If there has been a single consistent trend in the history of western criticism during the past half century, it has been a shift of focus from text to author to reader as the primary agent of interpretation. Literary theory during the 1930s and 1940s was dominated by the New Critics, whose aim was to endow interpretation with much of the objectivity and reliability of the natural sciences; this aim was to be achieved through a close reading of the text alone, without regard to historical period or author's purpose. I.A. Richards, in *Practical Criticism*, reduces the method to a handy tool for students of poetry, by proposing the four kinds of meaning (sense, feeling, tone, and intention) as criteria for interpretation.[1] E.D. Hirsch (*Validity in Interpretation*) approves Richards's insistence upon correct understanding,[2] but his step away from the New Criticism is his own postulation of the author's intention as the real object of interpretation. "No previously known normative concept other than the author's meaning" says Hirsch, has its "universally compelling character" (25). Hirsch does not discuss the role of the reader as interpreter, except for a curt dismissal of "what is loosely termed a 'response' to the text" (7). In this view, interpretation consists entirely in answering the question, What was the author's purpose?

The past twenty-five years, however, have witnessed a growing conviction among critics that the meaning of a poem or story must reside in the reading experience itself rather than the exact wording of the text or the intention of the author. Those theorists loosely classed as "reader-response" critics argue that meaning is not discovered in the text but is generated by the reading of it.[3] The best known among them is Stanley Fish. When Fish writes about the reader's "making sense" in *Is There a Text in This Class?* he intends the word "making" to be taken literally[4] and a few pages later he shifts the intent of the reading process from its conventional sense to the *writing* of the text, in that the reader "writes" as he or she reads (171).

The area of basic agreement among reader-response critics is that meaning is not inherent in the text but is generated by the interchange between reader and text during the act of reading. Wolfgang Iser argues that reading is an act in which textual material is processed by the reader under the guidance of the text. The reader, moving through the text and seeking answers to questions, encounters areas of uncertainty that depend upon the reader's interpretation for their meaning, at the same time raising new questions to which the reader must seek further answers (*AR* 96, 107). Hans Robert Jauss defines his task as describing the manner in which the first reading of a text becomes the "horizon" for a second, interpretive reading (*TAR* 145). Jauss's development of the "horizon," by which he means the totality of knowledge of literary conventions and norms that direct the reader's future expectations, is probably his most significant contribution to reception theory.

The approaches of both Iser and Jauss are helpful in understanding what happens during the reading of a tale of detection, with the special exception that a strongly conventionalized, hermeneutically specialized genre like literary detection requires a distinctive reading "mode" that is at least partially controlled by the detection formula. To the dichotomy of text and reader, or author and reader, must be added a third party, the genre itself, which supplies its own intentionality.

The terms *reader-response criticism* and *reception theory* are really interchangeable: both Iser and Jauss are usually classed under the "reader-response" rubric, but they have been pioneers in the development of reception theory. *Reader-response* is an umbrella term broadly applied to a variety of critics who agree in their opposition to the idea that meaning is inherent exclusively in the text. Jane Tompkins has arranged the better-known members of this group on a continuum based upon the importance each assigns to the text in the reading process. At one end she places Iser, who insists upon the guidance of the text in the act of reading, and at the other Fish, who calls the objectivity of the text an "illusion" (Tompkins in *R-RC* 201). She does not place Jauss, but I would locate him somewhat toward the Fish-y end of the scale, on the basis of his treatment of the text in *Toward an Aesthetic of Reception.*

Any critical theory that recognizes the place of the reader in interpretation should be prepared to explain how the reader's experience is organized or "normalized" in order for the interchange with the text to take place. The problem is much simpler if the norms of reading are implicit in the intention of the author or the logic of the text, but the problem of reader-centered interpretation is pointedly stated by Hirsch when he says, "As soon as the reader's outlook is permitted to determine what the text means, we have not simply a changing meaning but quite possibly as many meanings as readers" (*VI* 213). Hirsch's identification of the problem as one of validity, it should be noted, assumes a single valid interpretation, a view not shared by reader-response critics.

Iser holds that interpretation is just beginning to discover the limitations of its own norms; the role of the reader has been heretofore neglected, in spite of general recognition of the fact that no text has meaning until it is read. Both the reader and the act of reading are part of interpretation: "The study of a literary work should concern, not only the actual text but also, and in equal measure, the actions involved in responding to that text" (*AR* 20-21). In the interchange between text and reader, the signals to the reader may be incomplete, so that "something has to be imagined which the signs have not denoted—though it will be preconditioned by that which they do denote." The reader is compelled to transform denotation into connotation, and the signified becomes the signifier.

The example with which Iser illustrates these views is the character of Squire Allworthy in *Tom Jones*, where the signifiers (Allworthy's reputation for perfection) are in conflict with the signified (Allworthy's lack of judgment). The signifiers do not add up to perfection but designate conditions whereby perfection is to be conceived (65-66). The secondary meanings produced by this process introduce the necessity for some reading for implied meaning, a matter of considerable importance in the definition of the detection genre, where secondary meanings are often more important than the apparent ones.

The idea of secondary or implied meaning, which is at the heart of reader-oriented criticism, is also essential to the understanding of the detection mode. Iser assigns priority to this kind of meaning with respect to intentionality and reader expectations. He cites Husserl 's phenomenological conception of the effect of expectations (Husserl significantly calls them *preintentions*) on the reading process, which not only anticipate what is to come but actually bring it to fruition. The process needs the reader's imagination to give shape to reader-text interaction, which is not so

much "the fulfillment of the expectation as a continual modification of it." In this fashion, the reader's expectations determine
how the text will be normatively understood (Iser in Tompkins *R-
RC* 53).

Through experience, the reader of detective fiction develops a
feel for the structure of the detection formula, which is basically
that of transformed play. This structure expresses itself as a series
of expectations within the intentionality of the formula; these
expectations are preintentions, as Husserl calls them, in the sense
that they not only guide the reader in recognizing the detection
structure but also shape his interpretation of it. In the next chapter
we will have a great deal to say about convention building and
conventionalization, but a simple illustration should be sufficient
here. In a succession of detective stories, a theme is so regularly
repeated that it is no longer noticed as a theme but becomes part
of the structure of the genre, shaping, guiding, directing future
reading. The effect of preintention can be illustrated by the interchange between the reader and the text of a detective story upon
the appearance of one of those stereotypical situations in which
the genre abounds. When we read at the beginning of a story that
the detective is about to take a vacation, we are also able to imply
that murder or some other major crime will be committed just in
time to cancel that vacation. The theme becomes so natural that
we no longer feel it as theme; it becomes part of the structure,
which now guides the reader to perceive a secondary meaning
and to expect that the detective will not only miss the vacation
but will also solve the mystery.

The meaning of a detective story is not to be found in either
the author's intention alone or the interchange between text and
reader alone. That special meaning must include the detection formula, that is, the reader's *understanding* of that formula. Thus,
there will be no two interpretations of a given detective story
exactly the same, but no two widely different from each other.
When we say, however, that the reading of a detective story takes
place within the guidelines laid down by the detection formula
(or genre) we must be careful not to assume too much about the
reader's experience; what we are talking about is the reader's *perception* of that formula, born of reading experience. I will use the
term *individual genre* to designate this personal horizon, and an
understanding of its influence is necessary to complete the picture. Variations in reading are attributable to variations in selection and organization; Iser says two people look at the night sky,

and one sees the image of a plow, another a dipper. The stars in the sky of a literary text are fixed, but the lines that join them are variable.[5] The analogy is an apt description of the way a reader organizes or structures reading, but in a formulaic genre we must add the element of previous experience: the viewer will not see either a bear or a plow without having seen one before, just as an inexperienced reader will have no idea what is going to happen when a detective tries to take a vacation.

One of the determinative influences on reception aesthetics has been the interpretation theory of Gadamer, who taught both Iser and Jauss at Heidelberg. One can gain an idea of the nature and scope of that influence in a brief discussion of the literary implications of phenomenology and philosophical hermeneutics.

In an oft-cited statement in *Truth and Method*, Gadamer rejects the ideal of "objectivity" of both the New Criticism and author-intention: "To try to escape from one's own concepts in interpretation is not only impossible but manifestly absurd. To interpret means precisely to bring one's own preconceptions into play so that the text's meaning can really be made to speak for us" (397). Thus the reader's participation, once excluded on grounds of "subjectivity," becomes a necessary partner in interpretation, along with text and author. Prejudice is thus not a hindrance to understanding but a condition of the possibility of understanding (Holub *RT* 41), partly because of the effect of "preintentions" and the reader's expectations. Gadamer's reliance upon the prestructured nature of understanding derives from his phenomenological position, which was to become his philosophical bequest to both Iser and Jauss.

Phenomenological theories of response are primarily interested in the relationship between the consciousness of the reader and the perceived text, and how an object "intends" to be perceived. They also undertake to describe ways readers apprehend texts by losing themselves to the writer's own way of perceiving reality (Beach, *TIRT* 19).

The three critics upon whose work we are depending most heavily in the present study should be classed as phenomenologists, on the basis of their positions with regard to reader expectations and the relative weight they assign to reader and text in the achievement of meaning. In general, the effect of phenomenology, with its reliance upon incompleteness, negativity, and expectation, is seldom absent from the work of Gadamer, Iser, and Jauss. Phenomenological literary theory has had a marked influence upon all three, as in Gadamer's elevation of subjectivity, Iser's reliance upon indeterminacy as essential in literary interpretation, and Jauss's treatment of the "horizon of expectation," which is derived from Husserl's phenomenology of perception (de Man, Introduction *TAR* xii).[6]

As we will see presently, the method of the phenomenologist, which assigns priority to such factors as indeterminacy, negation, "blanks" in the text, and the partnership between reader and text in generating meaning, is eminently suitable to the interpretation of detective fiction.

Phenomenological literary criticism, as Suleiman points out, is necessarily centered on reading, or "aesthetic perception"; the phenomenological approach concentrates on the mental processes that occur as a reader advances through a text and "derives from it—or imposes on it—a pattern." The reader's activity, then, is centered upon an effort to make sense of the text, through "the complementary activities of selection and organization, anticipation and retrospection, the formulation and modification of expectations in the reading process." That the reader not only derives a pattern from the text but may also *impose one on it* raises the problem that is central to any phenomenological approach to reading, the relationship between the text and the individual realization of it, which introduces the whole possibility of idiosyncrasy in interpretation (*RinT* 22-23).The problem of the relationship between text and realization suggests the question of the degree to which the reader's store of earlier experiences affects the act of realization, and this question brings us to the matter of *programming*, an issue vital to the discussion of any strongly formulaic genre like detective fiction.

Phenomenological criticism supplies at least one justification for the concept of the programming of the blanks in the text, which will be examined in some detail in chapter 6. There are, says Suleiman, numerous statements in Iser to suggest that the reader's participation in filling in the blanks is programmed by the text itself, so that the pattern the reader creates for the text is "foreseen and intended by the author." One critical difference between the theme of the present study and Iser's argument is that Iser considers programming to be occasioned by the text (i.e., by the author's intention) (25). In chapter 6 we will see how, in detective fiction, programming cannot be realized in text or author alone; the major partner is the individual genre, the reader's own perception of the formula, which conditions the signals of the text into guides or expectations for further development.

The possibility of idiosyncratic interpretation is largely eliminated by the intervention of the individual genre; the text supplies signals, which the reader "realizes" or "makes sense of," in terms of what the reader already knows. In the reading of detective fiction, idiosyncratic interpretations are simply blocked out; no experienced reader will, for example, interpret Doyle's "The Red-Headed League" as an antibanking tract.

A reader undertaking to realize any text is concurrently formulating and being guided by expectations of what is to come. The function of these expectations and their formulation is central to any reader-centered criticism; it is also, as Horton says, one point at which the phenomenologist diverges from the method of the reader-response critic. For the reader-response critic, the experience of expectation is the whole meaning of reading, but for the phenomenologist it is only one step in a complex process that leads to meaning, "which is the accurate perception of the whole text." In the reader-response model of interpretation, the reader is kept busy being surprised and entertained, but the phenomenologist provides a different kind of job during the reading experience. For the phenomenologist, the reader is not occupied with forming expectations about how particular segments will work out but is rather employed with projecting a vision of what the whole text is, on the basis of each part (26).

One of the themes of the present study is that, particularly in detective fiction, the realization of any text is directed by the synthesis of reading experience, which Husserl calls "retentions" (memories, recollections), with present perceptions and expectations, Husserl's "protensions." The reader moving through the text develops a store not only of isolated recollections of events and impressions but of rules, structures, conventions, ethics, and the like (retentions), which become the reader's perception of the genre and which intervene in future expectations of texts (protensions). (*AR* 111). This influence is especially strong in the reading of a genre like detective fiction, with its conventional usages and its constant reiterations of narrative material like variations on a familiar theme. Instead of being bored by these almost endless repetitions, the reader feels comfort and security within a framework of familiar expectations.

Husserl balances expectation off against recollection as components of an interplay that will eventually generate meaning in reading (Rappaport, *TLT* 153). Throughout the reading process, he says, there is a constant exchange between modified expectations and transformed memories; the text formulates neither the expectations nor their modification, nor does it specify how the connectability of memories is to be accomplished. This, as Iser shows, is the province of the reader, and we thus have a first insight into the process by which the reader's synthesizing activity enables the text to be translated and transferred to the reader's own mind (*AR* 111-12).

Basic to the Husserl's phenomenological interpretation is the conception of a constantly changing and shifting *horizon of expectations*, which controls reader receptivity (Berg, *TLT* 263). He argues that every moment of reading is "a dialectic of protension and retention, conveying a future horizon yet to be occupied, along with a past (and continually fading) horizon already filled" (*AR* 112). He thought that consciousness suggested horizons or fields of expectation, a pointing toward. Each sequence carries its own set of potentialities, which enable the reader to look in one direction instead of another, with a consequent redirection of perceptions (Rappaport *TLT* 153). Each new new perception answers expectations and arouses new ones (*AR* 111).

Because it represents a combination of conventionality and hermeneutic structure, the detective story is rich in examples of the influence of the horizon of expectations upon interpretation. One such horizon surrounds the convention of the FBI agent, a familiar figure in the American police story. As a result of past reading, the reader's image of the FBI man is that of an overbearing bureaucrat, probably slightly stupid. For anyone who has read Stout's *The Doorbell Rang*, the reader's reception of an FBI appearance in any new story is bound to be influenced by the memory of the humiliation of two overzealous agents by Wolfe and Archie Goodwin in that novel. Confronting a new manifestation of the convention, the reader will impose upon it the pattern gleaned from the former ones, and the resultant expectation is that the FBI man will be disgraced again. Lest we generalize too quickly, there are two cautions that must be remembered. The first is that every convention is subject to variation, with the result that the appearance in a new story may not meet the reader's expectations: the new agent could prove to be unexpectedly congenial and reasonably intelligent. The second is that no two readers will respond to any convention in the same way, because the reception of the new appearance depends in large degree upon the memory retained from past experience. Finally, I want to stress the importance of horizons of expectation in the theory of popular formulas and the evolution of popular genres, which will be discussed in some detail in chapters 3 and 4.

Because Gadamer is best known for his contributions to philosophical hermeneutics, and especially because I will also be using the word *hermeneutic* in another sense during the rest of this book, some distinction must be made between the two.

Philosophical hermeneutics is a theory of perception that can be defined as the "study of understanding, especially the interpretation of texts" (Divver, *TLT* 54). Horton explains that the hermeneutic model of interpretation assumes that understanding takes place within a circle, in which the parts (the text and the reader's experience of it) take on significance only when each is projected into a whole, and the whole becomes meaningful and susceptible to interpretation as a result of one's perception of the parts and the interrelationships among them (*II* 16). Gadamerian hermeneutics questions the meaning and value of the interpreter and his procedures, as well as those of the objects of interpretation. It is an activity of the mind in which subject, object, and mental process meet and act upon one another, with the result that the interpreting subject is affected by the object of interpretation, which is itself never the same for two interpreters (Stowe, *PM* 374).

Hermeneutic code, as applied to suspense fiction and frequently used in criticism of detective fiction, can be simply defined as the reader's need to find out what happens next. It is the code that impels the reader to move along toward the resolution, in contrast with the proairetic code, which guides the organization of plot elements (Culler, *SP* 203, 210). Sometimes the tale of detection is simply called a hermeneutic story, on the basis of the assumption, as Kermode says, that "it is possible to tell a story in such a way that the principal object of the reader is to discover, by an interpretation of clues, the answer to a problem proposed at the outset" (*PM* 179).

The difference between the two senses is apparent in the two essays just cited, both in *The Poetics of Murder*. Stowe, in "From Semiotics to Hermeneutics," treats the detective methods of Sherlock Holmes as an instance of semiotic analysis, and those of Philip Marlowe as Gadamerian hermeneutics. Kermode, in "Novel and Narrative," explains hermeneutic specialization in the detective-story sense.

Iser's major contribution to reception theory is his exclusive development of the place of indeterminacy in reading, an outgrowth of his views on the relationship between text and reader. Reading, according to him, is a dialectical process,[7] during which reader and text interact (Berg, *TLT* 259), and he consequently sees meaning as the result of that interaction, an "effect to be experienced," not an "object to be defined."

The product of that interaction is neither wholly text nor wholly the subjectivity of the reader, but a merger of the two (Holub, *RT* 82). Interpretation, says Holub regarding Iser, "does not entail the discovery of a determinate meaning in the text, but the experiencing of the work as this [interactive] process unfolds" (155-56).

The interactive process, however, does not provide a point of reference between text and reader, and there is consequently no way for the text to answer questions; the reader must accept the leadership of the text, and the reader's inability to "keep up" naturally creates an imbalance or "asymmetry" between the two. This asymmetry produces the states of indeterminacy basic to most of Iser's reading theory. An indeterminacy in reading is any part of the text that demands the reader's interpretation in order to have meaning; Iser discusses three types, under the headings of blanks, negations, and negativity. The asymmetry in the reading process is created by the circumstance that the reader is always a few steps behind the text, and the resulting opening is what Iser calls a "gap" between the positions of the two. This gap or blank, however, is not a vacuum: it has structure, suggests conflicting interpretations, and as a matter of fact depends upon interpretation for its effect. But these interpretations create further areas of indeterminacy. "The moment we try to impose a consistent pattern on the text, says Iser, "discrepancies are bound to arise" (Tompkins, *R-RC* 64).

The nature of indeterminacy can be illustrated by reference to almost any mystery story. Carol Higgins Clark's novel *Decked* opens with this sentence: "Athena ran blindly down the dark country lane, her breath coming in short, harsh gasps." The text is miles ahead of the reader, whose natural reaction is to ask, What is this? Who is Athena? What is she running from? What we want to notice, however, is that this opening sentence is not a vacancy: its structure is evident in the fact that it does automatically raise questions. It needs interpretation, but it also suggests conflicting interpretations, as witnessed by the fact that no two readers would answer the questions in the same way. Further along in the novel, private investigator Regan Reilly receives word from the police that another character has been poisoned: "'Penelope was poisoned?' Regan gripped the receiver, not believing what she had just heard. 'But how?'" At this point, a number of developments have taken place that give the indeterminacy a more sophisticated structure. Since the text has established itself as a mystery story, the reader will not now ask, What is this all about? but more likely, Who is trying to kill Penelope? The possible interpretations will also conflict with each other. One is that the person who poisoned Penelope is also the one who murdered Athena, but there is also the possibility that the poisoning was accidental (94).

The method by which the text exercises control over the dialogue between author and reader is one of the most important aspects of the communicatory process, according to Holub, and Iser assigns this regulatory function to the blanks of the text (*RT* 92). A reader moving through a story will encounter areas that leave open connections between viewpoints in the text and is consequently spurred to close those connections and fill them in so communication can take place. These areas are the blanks, and they stimulate the reader to attempt to balance the asymmetry between text and reader. Blanks cause readers to make frequent switches between what they already know and what they expect from the reading; blanks regulate and organize connections and have a selective influence on the meaning produced by the reader's mental processes (*AR* 212).

Detective fiction abounds in these "areas of suspended connectability," which can be illustrated by any situation where the reader is excluded from what is going on, or where questions are raised that can not be answered immediately. Sometimes a detective novel begins with a blank, like the opening sentence of *The Nine Tailors*: "'That's torn it,' said Lord Peter Wimsey." In order for the text and reader to communicate, the reader needs to know first of all what "that" is, and why it has "torn it." The asking of those questions is the first step in bringing the perspectives of text and reader into balance with each other. The terms set by the text in this case must include the knowledge that, since this is the first sentence in the story, it must have some special significance. What is already known to the reader is that when Lord Peter says "That's torn it" he means "That finishes it," and that, since this is a detective story, one must always be on the lookout for programmed meanings and concealed suggestions.

The reader will also be frequently challenged by another "area of indeterminacy," in which familiar elements are invoked only to be canceled out; what is canceled remains in view, however, and brings about modifications of the reader's attitude toward the familiar. These areas are *negations,* and, like blanks, they control the process of communication. Negations situate the reader halfway between "no longer" and "not yet," and thus guide him or her to adopt a position in relation to the text. The reader is challenged to reconcile the old negated meaning (the "no longer") with the new one (the "not yet"), which returns to the conscious mind and is superimposed upon it; in order to assimilate the new meaning, the reader also needs the old one, because this old meaning has been changed by negation back into the material out of which new meaning is fashioned (Iser, *AR* 213). Negation dominates Patricia Wallace's *Deadly Devotion,* in which private investigator Sydney Bryant is engaged by a defense attorney to prove the innocence of Keith Reilly, who has been all but convicted of double murder. For most of the story, the reader is placed in a position midway between the "no longer" (the assumption of Reilly's guilt), and the "not yet" (proof of his innocence). The challenge to the reader is to break the paradox presented by the necessity of accepting irrefutable evidence, as opposed to the necessity for success by the detective protagonist. But, as Iser says, in order to assimilate the new meaning (innocence) the reader also needs the old one (the evidence), because the old evidence of guilt has been changed by negation into the material out of which proof of innocence can be fashioned, as we can see in Sydney's repeatedly asking herself, "What am I missing? What can't I see?" (144).

Blanks and negations are the missing links that permit the imbalance between text and reader to be balanced out. Text and reader begin to converge, allowing the reader to experience unfamiliar reality. Thus, the formulated text has an unformulated "double," somewhat like the "unwritten text," which Iser calls "negativity" (*AR* 225-26).

"Unlike negations and blanks, which receive specific formulation in the text," says Holub, "negativity cannot be defined or precisely determined. It is like the deep structure of the text, an organization principle whose 'abstract manifestations' the reader perceives" (95). Negativity exerts a two-fold influence on the act of reading: it initiates the interaction "whereby the hollow form of the text is filled by the mental images of the reader," and it conditions the formulations of the text by enabling the written words to transcend their literal meaning. It is, says Iser, "the basic force in literary communication." Negativity becomes the infrastructure of a literary text as a result of surface signs of a hidden cause, like the signs that alert the reader to an unformulated cause in literature (*AR* 225-26). Negativity makes possible the comprehension that comes about through the reading process; it enables the reader to perceive hidden or implied meanings. It traces out the nongiven by organizing things into meaningful configurations; the individual viewpoints of the text have meaning only when linked together. Negativity, then, is the blank sheet on which the "not yet" text is written by the reader, with the guidance of the "no longer" text; it is that which has not yet been comprehended. It involves both question and answer, and it thus becomes the condition that allows the reader to construct the meaning of the text on a question-and-answer basis. This process provides the meaning of the literary text with its unique quality, as the reverse side of what the text has presented.

Iser's characterization of negativity as the basic force in literary communication is specifically applicable to the understanding of detective fiction, with its special dependence upon the presence of unfilled space and formulaic guidance. Detective fiction is particularly rich in "doubles," which can occur at any point where the meaning in the printed text is not nearly so significant as the secondary meaning, and the reader is consequently invited to read between the lines. One such occasion occurs early in *Decked*, where Athena's friends, unaware of her murder, think only that she has run away from school and is still missing. "Wouldn't you think she'd at least send a postcard?" one asks, but the reader's unformulated double is already perceiving a structure that points to Athena's death (17). In a stylistic sense, negativity is an end-of-the chapter device, whereby, as Iser says, "the hollow form of the text is filled by the mental images of the reader." Much later in the novel, when the finger of suspicion is beginning to point to the man of mystery mentioned earlier as Athena's murderer, a woman claims to have seen him in Greece, although he denies ever having been there. "When was that, Veronica?" one of the other characters asks, and the reply, "Eleven years ago,"closes the chapter. It does not, however, close out the ideations of the reader, who traces out the nongiven by organizing things into meaningful configurations: it was just eleven years ago that Athena was murdered. Now the reader's "double" comes into play, reading between the lines for that secondary meaning, which surpasses the printed text in significance.

We now move on to the special treatment of the text that has set Iser apart from the other reception theorists, but I should first at least mention what he says about reciprocal transformation, which is one of the most important links in the interaction between reader and text. During reading, says Iser, two things take place. First, there is a constant "feedback" of information already in the reader's possession; second, and importantly, there is also an inevitable insertion of the reader's own ideas into the process of communication (*AR* 67). This feedback is what Iser calls *reciprocal transformation,* which modifies the influence of the reader's viewpoint. As a result of the switching and reciprocal conditioning of the reader's viewpoint, the feedback produces a vehicle for interpretation. "In this sense, the vacancy [i.e., indeterminacy] transforms the referential field of the moving viewpoint into a self-regulating structure, which proves to be one of the most important links in the interaction between text and reader" (201).

Reciprocal transformation is basic to the reader's individual perception of the genre, which is the real guide to the reader's interchange with the text, especially in formula fiction. This "individual genre" is more than just a storehouse of plots, characters, and effects; it is also the summation of the reader's reactions to books read.

Before one can adequately deal with Iser's treatment of the role of the text in the act of reading, we need to review what he says about the way in which the interchange between reader and text is accomplished, or the process by which the signals of the text are organized into meaningful structures. The approach, says Suleiman, is a phenomenological one, which seeks to describe and account for the mental processes a reader experiences while advancing through a text and deriving a pattern from it or perhaps even imposing one on it. "The act of reading is defined as essentially a sense-making activity, consisting of complementary activities of selection and organization, anticipation and retrospection, the formulation and modification of expectations in the course of the reading process" (*RinT* 22-23). The reader "realizes" or "concretizes" the text, says Iser, in order for the translation to take place. The process of realization is dependent upon the fact that the text can never be understood as a whole but only as a series of changing perspectives, each of which is restricted in itself and so necessitates additional perspectives. The creation of these additional perspectives is the process by which the reader realizes the work as a whole. Thus, text and reader converge by way of a situation which depends upon both for its realization (*AR* 68).

For Iser, as for all response and reception theorists, the act of reading is an interchange between text and reader, but for Iser most especially the text is the senior partner, the guide, the pacesetter. Texts are written to be read, and they dictate the terms of their readability (Holub, *RT* 90), and we are reminded that reading is a one-way street that runs like the direction of the text, from beginning to end (Iser *AR* 222).

The text is always out in front of the reader, and the resulting gap between their positions produces the indeterminacy that has so marked an effect upon subsequent reading.

The text-reader relationship, involving a continuing mutual modification, is dominated by the reciprocal transformation mentioned earlier. Reading is an activity that is guided by the text," says Iser; ". . . this must be processed by the reader, who is then, in turn, affected by what he has processed" (*AR* 163). Elsewhere, commenting on the subjectivist element in reading, he points out that the experience of the text is brought about by an interaction that is neither private nor arbitrary. "What *is* private is the reader's incorporation of the text into his own treasure-house of experience . . . " and "the aesthetic effect results in a restructuring of experience" (24).

Two of Jauss's contributions to reception theory are of special interest in the study of the reading of the detective story, his "horizons of expectation" and his conception of the development and nature of genres. Since the two ideas are interlocked (expectations create genres and genres create expectations), I will attempt to develop them together. Expectations are born of experience, and the expectations created by a first reading also become the "horizon of expectations" of future reading. The pattern holds when projected onto the level of the reading public: the expectations of the first audience become the familiar expectations of later readers. Jauss's horizon is a phenomenological concept, derived from Husserl's theory of perception. In familar terms, a horizon is a system of references or mind-set, a "range of vision that includes everything that can be seen from a particular point" (Holub, *RT* 59).

A book, says Jauss, even a completely new one, does not seem new but predisposes its audience to a specific kind of expectation. It awakens memories of past reading and arouses expectations that can be maintained or altered "according to the specific rules of the genre or type of text." A corresponding process of continuous establishing and altering of horizons also determines the relationship of the individual book to the succession of books that compose the genre. A new text evokes for readers the "horizon of expectations and rules familiar from earlier texts" which are then altered, varied, corrected, or just reproduced (*TAR* 23). Jauss's reference to the "specific rules of the genre" and "rules familiar from earlier texts" is especially significant, because *rules* in this sense refers to the reader's perception of the way things work, which can be carried forward from one reading to another and eventually form the backbone of the reader's understanding of the genre.

Just as the expectations of a reader become the context of future reading, so the expectations with which an audience meets a new book will supply a context for later readers. The disparity between a given horizon of expectations and the appearance of a new book Jauss calls "aesthetic distance," which is experienced by its first audience as either pleasing or alienating, and which "can disappear for later readers, to the extent that the original negativity [distance] of the work has become self-evident and has itself entered into the horizon of future aesthetic experience as a henceforth familiar expectation" (25).

The history of American detective fiction during the 1920s, '30s, and '40s supplies a clear enough example of the principle. Hammett's novels arrived on the scene with a considerable aesthetic distance from the old horizon of expectations. With the passage of time, and with further development and reinforcement by Chandler and others, this distance closed, until today the hard-boiled novel is well within the horizons of most readers.

As was pointed out earlier, negativity, indicating "distance" and roughly equivalent to "indeterminacy," is a key term in reception theory. For Iser it is the basic force in literary communication. He defines it as the "interaction whereby the hollow form of the text is filled by the mental images of the reader" (*AR* 225), and develops the idea a little further when he says that "the formulated text has a kind of unformulated double. This 'double' we shall call negativity. . . " (226). Negativity is not in the text, but is generated by the interaction between text and reader. It is important to remember, especially in the interpretation of detective fiction, that a reader unaware of the strength of the detection formula, will miss most of this quality in reading the story.

Not surprisingly, negativity is a key idea in detective fiction; the principle is essential to a number of the unique qualities of the detective story, such as deliberate concealment and programming, but it can be easily illustrated by two fundamental qualities, the one we will be calling the efficiency principle, and conventionality. Simply stated, the idea of the efficiency principle is that the detective story does not waste words. The natural corollary is that the presence of any element in the text is presumed evidence of its importance. The "blank page of negativity" is created by the condition that the element must be important; the "double" appears when the reader asks, Why is the author doing this? This is what happens in the Chandler novel *The Long Goodbye*, where the narrator continues to return to the story of the presumably dead Terry Lennox, and any reader familiar with detective fiction will naturally wonder if there is not more to be told about Terry Lennox.

The force of conventionality in detective fiction is reflected in the predominance of such recurrent situations as the dying message, so familiar to any experienced reader, and therefore certain to create a negativity. The very presence in the text of some cryptic signal left by a murder victim opens an unformulated area when the reader recognizes the convention and projects an expected development, whereby the reader's "double" achieves reformulation.

In sum, negativity produces secondary meanings and implied meanings. The principle is illustrated in Sue Grafton's *G Is for Gumshoe*, where the plot switches back and forth between two unrelated stories, one a tale of detection and the other an account of a series of attempts on the life of the detective; each of these switches creates a negativity. During the murderous attempts against Kinsey Millhone, while the detection plot is on hold, the reader continues to make mental projections into the detective story, regarding possible connections, questions still to be answered, and developments taking place in the absence of the detective. The reader is experiencing, in Iser's words, the "unformulated double" that conditions the exchange between reader and text. In the reading of detective fiction the negativity is stronger and the process is made considerably more complex by the presence of the "detective story sense" or hermeneutic mode.

In his discussion of temporality in detective fiction in *What Will Have Happened*, Champigny takes some important steps toward clarifying the relationship between mystery and negativity. The question of What did happen? or What will happen? dominates most fiction, especially mystery, but the detective story adds another basic one, What will have happened? The reader needs to know not only the facts of the murder and what the solution will be, but also what is happening on that blank page of negativity.

As was explained earlier, the hermeneutic code of detective fiction must be distinguished from philosophical hermeneutics. The term in its detective story sense was apparently introduced by Roland Barthes in his analysis of five "codes" that govern the text in reading, which are defined by Culler as follows: 1) the "hermeneutic" involves the logic of question and answer, enigma and solution; 2) the "proairetic" governs the reader's construction of plot; 3) the "semic" provides models that enable the reader to collect semantic features; 4) the "symbolic" guides extrapolation from text to symbolic and thematic readings; 5) the "referential" is constituted by the cultural background to which the text refers (*SP* 203). These codes are not mutually exclusive; several or all of them may guide the reading of any given text. Almost any work of fiction will be guided by the hermeneutic code, in the sense that we usually want to know how the story will turn out, but in a novel like Waugh's *Brideshead Revisited* the need for closure may be overridden by the reader's need to assemble the elements of the plot in order to understand better the complex relations involved.

The point to remember here, though, is that the dominant-code (or better, *mode*) in the tale of detection is always the hermeneutic.

From here on, I will deal with the *hermeneutic mode* and abandon the term *code* as being too closely confined to the text. As Culler puts it, Barthes's five codes are "one of the voices of which the text is woven" (SP 202). A further reason for the substitution is that the idea of code in the interpretation of detective fiction neglects the importance of the play mode, the "humbug" element in the genre.

I will apply Kermode's term *hermeneutic specialization* to detective fiction in order to distinguish the special case of the detective story from other fiction, most of which has hermeneutic content. Champigny equates *mystery story* with *hermeneutic tale*, and makes closure (resolution) its chief criterion (*WWHH* 13). Most critics agree that the distinguishing feature of the detective

story is its resolution, the closure of a mystery that is both compelling and artificial. Champigny calls it a narrative secret, not a
conceptual mystery, and Grossvogel even more dogmatically
states that the mode of the tale of detection is to create a mystery
whose only purpose is to bring about its "effortless dissipation"
(*MIF* 15). The clearest and most comprehensive statement, however, is Kermode's, that it is "possible to tell a story in such a way
that the principal object of the reader is to discover, by an interpretation of clues, the answer to a problem proposed at the outset." All other conditions are subordinated to this interpretative or
hermeneutic activity (*PM* 179). In the detective story, says
Kermode, the reader is busy sorting out the hermeneutically relevant from all the other material, and doing so much more persistently than would be the case in the reading of other fiction (181).
Commenting on the special reader activity involved in Bentley's
Trent's Last Case, he significantly describes the novel as preemi-
nently a "hermeneutic game" (184).

A reader sorting out the hermeneutically relevant from other
information in the narrative asks of any new element how it "fits
in" or how it will "work out." In the most important statement in
the essay with reference to the reading of detective fiction,
Kermode says, "An important and neglected rule about reading
narratives is that once a certain kind of attention has been aroused
we read according to the values appropriate to that kind of attention, whether or not there is a series of definite gestures to prompt
us" (181). The phrase "certain kind of attention" applies with special force to the detection reading mode: the reader may be compared to the operator of a bimodal keyboard, who upon opening a
tale of detection punches the mode-button that will transform the
reception of signals in such a way as to modify interpretation,
with the result that the reader's responses will be somewhat different from those in other reading. In most fiction, for example, a
murder victim is the object of pity, but in the tradition of the
detective story he or she is usually either a hate-object or a nonen-
tity whose murder inspires not the slightest sympathy in the reader.

Closure (resolution) is the major criterion, says Kermode,
with all loose ends tied up and everything "fitting in" or "working out," all enigmas solved. Closure is "sacralized": to give away
the conclusion is to give away everything, "so intense is the
hermeneutic specialization" (180). The opinions of readers and
critics vary with regard to the sacredness of closure; all probably

want to be surprised at the end of the story, but some editors even take such extreme measures as a warning at the beginning of a review that the solution of the mystery is revealed in the upcoming paragraphs, not unlike the Surgeon General's warning against cigarettes.

As a matter of fact, Kermode continues, "hermeneutic preoccupation is dominant at the expense of 'depth'" (185). It should be remembered, however, that comments on the absence of "depth" in detective fiction and the corresponding employment of two-dimensional characters and artificial situations is an oversimplification of the immanence of transformed play as the structure of the detective story. The degree of "depth" in detective fiction is that of the game, and it is implicit in the compact between authors and readers.

Most of these principles can be illustrated by a look at Max Allan Collins's novel, *Nice Weekend for a Murder*, which is as pure a demonstration of hermeneutic guidance in detective fiction as one could wish. It is a remarkably complicated story, in which a dramatized "Murder Weekend" at Mohonk Mountain House is complicated by a real murder. The resultant double-exposure mystery-within-mystery offers a possibility for demonstration of "classic" method unusual for the present decade. Most noticeably, the strong self-referentiality of the novel, with hundreds of allusions to detective fiction and writers, never allows the reader to forget for a moment that this is, after all, just a detective story.

It would be difficult, as a matter of fact, to find a more challenging problem than the one that faces "Mal" Malory, himself a mystery writer and a participant in the Mystery Weekend at Mohonk. Malory, who witnesses what is to all appearances a staged murder but which he believes to be a real one, is forced to carry on his own investigation assisted only by his companion Jill Forrest. When they find the body of the real murder victim, Mal is prevented from going public by the fact that Mohonk Mountain House, in the best tradition of the English country house mystery, has been isolated by a snowstorm. Malory is requested by the police to carry on, but, in the interests of his and Jill's safety, not to reveal the discovery until the police are able to reach the scene.

Thus the hermeneutic drive, the reader's need to know the outcome, is stepped up to accommodate both the real and the play story. The novel is structured and programmed to such a degree as to permit only the domination of the hermeneutic mode, with the repeated raising of the questions, Why? and How does this fit in? as when Malory finds himself puzzled by the presence at Mohonk of the man cast in the role of Most Likely Victim in the play and also (as it develops) in the real-life murder: "What was he doing here?" Malory wants to know, receiving only the reply, "Beats me" (114). This victim, we should add, is such a perfectly type-cast bastard (he is a mystery critic) that his death disturbs no one and serves to relieve the crime of any possible stress, allowing the reader to push on toward what happens next. The dominance of the hermeneutic mode, the "detective story sense," is summarized by Jill when she tells Malory, "This isn't real life. It's Mohonk. More precisely, it's the Mohonk Mystery Weekend" (120).

The mode of the story is perceived easily enough by the experienced reader, who proceeds in the knowledge that in the detective story things are seldom as they seem and that the logic of the narrative is more likely to be the rationale of the game than the logic of normal problem solution. Cultivating Kermode's "certain kind of attention," the detective story addict becomes proficient at reading between the lines, perceiving the secondary meanings in which detective fiction abounds. "This was a great place for a murder," Malory says of Mohonk, an isolated mountain house heavy with Victorian atmosphere (11). The reader catches the irony much more easily than would be the case elsewhere, for the reason that the detection fan knows that murder is indeed upcoming because it is programmed into the formula. Between-the-lines skill manifests itself again when it becomes evident that Rath (the Most Likely Victim) has not left Mohonk as he was supposed to; the position in the story (page 56, about a quarter of the way through) strongly suggests that the time is just about right for murder. Later, when an avalanche of clues and other information seems overwhelming (136-37), the reader must perceive that in a classic story like this one, the truth should lie buried in here somewhere.

The need for closure, or resolution, which is implicit in all detective fiction, is an especially powerful stimulant in *Nice Weekend for a Murder*, as a result of the impulse to solve two mysteries, because the play mystery is almost as demanding as the real one. Besides the assurance that the mystery is always solved in a tale of detection, the hermeneutic mode also demands that the solution not be revealed until the end of the story and that it be achieved by the detective.

Nice Weekend for a Murder is two hundred pages long, and although Malory announces on page 176 that he knows the solution to the real murder, he does not even hint at its nature until four pages later. The revelation does not bring complete satisfaction, however, because the reader still needs to know the solution of the play murder, which has been made even more interesting by the presence of one of the hoariest conventions of detective fiction, the dying message, in this case a note in an apparently secret code typed by the victim just before his death. This mystery is not mentioned again for another twenty pages, but the reader's expectation is that it will be revealed, because any unresolved element in a tale of detection is unthinkable. Malory does at last disclose it, near the bottom of page 200, and the last loose end is tied up.

Reading in the detection mode, however, involves elements that are much broader and more complex than simple hermeneutic relevance. For a more satisfactory view of the reading of detective fiction, we need also to consider briefly the impact on the detection formula of transformed play, conventionality, and programming.

The presence of play transformed into underlying structure is especially visible in *Nice Weekend for a Murder*, which is set in a frame of play, the Mystery Weekend, with mystery writers as its main characters. The atmosphere of the occasion is such that murder is entertainment, provided by the murder game and received by the participants. As was noted a little earlier, the scene is relieved of stress by the fact that the victim (who, we want to remember, is murdered in both the play and the real plot) is so universally despised that his elimination is no tragedy to either the participants or the reader. The novel offers an abundance of tasks, the neatest of which is the dying message in the play murder, giving the reader something to work on while the story of the real murder proceeds toward solution. Finally, the story carries no social or cultural message beyond that of transformed play; the shutting out of the rest of the world by Mohonk's snowbound isolation has become a metaphor for the exclusion of society and its problems.

Nice Weekend for a Murder comes close to being a catalogue of conventionality, with the recycled stereotypes of the genre in greater abundance than is usual with detective fiction in the 1980s and '90s. Besides the most likely victim and the dying message, we encounter the veiled secret (not merely a mystery to be solved but one deeply and doubly concealed); the trapped detective (Malory is forced to solve the real murder in order to keep from being considered a fool); undue complexity (this book is in the classic Grand Style, as complicated as Berkeley's *Poisoned Chocolates Case)*; restricted detection (at the request of the police, Malory must solve the mystery without letting any of the other participants know that a real murder has been committed); the summary (a formal review of the situation, more for the benefit of the reader than that of the detective); the assembly of suspects (Malory calls the whole group together for revelation and explanation of the solution); and the expression on the face of the murder victim. This last one deserves comment as a demonstration of the perseverance of convention in detective fiction. Despite repeated demonstration that a corpse in real life has no facial expression except repose, faces of fictitious victims continue to present clues to the nature of their murders, as does Kirk Rath's: "His face was passive, not contorted," says Malory of the late critic (182). Any experienced reader of detective fiction can think of dozens of examples of these conventions, used hundreds of times by writers from Poe to the present. As we will see in chapter 3, the answer to the question of what keeps them from becoming deadly bores after so many repetitions offers a key to the interpretation of the genre.

In the development of his indeterminacy theory, Iser argues that the blanks of the text are structured; that is, they are given inferentiality and definition and so challenge a closing of the space between the position of the text and that of the reader. In detective fiction, the dominant conventionality of the genre will frequently not only define the blank but offer some suggestions (born of past reading experience) for its filling. When, for example, the proceedings at Mohonk are momentarily interrupted by Rath's yelling at somebody, "Go away!" the blank is structured by the question it raises, What's this all about? It is not, however, *programmed*, because it is not bound to any convention. We have already seen one example, in Malory's early observation that Mohonk would be a great place for a murder (11). Here the distance between the positions of text and reader indicates that the direction of the text is toward a murder, because convention demands a murder in a book like this one. The blank created by the presence of a convention like the dying message is almost automatically programmed: the experienced reader senses that the message will offer a deep puzzle, which will be solved before the end of the story, probably by the detective protagonist. The program does not give away the solution, but it does prepare the reader for one. This is one of the hallmarks of the detective story.

Most of these principles, including both Kermode's hermeneutics and my own modifications in terms of play, conventionality, and programming, can be summarized by reference to Iser's treatment of negativity, which is basic to hermeneutic interpretation in the detective story sense. The negativity of the text produces a "hollow form," which invites the creation of an unformulated text as a "double" of the formulated one (*AR* 225-26). The concept is especially applicable to detective fiction, where "what is revealed appears to be a sign for what is concealed" (227). The unsaid is often more important than the said, and the art of inferential reading becomes a necessary skill.

Throughout *Nice Weekend for a Murder*, the reader's attention is repeatedly drawn away from the unfolding story of the play murder and into the unformulated "double" of the real one, the solution of which is essential for Malory and Jill. In this story negativity is especially enhanced by the isolation of Mohonk, and the whole outside world becomes the unformulated "double" of the text, with the reader left to write on the "blank page of negativity" the reader's own speculations as to where Rath has gone or what the police are doing. The relationship between negativity and the hermeneutic mode is such that the drive to fill the void assumes precedence over all the other possible approaches to the interpretation of the text.

Before leaving this discussion of reception theory and hermeneutic specialization, we need to return briefly to the question of intentionality implied in Kermode's statement that in detective fiction "hermeneutic preoccupation is dominant at the expense of 'depth.'" He develops the idea more fully in his later parallel between two types of fiction. On the one hand there are those novels not written or read in the hermeneutic mode; such novels attempt to cope with "the world as it is, as it simply *is*, lacking all meaning but that signified in our texts." In contrast, there is the tale of detection, guided by "the simple hermeneutic expectation that it will *work out*, because it can only work out if we accept the false implication that the world itself is simply coded, full of discoverable relations and offering closure" (188).

Does its hermeneutic specialization deprive the detective story of any claim to seriousness? In Iser, lack of depth becomes lack of distance between the positions of reader and text. He develops much the same idea as Kermode's in his definition of "light reading" as that in which the expectations of the reader are so close to the position of the text as to preclude those negations that spur the reader to perform the operations basic to interpretation "Whenever negations can be so motivated that their final outcome need not transcend the reader's own disposition," he says, "there will be . . . little or no effect on that disposition; having to motivate negation constitutes the dominant strategy in certain types of fiction which we would normally classify as 'light reading'" (219).

What Kermode treats as preoccupations and Iser as dispositions can be stated in terms of the anticipations with which a reader approaches a book. The expectations of the detective-story reader are those of the game, where old values (right vs wrong) are negated by new ones (our side vs the other side). The reader willingly accepts preoccupation at the expense of depth, as Kermode says, along with the simple assumption that things will "work out" and that "the world is simply coded, full of discernible relations and offering closure." The game of Monopoly is a fair application of the principle. In a meaningful participation in that game, real-world value systems involving compassion and fair play must be negated by the simple intention to gain the monopoly and break the other players.

This is not to imply that a reader of detective fiction must be drained of all normal human affections, but rather that in the "detective story sense" reception of the signals of the text produces a different horizon from that of the real world, where most detectives are uninteresting people doing uninteresting work, where most murders are never solved, and where investigations of theft, blackmail, and missing persons rarely develop into murder cases.

The perspective of the text does not exceed that of the reader, because the detection text offers almost no expectations that transcend the reader's horizon: all the constitutive conventions of the genre are affirmed, and the text has little or no effect beyond a transitory confirmation or denial of the reader's own perception of the genre.

Nor should any of this be taken to imply that the detection formula is immune to innovation. When we turn to the discussion of the detection formula as an instance of genre as consensus, we will note that there are two kinds of literary conventions. The constitutive conventions are those that define the genre: the protagonist is a detective, the main plot is detection, and so on. The others are those that renew themselves in constant repetition and are subject to endless variation. The appearance of one of these may take the reader through a straight rehash of some traditional structure and thus only confirm the reader's perceptions, as in all those instances in which the most likely suspect proves to be innocent. There are some cases, however, that work a variation upon the theme by allowing the suspect to be guilty, with consequent modification of the reader's sense of the genre.

3

The Detection Genre

A genre can be defined simply as a group or class of works that meet a given set of expectations. A different kind of definition starts from the assumption that the generic horizon is not exclusively in text or reader but in the interchange between the two, whereby the reader responds to the signals of the text on the basis of expectations inherited from earlier reading experience.

For two somewhat different treatments of genre or formula in popular fiction, we will turn first to the work of John Cawelti, whose *Adventure, Mystery, and Romance* is widely regarded as the most authoritative work in the field, and to Jauss's chapter on genre in *Toward an Aesthetic of Reception*. Cawelti treats literary formulas as cultural products, which become conventional ways of "representing and relating certain images, symbols, themes, and myths" (20). Jauss considers a genre as a "preconstructed horizon of expectations," which can also be understood as a "relationship of 'rules of the game' to orient the reader's (or public's) understanding" (79). Each of these writers has important things to say about the relationship between the public and private reception of literary works; the difference is one of methodology, in that Cawelti attacks the problem as mass culturist, Jauss as reception theorist.

First, some clarification of the terms *formula*, consistently used by Cawelti, and *genre*, as in Jauss and others. A formula, says Cawelti, is a "combination or synthesis of a number of specific cultural conventions with a more universal story form or archetype," and this definition also fits the common meaning of genre. For purposes of Cawelti's discussion it makes no difference which term is used, so long as the meaning is clear (6-7). For the same reason, I will use the terms interchangeably. The difference is insignificant anyhow in the case of detective fiction, generally regarded as the most tightly formula-bound of all popular genres.[1]

Cawelti sets two parameters that have special relevance for this treatment of the detection formula. The first of these is the centrality of convention, as when he defines a literary formula simply as "a structure of narrative or dramatic conventions employed in a great number of individual works" (5). The other is his recognition of the possibility of uniqueness in a genre. A formula, he says, tends to define its own limits, which "determine what kind of new and unique elements are possible without straining the formula to its breaking point" (10). This latter principle is essential to the interpretation of detective fiction, which is more consciously self-defining and self-regenerating than other popular genres as a result of its having inherited its major structures from a single model. Recollection of this point could prevent a great number of unnecessary arguments over such questions as whether the detective should be a man or a woman, or whether a detective story must include a solution to the central mystery.

Jauss considers individual works and genres in the perspective of history, as when he speaks of the concept of continuity, "in which every earlier element extends and completes itself through a later one" (88). A genre in this sense can be defined in diachronic terms as "a trajectory of expectations" from a "tradition or series of previously known works" (79). In this way he assumes an ongoing reciprocal exchange between a genre and an individual work: a genre is defined in terms of the norms or horizons of the individual works that compose it, and the horizon of the genre in turn becomes the horizon of a new work: "A new work evokes for the reader . . . the horizon of expectations and 'rules of the game' familiar to him from earlier texts." These rules, we want to note, are not immutable; they can be varied, transformed, or even canceled out (88).

The same kind of reciprocal exchange of expectation and experience takes place between the genre and the individual reader. A theory of genres grounded in an aesthetics of reception, says Jauss, adds to the study of the relationships between a work and its audience, where the "historical system of norms of a literary public" can be reconstructed "through the horizon of expectations of a genre system that preconstituted the intention of the works as well as the understanding of the audience" (108).

Jauss's theory of genres supplies several useful guides to the understanding of the detection genre, as when he suggests that what he calls the "rules of the game" are preconstituted by past experience. Unfortunately, the term *rules* has acquired a negative context in detection criticism, as a result of the efforts of certain rules-makers in the early part of this century. S.S. Van Dine's "Twenty Rules," which are in reality nothing other than a statement of norms of success as Van Dine saw them, flatly prohibited a love-interest in the detective story and just as dogmatically stated that nothing less than a murder will suffice as the mystery for a book-length detective story, and Ronald Knox's canon forbade the introduction of a Chinese suspect into a story (Haycraft *AMS* 189-96). Jauss's rules have been abstracted from use *all* past experience of the genre, not just contemporaneously successful experience as in Van Dine and Knox.

As has been pointed out earlier, the purpose of any detective story is essentially determined by the detection genre. The intention of a work, says Jauss, is preconstituted by the horizon of expectations of a genre system. The principle applies with special force in the detective story, where both the purpose of the author in writing and the expectations of the reader in reception are dominated by the intentionality of the genre, which guides the compact between author and reader. Collins's *Nice Weekend for a Murder*, discussed in the previous chapter, is a book-length illustration of the point; the "reality" of that highly artificial setup poses no problems for an experienced author or reader, because it is imposed by the genre. For a more specific example, we can turn to Beck's *Amateur Night*, in which the direction of the whole plot is determined early in the novel by a single directive in a letter to Jane da Silva from her late Uncle Harold, who left her his money, subject to a condition: "My instructions to the trustees are very specific. The tasks you undertake must be difficult ones, for there is no real satisfaction, I have discovered, in anything that is too easy" (10). Again, there is no need to question the intention of the plot, because it has come into usage in our own time as one of a preconstituted horizon of expectations.

In any genre in which survival is directly dependent upon sales, the expectations of the reader determine the preintentions of the genre, and in detective fiction especially it is the paradigms of expectation that modify the interchange between reader and text, not only anticipating but bringing to fruition the method by which the text will be normatively understood. We can illustrate the effect by reference to a pattern in Arthur Upfield's *The New Shoe*, in which his Australian police detective Napoleon Bonaparte ("Bony") goes to a small seaside village to investigate a murder. During the investigation he spends considerable time in the shop of Mr. Penwarden, a master woodworker who prides himself upon his beautiful coffins. Early in the story he offers to make one for Bony (24), and during the ensuing pages that coffin is so insistently reintroduced that anybody may begin to wonder how it "fits in," but a reader aware of the efficiency principle in detective fiction will expect it to have more than casual significance. The expectation is fulfilled on page 200, when Bony almost loses his life in that coffin.

The reader of *The New Shoe* who next turns to Janet Dawson's *Take a Number* will find the same pattern much easier to recognize. In that novel Jeri Howard, approaching a murder scene, has a number of impressions of her surroundings, including that of a very angry face in the crowd gathered in the street. After several more references to that angry face, the reader is prepared to expect the same kind of structure as in the episode of Bony's coffin. What happens is that the preintentions of the genre determine those expectations that define the norms of the text (including, in this case, the necessity for inferential reading). In time a reciprocal effect or feedback is established, whereby expectations born of reading experience shape the gestalt of the genre, which will in turn define future expectations.

In Chapter 2, I asked the question, What keeps a convention from becoming a deadly bore after so many repetitions? The fact is, that devices like the Most Likely Suspect, who looks so overwhelmingly guilty early in the story but is almost always cleared before the conclusion, seem never to wear out. The reason contains a key to the "differentness" of the detection genre.

There are at least two explanations, one of which has its basis in the nature of detective fiction as transformed play. The conventions of the genre, according to this view, are vitalized in what Gadamer calls renewal via repetition, which in fiction is accomplished by variation on a theme. Jeri Howard's angry face eventually leads to the apprehension of the murderer instead of putting the detective in jeopardy, as does Bony's coffin. Variation on a theme, says Cawelti, is "one of the fundamental modes of expression in popular culture, as can be seen from the tremendous importance of performance in almost all the popular media." He uses the example of a revival of *Hamlet*, where there must some innovations to make the performance worth seeing, without lessening the quality of the original (10).

In his early essay on the concept of formula in popular literature Cawelti says that all cultural products contain two kinds of elements, convention and invention. The conventions are those elements already familiar to authors and readers, such as favorite plots and accepted ideas. Inventions are the products of the writer's imagination.[2] In this study we will treat the conventions as tradition, structure, those things that change very little if they change at all (the recurrent structure). The inventions are the variations, the innovations that give each story its special character (Bony's coffin and Jeri's angry face). The convention renews itself in constant repetition, but, as in the endless replays of hopscotch, it never becomes boring.

The second explanation is based upon a concept of convention as celebration; that is, each experiencing of a literary convention is the renewal of an old acquaintance, like a familiar holiday. Popular conventions, say Hall and Whannel, have three characteristics: they are known, accepted, and endlessly repeatable; it might be added that their endless repeatability is made possible by the fact that they are endlessly repeatable because they are known and accepted (PA 57). At least a part of the freedom from stress in detective fiction stems from its conventionality; we feel comfortable with what is already familiar. It is, says Gadamer, the "nature of a festival to be celebrated regularly. Thus its own original essence is always to be something different (even when celebrated in exactly the same way)" (TM 122-23). This is the reason why we greet the Most Likely Suspect as an old friend and wonder how the author will handle him this time, instead of yawning and putting the book aside.

As we have seen, expectations arise from earlier reading experience, and these expectations intensify our perceptions of conventionality. The realization of a book is directed by the synthesis of memories and recollections from past reading with present perceptions and expectations. Thus the reader develops a store of recollections, of not only events and impressions but also rules, structures, conventions, and the like. This store shapes the reader's perception of the genre and intervenes in future expectations of reading. Its influence is especially strong in a genre like detective fiction, with its conventional usages and constant reiterations.

The word *convention* is used in several different ways, resulting in no small confusion and dispute among critics. To distinguish between three types or levels of convention, there are , first, constitutive conventions, which define the genre and are essential to it (a poem that is not fourteen lines in length is not a sonnet, and a story that does not have a detective is not a detective story); second, regulative conventions, which characterize a genre but are not essential to it (there is almost always a murder in a detective story, but it is perfectly possible to have a detective story without a murder); and third—by far the largest in detective fiction—the recurrent stereotypes like the Most Likely Suspect, the Most Likely Victim, and the Death Warrant. *Convention* will be a blanket term here, covering all three classes.

The constitutive conventions of literature are not intended to limit the creative efforts of writers but rather to draw the boundaries of the genre. They serve much the same purpose as rule books for games, which, as Straus aptly puts it, "don't just regulate those games but create the very possibility of playing them" (*TLT* 215). For our purposes, there are only four in detective fiction, the "imperatives" of the genre: the protagonist is a detective, detection is the main plot, the mystery is an inordinately difficult one, and it is always solved. These four, like so much else in detective fiction, originated in Poe's "The Murders in the Rue Morgue."

The first of the imperatives is that the tale of detection is not just a story about a detective: it is *the detective's story*. From the moment he appears on the scene in "The Murders in the Rue Morgue" Dupin is not only the main character but also the prime mover of the action. The detective may be a strong personality like Sherlock Holmes, who dominates the story to the degree that his author found it almost impossible to keep him off the stage, or it may be a more modest figure like Marcia Muller's Sharon McCone, who is seldom quite sure of herself but whose centrality in the narrative is beyond question.

Second, the same degree of centrality has governed the nature of the main plot since the first of the Dupin stories: there is no competitor to the investigation of the strange business in the Rue Morgue. Some detective novels develop strong secondary themes (like the church lore in Dorothy Sayers's *The Nine Tailors* or the Wall Street lore in the novels of Emma Lathen), but these considerations may not overshadow the detection.

Third, the hermeneutic specialization of the genre demands that the mystery be not merely a problem to be solved but one deeply veiled and doubly wrapped.[3] The problem in the Rue Morgue was not a pair of run-of-the-mill murders of two women but a crime impossible to commit and hopeless to solve. Many of the older classics of detection involved incredibly complex problems (like the one in Anthony Berkeley's *The Poisoned Chocolates Case*, which is solved eight times), but the need for complexity was continued into the private-eye tradition: in Ross Macdonald's *The Drowning Pool*, Lew Archer must solve not only a case of blackmail but a murder, both deeply veiled.

Finally there is closure, which according to Kermode, is "sacralized": to give away the conclusion gives away everything,"so intense is the hermeneutic specialization" (*PM* 180). It is part of the intentionality of detective fiction that the only acceptable closure is solution of the mystery. The solution may be concealed from the police, or it may not even be known to the detective, but it must be known to the reader. Ed McBain's police procedural story *Ice* does actually end with one murder unsolved, but it is so minor a matter that most readers will not even notice (316-17). Stan Cutler shows how it is possible to push the bounds of genre even a little further in *The Face on the Cutting-Room Floor*, which concludes with a suggestion that the Mafia had more to do with the case than even the reader has been allowed to know: structurally, however, the stated solution is completely satisfying.

As a result of its play structure, some constitutive conventions or rules are necessary to detective fiction, in order to define the space that is, as Gadamer says, "specially marked out and reserved for the movement of the game." This game, however, is played not for the sake of winning it but of seeing it won: " . . . the purpose of the game is not really solving the task but ordering and shaping the movement of the game itself" (107). E.D. Hirsch is not quite so comfortable with the rigidity of the idea of "rules" and reminds us that "slight alterations in the system of conventions are possible." He suggests that a genre is more like a code of social behavior, and he suggests that a better word than "rules" might be "proprieties" (*VI* 93). This brings us to our second class, the regulative conventions, those that do not define the genre so much as describe it, that give it its special sense or feel. Unlike the constitutive, these regulative conventions are subject to variation and innovation. They are the ones that, as de Beaugrande says, "become stabilized as integrative frames for managing the complexity of individual acts of writing or reading. In exchange, authors and readers feel impelled to innovate against these frames, at least over longer periods of time" (*CD* 11).

One effect of the principle is that anything mentioned in a story must be important to the forward movement of the plot. The reader of *The Nine Tailors*, for example, may wonder why, fairly late in the novel, Sayers digresses into a detailed description of a flood-control project in the fen country (341-46). As that reader discovers shortly, however, the apparent digression becomes vital in the final resolution. The dominance of the genre compels the reader into a different mode of reception. The same kind of situation occurs in *The New Shoe*, when Bony takes time off from his investigation to accompany some of the local men on a logging expedition (125 ff); the reader with previous experience of the efficiency principle will recognize the importance of the episode, which shortly becomes manifest in the solution of the mystery.

The convention is regulative, however, not constitutive. Some readers of the Nero Wolfe novels by Rex Stout claim as much enjoyment from Wolfe's obsessions with food and orchids as from the detection. In general, the principle is considerably relaxed in the private-eye tradition, as in Bill Pronzini's *Jackpot*, rich in descriptions and discussions of the countryside around San Francisco, which are not relevant to the plot except as atmosphere. Spenser's long digressions into food, sex, and physical combat contribute very little to the hermeneutic impact of Robert Parker's series, but readers tend to cite them more often than they do Spenser's efforts as detective. At the same time, Patricia Wallace's *Deadly Devotion*, a private-eye story, is as tightly efficient as the strictest classical novel.

A somewhat more extensive regulative structure is the standard seven-step plot of detective fiction, another of the bequests of "The Murders in the Rue Morgue," generally practiced a century and a half after its appearance. These seven, which are subject to almost infinite innovation and variation, are the Statement of the Problem (the newspaper accounts of the murders of Madame L'Espanaye and her daughter), the first solution (the arrest of Adolphe LeBon, the Most Likely Suspect), the complication (Dupin points out flaws in the police solution), the period of gloom (the evidence appears to be hopelessly contradictory), the dawning light (Dupin discovers evidence of the presence of an animal at the murder site), the solution (the sailor explains the behavior of his pet orangutan), and the explanation (Dupin outlines the reasoning that led him to the correct solution).[4]

The applicability of this structure, subject to variation, to any kind of detective novel, can be seen in a step-by-step parallel between a typically classical novel, *The New Shoe*, and a standard private-investigator story, *Take a Number*. The problem in *The New Shoe* is introduced early, in the account of the body found mysteriously walled up in a lighthouse (3). The first solution and complication come very close together: the first solution is that the murder was a gang-killing, but the complication is that the body has remained unidentified for some time after discovery (10). The period of gloom extends over a series of blind alleys and contradictory clues, which leave Bony considerably puzzled. The light dawns twice: on page 67 Bony discovers the new shoe that leads him on a new line of reasoning, and on page 124 he makes a highly significant discovery about three local boys and a girl. The solution comes from old Mr. Penwarden, who confirms Bony's conclusions about the nature of the shooting (212). Finally, at the point of the explanation, Bony reconstructs the whole picture of the crime (222), and the novel ends shortly afterward. The construction is representative of the classical, especially in the early presentation of the problem, the exploration of all clues, and solution by the detective at the very end.

The plot of *Take a Number* follows the same pattern: the problem, Sam Raynor is murdered (111); the first solution, Ruth Raynor (Jeri Howard's client) is arrested (120); the complication, Sam Raynor was so unanimously hated that anybody who wanted to murder him would have to get in line and take a number (129); the period of confusion, in reply to the question, "If Ruth didn't shoot her husband, who did?" Jeri can only reply, "I wish I knew" (169); the dawning light, Jeri tells another woman, "You can help me catch a murderer" (325). The solution, the guilty party is identified (334), and Jeri presents her explanation (341)..

As a private-eye or hard-boiled story, however, *Take a Number* follows the Hammett-Chandler as well as the Poe tradition. In this story a second set of conventions is superimposed upon the structure common to all detective fiction. In the private-eye story, the detective is usually engaged upon some noncapital investigation, such as blackmail, theft, or a search for a missing person (the original commission). Later, however, a murder is committed in connection with the first problem, and the detective becomes involved (the expanded commission). This, we might note, is one of the few concessions the detective story makes to reality: in real life, private investigators are not called in on murders, but there must be a murder later in order to keep the story alive. In *Take a Number* Jeri Howard is originally called upon to gather evidence to be used by Ruth Raynor in her divorce case against the abusive Sam Raynor, but when Sam is stabbed and Ruth arrested, Jeri is compelled to solve the murder. Incidentally, in keeping with the hard-boiled tradition, Jeri tells her own story; the classic novel usually employs a third-person narrator.

We are not treating the police procedural novel as a subgenre; although it shares the themes of the grubby world of the hard-boiled story, its plot structure is classic. The problem presented to Staff Inspector Charlie Salter of the Toronto police at the beginning of Erich Wright's *A Fine Italian Hand* is the murder of an actor known to be in serious trouble for some unpaid gambling debts (15, 25), unlike the private-eye story, which typically opens with a noncapital crime that is later converted to a murder case. The first (and easy) analysis is that the murder is a mob killing (28), but the complication comes in the form of a message through a reliable pipeline that the Mafia disavows any connection with this one (67, 130).

In keeping with classic structure, the period of confusion is long and complex, consisting partly in the unavailability of hard factual information and partly in the conflicts within the little evidence the police have to work with (94, 172, 191); at one point the confusion is compounded by the introduction of one of the minor conventions of popular formula fiction, when Salter learns that somebody else is seeking the same information that the police are after (191). The dawning light begins to appear when Salter becomes suspicious of the involvement of drugs (230), and the Solution follows a few pages later when the police arrest a person previously unsuspected (238). At this point, however, the reader is reminded that there are two solutions involved in a police case, the logical one resulting from the employment of police investigatory procedures, and the actual one reached by a jury: "The main job was done. They had the man who killed Hunter. What happened in the courtroom would be another story . . . " (242). The explanation is shared by Salter and the murderer, with the guilty person admitting part of the truth and Salter supplying the rest (240).

Two other regulative structures give the detective story its special quality, namely its habit of self-reflexivity and its remarkable temporality.

In brief, self-reflexivity is the detective story's habit of calling attention to itself, the one we encountered in *Nice Weekend for a Murder*, where the reader is not allowed to forget that this is merely a tale of detection. In its simplest form it consists of the habit of fictional detectives commenting, usually unfavorably, on other fictional detectives in other stories. As with so many of the other conventions, this one originated in "The Murders in the Rue Morgue," where Dupin takes occasion to criticize Francois Vidoq, a police detective whose largely fictional *Memoires* were popular in Poe's time. Vidoq, says Dupin, was "a good guesser and a persevering man" who lacked "educated thought" (175). Later Sherlock Holmes disparaged Dupin, and the convention became one of the established traditions of the genre, to the extent that today it is still difficult to find a story in which somebody does not refer to Sherlock Holmes, Perry Mason, Columbo, or to detectives in print and on television generally. Thus in *Amateur Night* attorney Calvin Mason "envied the detectives in books and on TV who had terrific sources in the police department" (37), in addition to references elsewhere in the book to Inspector Clouseau and Nancy Drew; in *Decked* the narrator tells how in college two classmates would read the same book at the same time, and whoever figured out the murderer bought the first sherry of the day (24). The self-reflexivity of the novels of the Golden Age was even more obvious, as in Ellery Queen's memorable challenge to the reader, where the author stepped onto the stage and laid out an invitation to the reader to solve the problem ahead of the detective, or in Dr. Fell's oft-cited lecture on locked rooms in John Dickson Carr's *The Three Coffins*. In the stories of our own time the convention is likely to use a softer touch, as when Detective Toby Peters in Stuart Kaminsky's *Poor Butterfly* regrets that everybody has an alibi for everything, to which his companion replies, "As is always true in detective fiction" (76). Although prevalent, the quality of self-reflexivity is not essential to a detective story; its regulative function rests in its describing or characterizing the genre without defining it.

The other regulative structure that contributes to the "differentness" of the detective story is its unusual temporality: traditionally, it tells two stories simultaneously, that of the investigation (present) and of the crime (past). Grossvogel calls it a "curiously articulated fiction, in which what happened is kept from the reader, while what he is told is less than relevant to what has happened" (*MIF* 15). This feature of detective fiction has occasioned more comment from critics than most others, as attested in the studies; cited earlier; by Todorov (44-45), Porter (328-29), O'Toole (152), and Kermode (185). It is relatively easy to find illustrations of dual chronology in detective fiction. In Christie's *Cards on the Table* there are three levels of time: the remote past (the four original murders), the recent past (the murder under investigation), and the present (the current investigation). Even when the remote past has been uncovered, the recent past remains veiled. The three-level-time plot survived into the private-eye school of detection, practically becoming a staple of the Lew Archer novels of Ross Macdonald. Archer must sometimes solve a murder mystery fifty years old before he can make sense of the current one.

The most complete analysis of the temporal element in detective fiction is the one developed by Champigny in *What Will Have Happened.* "Unlike texts called 'adventure stories' or 'suspense stories,'" says Champigny, "mystery stories sharpen the interest not just for what will happen but for what will have happened. To some extent, in any narrative the description of an event further determines events already described. Mystery stories, however, radicalize the tension, or complementarity, between progressive and regressive determinations. This is what the future perfect in the phrase 'what will have happened' is designed to suggest." The narrative finally produces a denouement that is designed to transfigure the whole sequence (13-14).

One other aspect of the temporality of the detective story further complicates its "turbulent flow": sometimes the movement of the narrative is projected not only into the past but also into the future. This is the case with what may be called the preprogrammed murder, in which the reader's expectations may be well along in anticipation of the investigation some time before the murder is committed. This is what happens in Christie's *The Murder at the Vicarage:* not only the prospective victim but four plausible suspects and the murder weapon have been identified. This happens frequently in the English "soft-boiled" tale of detection, and the phenomenon serves to complicate the innate negativity of the genre.[5]

One of the most informative principles of the conventionality of the detection formula is that the conventions themselves have structure, and that they are absorbed into the structure of the genre as a whole. The structure of the convention, as we will see in the next chapter, has some bearing upon its value as a narrative device. A good example of a useful, well-structured convention is the one we will call the death warrant.

The death warrant should be recognizable to any experienced reader: a detective in a story, working on an especially difficult case, receives a call from someone who has something vital to the solution of the mystery and is willing to pass it on; they make an appointment for a meeting, which the detective keeps only to find the prospective informant murdered and the important evidence missing.

Raymond Chandler seemed to like this one especially. In *The Little Sister* Marlowe receives a call from a person who refuses to reveal his identity but who wants Marlowe to pick up something very important and very mysterious. They make an appointment for the pickup, at a specified room in a certain hotel (45). Ten pages later Marlowe keeps the appointment and finds the caller murdered. Much the same thing happens in *The High Window*. A man named Phillips, who has information badly needed by Marlowe, gives the detective the key to his apartment and agrees to meet him there (43). Once again Marlowe goes to the apartment, only to find Phillips dead (56). Once a reader has become familiar with the pattern, it is easy enough to recognize. Thus when in Richard Prather's *The Trojan Hearse* a woman calls Shell Scott about a recording that contains a vital clue and offers to bring it to him at a specified time (99), nobody should be surprised when Scott returns to the hotel, finds her murdered and the recording stolen (107). One reason why authors love this device is its hermeneutic value. Note how it serves a dual purpose: it prolongs suspense, and at the same time it justifies the delay. It has proved equally useful in hard-boiled and classic literary detection.

A reader inexperienced in the genre will walk right into the development without a hint of what is to come, but to the veteran reader the very appearance of a cooperative informant is a signal that a familiar complication is about to take place. The phenomenon can be understood in terms of Jauss's horizon of expectations: the experienced reader brings to the text a mind-set or system of reference that includes a programmed response to the special signals of the death warrant convention.

It is not surprising that a lover of complexity like Ellery Queen uses the Death Warrant twice in *The Tragedy of X*. Early in the story the district attorney receives an anonymous letter offering vital information, with the exact time and place of meeting specified (64). The police keep the appointment, just in time to see the informant mysteriously killed (68). Somewhat later a suspect named DeWitt tells Drury Lane he has something important to pass on to him the next morning (172-73). Morning comes, and DeWitt is found murdered (189).

After a few experiences of the death warrant, the reader will develop a set of expectations for it. Mark Bradley, in Stan Cutler's

The Face on the Cutting-Room Floor, summarizes the idea as follows: "You know what happens. Whenever anybody's going to give you the name of the killer only later . . . they turn up murdered" (100). "Anybody who says 'The name of the murderer is . . . ' in Hollywood is not going to make it to the closing credits" (150-51). As a matter of fact, this convention does have a well organized structure, with the following rules:

1. The offer of information is volunteered by the prospective informer, not solicited by the detective.
2. The information is represented as vital to the solution of the case.
3. Circumstances make it necessary to postpone delivery of the information.
4. A meeting is arranged between detective and informer, with exact time and place stated.
5. The detective keeps the appointment.
6. The detective learns that the informer has been murdered and the information is unavailable.
7. The information ultimately becomes available as part of the solution of the mystery.

The death warrant belongs to the class of those recurrent and preconstituted themes like the most likely suspect (who is almost never guilty) or the dying message (which requires the attention of a master sleuth and the rest of the novel to work out). A familiarity with these conventional structures is essential to the understanding of detective fiction, because they dominate the genre to a far greater extent than is the case with any other popular fiction.

In Cutler's *The Face on the Cutting-Room Floor,* for example, the promise of information is not delivered over the phone but rather by a heavily disguised suspect, who secretly slips a card to one of the detectives, with a proposed time and place of meeting. The rest of the pattern is conventional; the informant fails to show up because he has been murdered. The variation is in the use of the disguise, which in this case replaces the phone call as a means of concealment, but we do not want to miss the point that the limit on revelation is still accomplished by the inability of the participants to talk at that point.

In Stuart Kaminsky's *Poor Butterfly,* a woman with vital information calls detective Toby Peters and leaves a message for him to come to her apartment (93). He goes there and finds her dying after a brutal attack, but still able to talk a little (103). Her message, however, is so badly garbled that it puzzles Peters (and the reader) for many pages to come. Kaminsky is able to preserve the suspense value in this case by introducing a second, and similarly structured, convention, the dying message.

Trella Crespi gives the convention a slightly different twist in *The Trouble With Moonlighting,* when a woman movie star tells amateur detective Simona Griffo, "Come to my place at six-thirty, the Mayfair, 115 Central Park West, nineteenth floor," and Simona wonders what she wants (58). She keeps the appointment and finds the woman murdered (66). Here the variation is that the purpose of the appointment is ambiguous, with no actual promise of information, but still recognizable as the death warrant and should touch off the programmed response in an experienced reader. That response is reinforced much later when Simona learns that the woman did as a matter of fact have something important to tell her.

One more example, this one from Rex Stout's *Gambit:* Archie Goodwin and Sally Blount go to the apartment of a lawyer named Daniel Kalmus, who is at this point the most likely suspect in the case under investigation (85) and find him murdered (87). Too late, Archie discovers that Kalmus did have important information, which is now missing (92). Here the variation involves a reversal of the time element: the murder is discovered before the importance of the information is revealed, but once again, the convention is sufficiently recognizable to touch off a predictable set of expectations in the detection fan.

It would be difficult to trace the origin of the death warrant. It was not one of the Poe conventions: the sailor keeps the appointment with Dupin in "The Murders in the Rue Morgue," and I do not remember it anywhere in Doyle. Henry Baker shows up alive and well in "The Blue Carbuncle," and so do the other people with information in the Sherlock Holmes stories. If this one followed the usual dictates of the market, somebody used it successfully, readers liked it, other writers picked it up, and still others worked variations on it. The death warrant entered the readers' horizons of expectations and thus became an accepted ingredient in the detection genre.

Whatever its history, the Death Warrant presents an unusually clear example of transformation of theme into structure. The structure itself becomes permanent, but it is subject to infinite variation of both theme and rules. After several recurrences, the material is no longer experienced as theme but becomes part of the structure: it not only gives shape or form to the material repeated but also directs the reader's future responses to the same sequence.

After sufficient repetition, each of the recurrent themes of detective fiction will develop not only a set of rules but a hermeneutic structure, and it shares with other recurrent themes the deep structure of transformed play. The principle can be illustrated by continuing our analysis of the death warrant, starting with a parallel between the rules of the convention and its structure, discussing several other recurrent themes that share the same structure, and finally noting the relationship between the deep structure of these conventions and that of transformed play.

The correspondence in the death warrant can be represented like this:

Structure	Rules
Initial availability	Offer by informant
	Important material
Appointment	Present transmission
	impossible
	Precise time and place
Rendezvous	Kept by detective
Unavailability	Impossible transmission
	continued
Final Availability	Resolution: transmission
	completed

The structure of the convention is obviously hermeneutic because, in Kermode's words, "the principal object of the reader is to discover by an interpretation of clues the answer to a problem proposed at the outset" (PM 179). The textual motivation of the death warrant is to discover not only the nature of the information but also who killed the prospective informant and why. After a few experiences with the convention, the reader will develop a feel for its structure, knowing that the pattern of development will be anticipation, followed by disappointment and finally relieved by fulfillment.

The structure of the death warrant is virtually the same as that of the dying message, mentioned earlier. In *The Tragedy of X* the gifted amateur detective Drury Lane tells a story that will serve as an illustration of its classic form: An important underworld figure who is known to have served as a police informer is found shot to death in his hotel room. Indications are that after receiving the fatal shot he crawled seven feet, overturned a table, upset the sugar bowl, and died with a handful of sugar tightly clenched in his fist. From these facts Lane is able to deduce that the dying man was leaving a message that his murderer was a cocaine addict (182-83). The rules of the convention are, first the message has some special significance; second, it represents a considerable effort on the part of dying person; third, it is coded in some distinctive way that the murderer will not recognize; fourth, the coding has special meaning for the detective. The same rules characterize a murder in Martha Grimes's *The Man with a Load of Mischief*, where a vicar is found murdered and on his desk what appear to be some sermon notes, largely undecipherable gibberish (242). Twenty-five pages later those notes supply Inspector Jury with a clue to the murderer.

Sue Grafton uses a variation of the convention in *G Is for Gumshoe*, where private detective Kinsey Millhone fails to reach an elderly woman in time to receive her dying message, but the doctor who was present tells her the woman said, "Tell her it used to be summer" (220-21). Kinsey is puzzled for fifty pages before she realizes what the dying woman really meant. The structure is unchanged, but the rules are amended to introduce an unintentional coding (faulty transmission) as a substitute for an ingenious coding of the classic original message. There is another variation of the theme in the episode just cited in Kaminsky's *Poor Butterfly*, where Toby Peters reaches the dying woman in time to hear her say what sounds like "shave" (104). Here the unintentional coding is the result of the victim's condition, but in both of these instances the structure is still that of the death warrant.

Another popular convention that shares the structure is that of the missing person. The rules of this one are as follows: the absence of the person is unexplained; the person is also a suspect; he or she is found murdered; the body of the missing person was close at hand all the time. Early in Van Dine's *The Kennel Murder Case*, while Vance and others are investigating the murder of Arthur Coe, it is revealed that the victim's brother is attending a meeting in Chicago, and Vance is prompted to remark, "Ah! Most convenient" (21). Somewhat later, the body of the murdered brother is found in a closet of the same house (106). The convention appears in much the same form in Hammett's *The Thin Man*, in Sarah Shankman's *First Kill All the Lawyers*, Harry Kemmelman's *Sunday the Rabbi Stayed Home*, and dozens of others. Ross Macdonald varies the rules in *The Blue Hammer*, where the missing artist Richard Chantry has been close at hand throughout the story, living under a false identity (192). Tony Hillerman uses two missing persons in *The Ghostway*, one of whom turns up alive (59), but the other has been murdered (235).

In general, the dying message and the missing person share the structure of the death warrant: first, there is information available, in the message of the dying victim or the presumed guilt of the missing person; an appointment is kept in the form of an investigation by the detective, in the rendezvous with the dying person or the search for the missing one; the information is unavailable because of the coding of the dying message or the absence of the presumed suspect; the information becomes available when the message is decoded or the missing person found. The one feature shared by all of them is their hermeneutic value: the conventional structure of each is recognized by the experienced reader, whose participation in the story is pushed toward the unraveling of the mystery.

Several other frequently used conventions share not only the hermeneutic mode of these three but also their deep structure, which I will characterize as the stages of anticipation, disappointment, and fulfillment. This brings us to a brief consideration of three other frequently employed recurrent themes that share this structure, the unidentifiable victim, something bothering the detective, and the detective on vacation.

A convention with especially strong hermeneutic value is the unidentifiable victim: the victim has been mutilated in such fashion as to be unidentifiable; after considerable effort on the part of the detective the victim is identified, but the first identification proves to be mistaken. This is the case in *The Blue Hammer*, in which the face of the victim has been eaten away by desert animals, in *The Nine Tailors*, where the facial features have been purposely mutilated by the murderer, and in Ellis Peters's *The Potter's Field*, where the victim has only a faceless skull. In each of these cases the original tentative identification of the victim is later proved to be mistaken. This convention illustrates the effect of the hermeneutic mode in the reading of a detective story: the potential gruesomeness of the situation is canceled out by the challenge of the mystery.

Another favorite hermeneutic structure is the instance in which something keeps nagging at the back of the detective's consciousness, something he or she can not identify at first but which later proves highly significant. The signal is a remark by the detective, such as Jane's in *Amateur Night*, "The picture was there for a frustrating second" (111), or Kinsey's "Something about it bothers me, but I can't figure out what it is" in *G Is for Gumshoe* (255). The convention receives more extensive development in *The Ghostway*. As Jim Chee looks at the cabin in which the murder was committed, "something a touch out of harmony with things as they should be" bothers him (23). The signal is influenced by previous experience of similar cases, like the ones just mentioned, and the reader senses the feel of the structure. When it is reinforced by repetition on the next page, "Something didn't fit" (24) and again on the next one, the reader should begin to experience the negativity that will become the theme of the novel.

The rules of the detective on vacation, are simple: no detective is ever allowed to take a vacation or to retire. Sherlock Holmes in "The Adventure of the Reigate Squire" is desperately in need of a complete rest, but even on his holiday he must solve a murder. The same thing happens to Peter Wimsey in Sayers's *The Five Red Herrings*, to Alan Grant in Tey's *The Singing Sands*, and dozens of others. The theme is varied in *The Trouble with Moonlighting*: there, Simona Griffo must interrupt her moonlighting job to solve a murder. By the same convention, no detective is ever allowed to retire, as Nick Charles discovers in *The Thin Man*, where he must not only interrupt a holiday but even come out of retirement to investigate a homicide.

As a result of the hermeneutic mode of detective fiction, the reader knows that not only will the vacation or retirement be interrupted but the detective will successfully arrive at the correct solution.

This review of a few of the conventional recurrent themes of detective fiction should demonstrate the two qualities of a convention that are essential to the structure of the genre, its hermeneutic structure and its capacity for repetition. As a result of the persistence of the hermeneutic mode, a convention develops its own expectations, which then merge into the horizon of expectations of the genre. A genre is more than a simple collection of conventions, but there seems to be little question that the conventions of detective fiction collectively supply much of its context. In a succession of detective stories, as noted earlier, a theme can be so regularly repeated that it is no longer experienced as a theme but becomes part of the structure of the genre.

As a result of the process of reciprocal transformation, the horizon of expectation of the convention merges into the horizon of the genre, and the genre takes shape as experience breeds expectations, which in turn guide subsequent experience. For a formula to be successful, says Cawelti, conventions must impress themselves on the general consciousness, becoming accepted vehicles of attitudes and aesthetic effects. A convention "appeals to previous experience of the type itself; it creates its own field of reference" (*AMR* 9-10).

To a greater degree than any other popular fiction, the detection genre creates its own field of reference, with the result that conventional structures dominate detective fiction and determine the special reading mode of the genre. As the reader learns to read between the lines and develops a feel for convention, a theme like the missing person will tend to fade as theme and to be increasingly felt as structure. Probably the ultimate instance of such transformation is the recurrent structure convention, discussed earlier in regard to the three images, "chocolate" in *The Main*, Bony's coffin in *The New Shoe* and the angry face in the crowd in *Take a Number*, where the patterned repetition of the theme signals its own importance. The difference in this convention is that an element already structured (the position of the theme) is transformed by repetition into "pure" or deep structure. There is another example in S.S. Van Dine's *The Kennel Murder Case*: early in the investigation of the murder of Archer Coe, Philo Vance and his associates discover a small wounded Scottish terrier in the house, and the importance of her presence is signaled in Vance's exclamation, "That's the thing I've been waiting for!" (69). The image is reinforced on page 77, mentioned briefly on 140, then several times more until 255, when its importance is fully developed. The perceptive reader will develop a sense of pattern in which conventionalization depends upon position rather than thematic material.

In time, the "rules of the game" of any of the conventions will be transformed into the hermeneutic structure of detective fiction. In the convention, as a result of the deep structure of transformed play, the element of stress is eliminated, the reader is invited to undertake any of the voluntary tasks offered by the text, the story refuses to "go anywhere" in a social or cultural sense, and the convention renews itself through constant repetition.

All sense of stress is eliminated from the convention by the generic assurance of literary detection that everything will finally "fit in" and "work out," including the solution of the mystery. The death warrant and the dying message carry with them the assurance that the information needed by the detective will inevitably become available; likewise, the detective on vacation will solve the mystery (and will feel much better for having done so), and the unidentifiable victim will inevitably be identified.

As a result of their hermeneutic structure, most of the conventions of detective fiction offer the reader an opportunity to undertake tasks that are inherent in the convention. The challenge in the convention of the death warrant, for example, is to reconstruct the information made unavailable by the murder of the informer, and in the most likely suspect to measure that suspect's prospects against those of the other people in the story. However, the tasks are always optional: the reader can actively undertake to work out a solution or relax and wait for the detective to do so. In the next chapter we will examine a convention that is entirely thematic and lacking hermeneutic structure, justice thwarted, which enjoyed some popularity for a time and then faded from the scene as a result of an absence of challenge.

As a rule, the conventions of detective fiction are lacking in social or cultural relevance because of the disinclination of the convention to "go anywhere" in the real world. Conventions such as something bothering the detective, the unidentifiable victim, and the detective on vacation are consistently strong hermeneutically but completely lacking in social values.

Finally, the to-and-fro motion of play is transformed into a capacity for self-renewal in constant repetition. The viability of a convention lies in its being known, acceptable, and endlessly repeatable (*PA* 57), a fact we have already noticed in the almost inexhaustible capacity for variability in structures like the death warrant and the dying message.

As a result of this ongoing process of transformation, the structure of the convention becomes part of the structure of the genre, shaping and guiding the nature of the reader's expectations, which determine how the text will be understood. In the phenomenological view, the effect of expectations on the reading process is that they not only anticipate what is to come but bring it to fruition.

The perceptive reader of detective fiction should sense in the genre the presence of two definitional forces, and the dialectic of the two endows the detective story with its aesthetic quality. The first of these is hermeneutic drive, the need to reach a resolution, and the other is the conventionality of the story, including its unusually heavy accumulation of tradition.

Because of the dominance of hermeneutic specialization, indeterminacy is more nearly basic to the formulation of meaning in detective fiction than in any other popular genre, and most of that indeterminacy is created by the dominance of the two elements Iser calls negation and negativity. Of the two, negation (contradiction, denial) is the more useful, as we can see in those numerous cases where a system of values in which the reader has been led to believe is canceled out by contradiction. There are times when the genre seems to use its established conventionality to heighten its own indeterminacy, as when the convention declines to follow its set program: the most likely suspect turns out to be guilty, the missing person shows up alive and well. Such is the case with the disappearance of Tiffany Collins in *Take a Number*. When Tiffany is repeatedly reported missing (192), the experienced reader will rely upon the system of the convention to assume she has been murdered, but instead she returns safe and unharmed (243). Negations, says Iser, invoke familiar elements only to cancel them out, and in so doing it creates new blanks, thus heightening hermeneutic specialization. The unpredicted return of Tiffany Collins is such an example, as well as an illustration of the convention's capacity for infinite variation, which minimizes the danger of boredom in the endless repetition of a theme. If the impetus of the detective story consisted only of a need to solve problems, it would become a sheer "whodunit" indeed, a puzzle story; its aesthetic completeness requires the whole context of convention and tradition, as does any game with a well-founded tradition.

In considering the mutual interchange among reader, author, and genre, we need to distinguish between two uses of *genre*. The term really has two conceptual frames of reference: the idea of genre as the total of works customarily subsumed under that category by historians, publishers, and librarians; and the reader's individual conception of genre, which arises from his or her own experience with books, the "horizon of expectations" and "rules of the game" familiar from earlier texts. To avoid confusion, I will refer to them as *historical* and *individual* genres respectively.

The historical genre is the one that has developed during the period since "The Murders in the Rue Morgue," and it is built of the acceptances, rejections, consolidations, and rearrangements of tradition. The individual genre, on the other hand, is not the same for any two readers; it is built of the reader's own horizon of experiences and expectations. In the context of this book it is important to bear in mind that it is the individual, not the historical, genre that conditions the guidance of the text. Thus a simple assertion that in the reading of detective fiction, the formula intervenes and transforms the reaction between reader and text needs some reinterpretation. The reader may form a conception of the historical genre by reading Haycraft, Murch, Symons, or any of the other historians of the genre, but it is the individual genre that will dominate that reader's perceptions. With additional reading of detective fiction, the individual will tend to merge with the historical, except that the sequence of experience will vary from the historical: nobody reads Poe first and then proceeds chronologically to the latest on the market.

In chapter 4 we will discuss in greater detail the relationships between the two, as readers' personal preferences (and buying instincts) tend to determine the directions of development of the historical genre, and these in turn guide the development of consensus between authors and readers.

For purposes of this discussion, the detection genre can be defined in terms of consensus among readers, writers, and the genre itself, where the rules of the game represent a synthesis of the horizons of expectations of its participants. No genre, however, can remain permanently static; if it simply recycles its old material, its conventions tend to become mere stereotypes. The development of a dominant genre, says Jauss, involves three steps: canonization (legitimization), automatization (conventionalization), and reshuffling (testing of the old rules) (*TAR* 106). The next chapter will discuss reshuffling, the kind of probing and testing of boundaries done successfully by Hammett and Chandler in the earlier part of the twentieth century and undertaken by several creative writers of our own time.

4

Conventions, Inventions,
and the Bounds of Genre

A reader of the critical anthology *The Cunning Craft* may be struck by the two markedly different treatments of the historical environment of popular formulas. First, there is a tendency to consider the genre a social/cultural phenomenon, as when one of the writers points out that "the popular text is sensitive to its environment and provides what amounts to a social seismograph,"[1] and another refers to Jameson's characterization of a genre as a social contract between a writer and his readers (Lovitt, "Controlling Discourse in Detective Fiction, or Caring Very Much Who Killed Roger Ackroyd" 68). Other references in the same essays, however, specifically address the detection formula as a separate entity, with its own dynamic, its own values and logic. These references employ such expressions as "the powerful generic logic governing the text" (Lovitt 76) and refer to the novelistic element as "a realm at odds with the ethos of detective fiction" (Wald, "Strong Poison: Love and the Novelistic in Dorothy Sayers" 102), as if the detection formula tended toward self-definition instead of simple response to the social/cultural environment. These two ways of looking at the formula provide a useful setting to the question of change and stability in detective fiction. In practice, the detection formula responds far more readily to its own generic logic than to its popular role as social seismograph. There is indeed a compact between the writers and readers of detective fiction, but it does not in itself constitute the genre; rather, the terms of the compact are dictated by the genre.

The theoretical position of this chapter, which will deal with the nature and conditions of change in the detection genre, begins with an acceptance of Jauss's historical view and his treatment of genre in terms of horizons and rules, preconstituted by tradition.

Some critics describe the nature of a genre by referring to its bounds. Thus the literary theorists whose work we are using in this study speak of a genre's "set of limits" with a "breaking point," or of the bounds of genre as integrative frames within which generic traditions and rules are effective. Jauss especially treats a genre as a trajectory or horizon of expectations, whose norms can be defined as "everything expected." This quality in particular should be kept in mind in any discussion of the detection genre, which is in a sense a tension of conventionality and expectation.

Before moving into the question of change, it should be noted that there are two ways of defining a genre. One, the *synchronic*, stops the action and bases its description upon a cross-section of a class of works, disregarding developmental history and tradition. Such a definition of the detection genre might hold to a consideration of living authors and their books only, and of the condition of the detective story as it is in the 1990s. The other, the *diachronic*, views the genre in terms of its history and background. A diachronic study of detective fiction would see the stories of the 1990s as products of a history that would include both the heritage of Dupin and Holmes and also that of Sam Spade and Philip Marlowe. The diachronic or historical perspective is the one accepted by Jauss and most of the other critics cited here. Such a dynamic as this second view suggests, with its acceptance of the horizon of genre as a "trajectory," does not allow for a static genre. The historical concept of continuity, says Jauss, "is one in which every earlier element extends and completes itself through a later one" (*TAR* 88).

The bounds of a genre naturally offer a challenge, to which creative authors respond by probing those limits and seeking points of breakthrough. What takes place then is a continual founding and altering of horizons. If the reading public accepts these alterations, the rules of the game will be revised and new horizons of expectations established. To a great extent, the success or failure of an innovation will depend upon the nature of genre preconstituted by tradition, because, in phenomenological theory, both the genre and its susceptibility to change are guided by generic preintentions. In the case of the detective story, those pre-intentions were coded into the formula by Poe in the Dupin tales.

One element that must not be overlooked is the crucial position of expectation in this conception of change in genre. Iser cites Husserl to the effect that "every originally constructive process is inspired by pre-intentions, which construct and collect the seed of what is to come and bring it to fruition." Iser goes on to point out that the interactions within a text "will not be a fulfillment of an expectation so much as a continual modification of it."[2] The principle is easily illustrated in detective fiction, specifically in the way in which the hermeneutic structure of a convention anticipates the structure of the whole genre, discussed in chapter 3. This is the reason why the hard-boiled private-eye story, thematically different from the classical in a number of ways, nevertheless preserves not only the four constitutive "givens" but also the seven-step plot structure and several other regulative conventions instituted by Poe. Hammett wisely declined to depart from the tradition, because he knew that his readers would hold these expectations of *The Maltese Falcon*, *The Dain Curse*, and *The Thin Man*.

Certainly one of the best examples of the degree to which the detection genre is preconstituted by the expectations of readers is the account of the death and resurrection of Steve Carella in the 87th Precinct novels of Ed McBain. McBain explains that he intended his police procedural series to reflect the realities of police life, in which there are no heroes but teams of law officers who share the work of investigation, where policemen lead hard, dangerous lives and are frequently killed on duty. In the first three novels, several policemen are killed, including Steve Carella, who figures prominently in the first book, is absent from the second, and then dies at the hands of a drug dealer at the end of the third. In the terms used earlier, McBain was probing the bounds of the genre, seeking a point for successful innovation. "To my knowledge this had not been done before," he says, "and I felt it was unique." What happened was that he immediately found himself stopped by the "powerful generic logic" of the detective story in the person of his editor, who informed him that he could not kill Carella: "He's the hero. He's the star of the series." The ending was rewritten, Steve Carella was restored to life and is quite active in the continuing series almost forty years later.[3]

This episode illustrates several elements pertinent to convention, invention, and change in the detection genre, including the unusual relationship among author, reader, and genre. Here the detection formula was preconstituted by the expectations of readers, based upon tradition and expressed in terms of sales, the only criterion of success in popular fiction. There is, however, an equilibrium in the process, between the conservatism of the reading public, who want to keep things much as they are in the formula, and the need for creativity to prevent stagnation. Thus writers continue to test the limits of the genre, sometimes forcing a successful breakthrough, as Hammett did with the innovations of the private-eye school. In general, what these writers have found is that the bounds of formula will reject any violation of the constitutive norms of the genre: the hero must be a detective, the book must be mainly about detection, the mystery must be a difficult one, and it must be solved. The regulative conventions, however, are always subject to testing: the seven-step plot is subject to all kinds of variation, as are the principles of efficiency, temporality, and self-reflexivity. As far as the recurrent themes are concerned, they are always available and subject to revision to fit any innovation. One point not to be missed: these determinations are made by readers and writers, not by academics, critics, or the historians of the genre.

Part of the dynamic conception of genre is that its limits not only allow but continually invite probing and testing. Jauss describes the challenge and response in terms of the introduction of a new work into an established genre. "If the artistic character of a work is to be measured by the aesthetic distance with which it opposes the expectations of the first audience, then it follows that this distance, at first experienced as a pleasing or alienating new perspective, can disappear for later readers, to the extent that the original negativity of the work has become self-evident and has itself entered into the horizon of future aesthetic experience as a henceforth familiar expectation" (*TAR* 25).

According to Jauss, the new work and the genre maintain a reciprocal relationship, whereby the horizon of the genre sets the terms of reception of the book, which upon acceptance becomes part of the "henceforth familiar expectation." Thus, when a Mary Roberts Rinehart or a Dashiell Hammett publishes an innovative novel, the disparity between the "newness" and the reader's expectations becomes a "negativity," a *distance* between the horizon of the new book and that of the reader. Over a period of time, and after further experience with the innovation, the negativity of the new approach disappears, and the innovation itself has become part of the reader's own expectations. In a rigid genre like detective fiction, however, an additional step enters the process: before it can be absorbed into the reader's horizon, it must demonstrate its compatibility with the formula. If the distance is too great, as with Rinehart's "Had-I-But-Known" story, readers will eventually reject it; but if, as history demonstrated in the case of the hard-boiled innovation, the new work is consistent with the constitutive elements of the genre, it will not only gain acceptance but will be incorporated into the formula.

I have already referred to the unique compact between authors and readers of detective fiction, wherein each is familiar with the "common law" of the genre, which serves much the same purpose as a book of rules for a game. The relationship between these writers and readers is much like that among experienced bridge players, two of whom, having never met or played each other, will have such an adequate understanding of the rules and conventions that unspoken communication between them is easy. Each knows to depend upon the other to the extent that they can anticipate each other's strategies.

This relationship is what Gadamer calls *Verstandnis*, or pre-understanding. In order for genuine conversation to take place, he says, the partners must open themselves to each other, accept each other's points of view as valid, and "transpose themselves into each other" to the extent that each not only understands the other but what the other is saying. "What is to be grasped is the substantive rightness of [the partner's] opinion so that we can be at one with each other on the subject" (*TM* 385). Thus an experienced reader of detective stories coming across an unfamiliar detective novel will know without opening to the first page that certain things in the book can be depended upon: the story may deal with a number of themes, but it will be primarily a tale of detection, it will contain a mystery, and the mystery will be solved. Here our bridge-player analogy can be extended: just as each player will know that the other understands that the partner's ace is not to be trumped, except under unusual circumstances, so the reader will be able to depend upon the new book's containing a detective protagonist. There are, however, some variations in the conventions of bridge, depending upon whether the game is contract or duplicate, or whether the other player uses the "false club" convention. The same kinds of variations hold for the detection genre: the reader might do well to note whether the novel was written in 1940 or 1990, and whether the author is man or woman, American, English, or Swedish. Now, however, the analogy ends. Creative writers are constantly testing the conservatism of the detection genre, probing its bounds and violating its conventions whenever possible, and even changing the rules to the extent that other writers pick up their innovations. Bridge players, however, enjoy no such flexibility: a player who repeatedly fails to follow suit will probably not be invited back.

In one sense, changes in the detection genre take place in response to the state of tension that exists between tradition and creation, or as Cawelti implies in an early essay, in the distinction between convention and invention. Conventions, he says, are "elements known to creator and audience," such as stereotypes, accepted ideas, favorite plots, and the like. Inventions he defines as "elements uniquely imagined by the creator," such as new characters, ideas, and linguistic forms ("Concept of Formula" 113). The natural tension between the two, as we will see, becomes a determinant in the changing detection formula: authors constantly test the conventional forms, threatening to transcend convention, sometimes backing off short of real innovation, sometimes breaking through and effecting a modification of tradition, or even a new form. The result of generic change is increasing complexity and enrichment of the genre. Literary signification, says Horton, rests on institutionalized conventions, which an innovative writer will try to violate. Ultimately, those attempts will "lead to changes in the system itself, which will inevitably lead to more interpretations" (*II* 30-31).

Of course the most dramatic and most often discussed set of innovations in the detection formula was that undertaken by Dashiell Hammett in the late 1920s and expanded and enriched by Raymond Chandler some ten years later. The hard-boiled or private-eye novel did achieve some constructive changes, but all of them were thematic, not structural; the private investigator is still the prime mover of the narrative, detection is still the main business of the plot, the mystery is deep and apparently impenetrable, and the case is always solved. Hammett observed these "givens" in his three detective novels, *The Dain Curse*, *The Maltese Falcon*, and *The Thin Man*. There can be no question about the status of the Continental Op, Sam Spade, or Nick Charles as protagonists, nor any with regard to the centrality of the detection plot in each story. The mystery is both deep and complicated: the tangled relations in the Leggett family, the genuineness of the falcon, and the involvements in the disappearance of Clyde Wynant. Each of them is solved, however, by the detective, near the end of the novel, in classic style.

Hammett did introduce one innovation, which was more a response to the demands of real life than a creative breakthrough, but it has become a staple regulative convention of the private-eye story. In each of these cases the detective is called in on a case that does not involve murder, the Continental Op to find some missing diamonds, Sam Spade to locate the mythical partner of Brigid O'Shaughnessy, Nick Charles to find Clyde Wynant. Later, however, murder is committed and the detective finds himself involved in its solution. Hammett made one other change that has been widely imitated by his successors, in the progressive relaxation of the efficiency principle in the three books. It is not particularly noticeable in *The Dain Curse*, but is much more so in *The Maltese Falcon*, especially in the problematic Flitcraft narrative, which represents an intrusion into the main business of the plot.[4]

The relaxation is most noticeable in *The Thin Man*, in the antics of Nick and Nora Charles during their alcoholic Christmas holiday in Manhattan. Hammett's private investigators were as a rule less cerebral and more practical-minded than their classic predecessors, and usually more inclined to take matters into their own hands and manipulate outcomes, but their stories tended generally to conform to the classic structures.

The probings and testings of the limits of the genre are not confined to the private-eye story, as a brief examination of two recent popular novels with classic amateur detectives will demonstrate. The first is from one of Ellis Peters's Brother Cadfael stories, *The Potter's Field*, and the convention violated is that of the unidentifiable victim. Early in that novel a woman's skeleton is uncovered in a field belonging to the monastery, and it is at first feared that she may be the erstwhile wife of one of the monks.

The blank created is immediately programmed by the experienced reader, who knows the convention is that a faceless murder victim is never correctly identified at the outset. Shortly afterward, the convention is confirmed (the skeleton is believed to be that of another woman), but then toward the end of the story this confirmation is canceled (the other woman is still alive), and we learn that the skeleton was indeed correctly identified from the first. The integrative frame in this case, the expectation with which the reader proceeds, is that of mistaken identification, because that is always the case when a corpse is unidentifiable; the innovation consists of the breaking of the frame. Now this is hardly cataclysmic; the reader is guided by the bounds of the genre, and the outcome actually makes no big difference, except that within the reader's own horizon of expectations the probability of the convention of the unidentifiable victim is modified from "always incorrectly identified" to "usually incorrectly identified." Regulative conventions, as we have seen, are subject to constant testing and revision of this sort, with the result that a critic speaks of them in terms of "always" and "never" only at extreme peril.

The second illustration is *The Players Come Again*, one of Amanda Cross's novels featuring the academic detective Kate Fansler, in which the challenge is extended to three frames, the well-made plot, the efficiency principle, and solution by detective protagonist. The convention of the well-made plot is that the problem stated at the beginning (modified, expanded, or contracted, as suits the story) is the one solved at the conclusion. The problem presented to Kate at the outset is to determine the truth about the role of the wife of a famous writer in that writer's career. Kate, as we will see in a moment, does not really "solve" that one, but she does come up with a bombshell solution of the murder of the writer himself, thus unveiling not the veiled mystery at the center of the story but a different one not introduced until the moment of resolution. The second point of challenge is the efficiency principle, which holds that everything in the story is likely to be important; traditionally, the tale of classic detection wastes few words. The challenge in *The Players Come Again* is a fifty-three page narrative that is in itself a fascinating story, but serves as little more than background to the detection plot.

The third convention challenged is also regulative, solution by the detective protagonist. The rule is that the problem is not only solved but is solved by the detective at the end of the story. Kate actually does very little detection, with the exception of her nearly gratuitous solution of the previously unsuspected murder. The solution of the main problem results almost entirely from the voluntary revelations of three friends, who have decided that Kate shall have the truth about the wife of the famous novelist. Notice that there is no question here about the breaking of a constitutive convention; the only challenge is to the regulative solution by detective protagonist, which is one of the conventions repeatedly tested by writers of our time, as in Clark's *Decked*, where the mystery is solved by the police. As we will see, however, not even the constitutive necessity for solution is exempt from the probings of a creative writer.

Changes in genres result from the interaction of two forces, the violations of conventions by writers and the acceptance of those violations by readers. According to Horton those conventions are *institutionalized*, however, and the readers' willingness to accept them will depend to a great degree on the strength of tradition in the genre through which they are institutionalized (15).

This brings us to consideration of the effect of the interaction between text and reader upon the nature of change in the formula. It is almost impossible to discuss the tension between invention and convention without reference to the pivotal position of the reader, whose acceptance or rejection largely determines the history of popular genres. We want to note especially how the reader of detective fiction is doubly conditioned, in the process of reading, by the social/cultural milieu on one hand and the prevalence of the formula on the other. It is this dual conditioning that creates the dialectic of Horton's institutionalized conventions, which represent the conservative aspect of the formula, and the creativity of authors, which supplies the counter-influence.

The historical view, says Jauss, poses a genre "in which every earlier element extends and completes itself through the later one." Thus, the relationship between a new book and the genre "presents itself as a continual founding and altering of horizons. The new text evokes for the reader . . . the horizon of expectations and 'rules of the game' familiar to him from earlier texts, which as such can be varied, extended, corrected, but also transformed, crossed out, or simply reproduced" (*TAR* 88). In this view, the amenability of the genre to the founding of new horizons and the altering of existing ones is dependent upon the strength of those earlier elements that persist in later expressions, and upon the strictness of the inherited rules of the game.

Because of its nature as transformed play, the detective story has developed a special set of limits, which welcome and even encourage innovation in certain conventions but not in others. The constitutive conventions, such as the necessity for solution, permit essentially no change. "Each formula," says Cawelti, "has its own set of limits that determine what kind of new and unique elements are possible without straining the formula to the breaking point" (*AMR* 10). Regulative conventions, on the other hand, are open to some innovation and even invite experiment: the seven-step plot is standard, but writers have always tried variations in the chronology, like converting the sequence of complication–period of gloom–dawning light into a cyclical structure that can be repeated several times without ruining the suspense element in the story. There is even greater flexibility in the recurrent themes, such as the most likely suspect and the death warrant: in these, as we noted in the last chapter, the structure of the convention remains the same, but the thematic material is subject to almost unlimited variation. The dying message is frequently recycled, but usually renovated in such fashion as to conform to the demands of reality.

The practice is especially visible in the private-eye story, which established some conventions of its own, notably the expanded commission, where a noncapital problem is later converted to murder: in some recent stories, private investigators are invited to help in murder investigations (*Dangerous Devotion*), or they may be excluded from the solution of the major mystery (*Decked*). Another liberalization is the freedom with which writers choose their narrative points of view. The old rule was that the story of the classic supersleuth is always told by someone else than the protagonist, because first-person narration would give away the workings of the detective's mind, but stories about private eyes, following the lead of Chandler, read better with the protagonist as narrator. The rule is now frequently disregarded by writers of both schools. The private-eye genre is also open to relaxation of such classic standbys as the efficiency principle, in the introduction of lengthy passages of nonhermeneutic material, like the politics in Prather's *The Trojan Hearse* or Spenser's love-life in Parker's series. Much the same can be said for the convention of self-reflexivity; private-eye readers are reminded much less frequently that what they are reading is a detective story.

As we saw in chapter 3, recurrent themes like the death warrant are subject to almost infinite variation, as are the missing person, the dying message, and most of the others. There seems to be a rule for the retention or rejection: those conventions with strong hermeneutic structure (anticipation-disappointment-fulfillment) are retained, those lacking it are discarded. This structure dominates the ones just mentioned, plus such other perennial favorites as the most likely suspect, the unidentifiable victim, and something bothering the detective. One especially pertinent illustration of the principle is the expression on the face of the victim, which recurs on occasion because of its suspense value, in spite of the fact that it has no basis in reality. In contrast, the justice thwarted convention, which we will examine shortly, did not outlast its own generation, apparently because of its weak hermeneutic structure.

Some critics object to the idea of the inherent conventionality of detection fiction, notably David R. Anderson, who in his afterword to *The Cunning Craft*, writes that "most of us [academics[still tend to treat the conventions of detective fiction as stable and authoritative despite our attention to real or perceived challenges to these conventions." He goes on to discuss the nature of some of these challenges and to question the conventional rigidity of the formula, and he calls upon the academic critic especially to give attention to some of the artificial restrictions we have placed upon the interpretation of the genre. "In doing this," he writes, "I believe we will find ourselves more and more uncertain about the possibility of any 'master' conventions for detective fiction and reluctant to speak with too much assurance about the rules of even the subgenres." He concludes with a reference to "walls" around the genre that we ourselves have erected, and adds, "Perhaps it is time they came down" (CC 188-90). While we can only applaud Anderson's call for more attention to the challenges to convention, we must remind ourselves not to be overeager to tear down the walls around detective fiction, because those walls have for the most part been erected by the fans, not the academics. Changes in the formula come about as a result of a writer's challenge, which if successful is imitated by other writers and is incorporated into the horizons of expectations of the readers. If some conventions seem overly rigid, we must remind ourselves that they are so because the readers like them that way. At several points in the preceding pages we have compared the rules of detective fiction to those of a game, and if the parallel is valid, we must not forget that the rules of a game are changed only with great reluctance, because without them the game would lose its meaning. Constitutive rules, whether in a ball game or in literature, do not simply regulate nearly so much as they make it possible to play the game (Straus *TLT* 215).

In the detective story, as in McBain's attempt to kill off Steve Carella, the tension between tradition and creation is inherently out of balance. Because of the essential conservatism of the genre, pressure is always stronger in the direction of the traditional and conventional. The formula's resistance to innovation becomes part of its horizon of expectations, with the result that the detection addict is conditioned toward keeping things as they are. The idea is well illustrated by Thomas J. Farrell in one of the essays in *The Cunning Craft.* Farrell comments upon the various efforts to "deconstruct" the Professor Moriarity of the Sherlock Holmes stories; according to one kind of reinterpretation, Moriarity is no Napoleon of crime at all but, as in Nicholas Meyer's *The Seven-Per-Cent Solution,* a harmless elderly teacher of mathematics. Farrell writes, "Popular literature usually gets a lot of cooperation from the reading public, and the popular reading mind clearly wants Moriarity to be as he is postulated" ("Deconstructing Moriarity" CC 60).

The prevalence of the detection formula and especially its influence upon the reader's reception of innovative practices are illustrated in the history of the genre. During the early years of the twentieth century the reading public rejected the "Had-I-But-Known" school of detective fiction (per AMS 319), which was the innovation attempted by Mary Roberts Rinehart and her imitators, but just a few years later accepted the hard-boiled school of Dashiell Hammett and his successors, in spite of the fact that, thematically, the hard-boiled approach appears to be a much more radical departure than the relatively innocuous ambience of the Rinehart school. Rinehart's *The Circular Staircase* (1908), with its artificially imposed limits, its postponements, missing witnesses, mysterious figures and concealed identities, is a classic of the "Had-I-But-Known" type, which earned its title from its habit of blocking the reader's access to the realities of the story, and which in this novel serves to bolster a weak hermeneutic structure.

The Circular Staircase challenges two of the constitutive conventions of the formula, the detective protagonist and the primacy of the detection plot. The real protagonist, the narrator, can hardly be called a detective because she spends most of the story in as much of a fog as anyone else, and the real detective, a policeman, actually plays a minor part. At the same time, most of the real detection takes place offstage, in a position decidedly secondary to the muddlings of the narrator and her associates. The challenge did not succeed: despite Rinehart's own popularity as a storyteller and the number of her imitators, the "Had-I-But-Known" formula did not outlive its generation (Haycraft, *MP* 89).

How, then, did Hammett succeed where Rinehart did not? Hammett's novels of detection challenge the regulative conventions of the detection formula, but not the four "Murders in the Rue Morgue" basics, and the hard-boiled conventions not only gained acceptance but were incorporated into the readers' horizons of expectations as an acceptable variation on the classic theme.

Thus, when a Rinehart or a Hammett publishes an innovative novel, the disparity between this newness and the reader's expectations becomes a negativity, an aesthetic distance between the horizon of the work and that of the reader. Over a period of time, and after further experience with the innovation, the negativity of the new approach disappears, and the innovation itself has become part of the reader's own expectations. In a rigid genre like detective fiction, however, an additional step enters the process: before it can be absorbed into the reader's horizon, it must demonstrate its compatibility with the formula. If the distance is too great, as with the "Had-I-But-Known" story, readers will reject it; but if, as history demonstrated in the case of the hard-boiled innovation, the new work is consonant with the constitutive elements of the genre, the distance disappears.

While the history of detective fiction does not reveal a clear pattern of adoption, cultivation, and rejection of conventions, it does display a tendency to retain useful standbys or to revive old ones on the basis of hermeneutic value. Consider, for example, the locked-room convention, which Poe introduced in "The Murders in the Rue Morgue" and which has been so frequently recycled by detective-story writers as to have assumed a mystique of its own and to have almost achieved the status of subgenre.[5] The locked-room story is especially distinguished by two characteristics: it has terrific suspense value, and it represents such a marked departure from any pretense at realism as to appear completely incompatible with hard-boiled detection. The prevalence of hermeneutic value over the demands of reality is demonstrated in its successful employment by Henry Kane in the private-eye novelette *The Narrowing Lust,* and by Ed McBain in a police procedural novel, *Killer's Wedge.*

We can summarize the rule of change in detective fiction with two statements: first, the weight of tradition is heavier than it is in most other genres, and second, hermeneutic value is the arbiter of innovation. The bounds of the detection genre not only invite challenge but will yield to testing and may even produce a new variant, provided that the innovations conform to the hermeneutic intention of the formula. The primacy of hermeneutic specialization is historical, one of those elements which, according to Jauss, "extends and completes itself" in later manifestations.

"A theory of genres grounded in an aesthetics of reception," says Jauss, "necessarily will add to the study of the structural relations between literature and society, work and audience, where the historical system of norms of a 'literary public' lies hidden in a distant past; there it can most readily be reconstructed through the horizon of expectations of a genre system that preconstituted the intention of the works as well as the understanding of the audience" (*TAR* 108).

The statement reflects the influence of both reception theory and phenomenological criticism. The norms in reading (the understandings or assumptions with which the reader proceeds through the book) are in neither the written work alone nor the reader alone; they are preconstituted by the genre system which predisposes both the intent (the aims or purposes) of the book and the understanding of the reader (that is, what is understood by the reader as acceptable). The system of norms of the reading public "lies hidden in a distant past"; the historical system is the product of both past reading and social/cultural experience.

I want to note especially the use of the word *intention*, one of the most controversial terms in literary theory: Is the purpose of the work in the mind of the author or the interpretation of the reader? Jauss's theory, like that of Iser and many other reception theorists, locates the source of intent of the book in the interaction between text and reader, within the generic horizon of expectations. The concept satisfies the intentionality of the detective story except that, in the special case of detective fiction, the only acceptable intention must meet the demands of hermeneutic specialization, which places upon the reader the special necessity for being alert for secondary meanings. In any other kind of fiction, the fact that a half-forgotten idea is annoying a character may or may not be significant, but in a tale of detection the presence of something bothering the detective is practically guaranteed to develop into a clue, as it does in *The High Window* when Marlowe says, "Something squirmed at the back of my mind": a few pages later the squirming thought starts him onto a new and profitable line of inquiry (113, 118). The intention of detective fiction is hermeneutic to the degree that a loss of hermeneutic drive is the loss of genre itself.

As a result, most of the changes in the detection genre are thematic, very few structural. The principle is clear in the history of the dying message convention, which we cited a little earlier as one of those old conventions rich in suspense value and also amenable to endless revival, because the device may assume either of two forms, one decidedly nonmimetic and the other quite plausible. The implausible version is the one in which the murder victim, in the last seconds before death, concocts a clue so abstruse as to require all the powers of the protagonist detective to solve it, like the crossed-fingers signal of the murdered man in Ellery Queen's *The Tragedy of X*. There is another, closer to reality, in which the obscurity of the message results from the victim's inability to communicate clearly; this is the device employed by Kaminsky and Grafton in the instances cited, where the hermeneutic structure of availability-disappointment-fulfillment remains intact, even though the thematic material is considerably different.

In a genre with a strong history of hermeneutic domination like detective fiction, two conditions result from the fact that the expectations of the genre preconstitute both the intention of the book and the understanding of the reader: the readers want to keep most of the narrative structures much as they have been, and the intention of the genre consequently becomes what Lovitt calls its intolerance toward innovation (CC 71). Thus a reciprocal feedback develops, where the intolerance of the genre is absorbed by the detective story addict, who is further conditioned in the direction of leaving certain things as they are. They do not, as Farrell says, want Moriarity "deconstructed": they find the Napoleon of Crime more acceptable than the wimpy mathematics teacher of the revisionists. Quite often this intolerance toward innovation asserts itself in the very techniques of storytelling that characterize the detection formula. One of the hallmarks of the traditional detective story has been its habit of repeatedly reminding its readers to pay attention to such details as the exact time at which a crime was committed, and the same textual guidance is preserved in hard-boiled detection. Thus, when Travis McGee in MacDonald's *The Lonely Silver Rain,* speculating about the past of one of the other characters, remarks on "something a little out of focus" (16), the signal is clear: Watch it, something will come of this.

Indications are that the direction of change in the detection genre has been determined almost exclusively by the innate intention of the genre, expressed in its resistance to innovation, and very little by changes in the social/cultural milieu. Because of the book's tendency to minimize stress, for example, the detective story responds to an inner need to get away from reality. In times of great crisis like war and economic disaster, people read detective novels in order to escape from rather than to participate in reality. The need was dramatically manifest in London during the blitzkrieg in the early 1940s, when people spending the night in air-raid shelters could not get their fill of classic prewar detective fiction. During that war several writers incorporated military themes into their books, like Rex Stout, whose Nero Wolfe and Archie Goodwin became involved in the war effort. When the war ended, however, the genre returned to its customary negation of external reality. The principle is well illustrated in Josephine Tey's *Miss Pym Disposes,* which, although it was published in 1947, carefully avoids any mention of the just-ended war and the severe economic conditions that were affecting the lives of all British people. Another, and more general, application of the principle can be found in the way in which the reader of the novel is asked to accept the idea that Lucy Pym, with no formal training in the field, writes a book on psychology that not only is a bestseller but wins the praise of professionals in the field.

We have discussed two principles that determine the degree and direction of change in detective fiction. The first of these is the premise of the genre with its special dynamic, which responds to its own values and limits. The second is the conception of hermeneutic value as the determinant of the survival and continuation of conventions.

The operation of both principles can be illustrated with a narrative device that enjoyed considerable popularity for a time, then faded and has generally failed to reappear in more recent writers. We will call it the justice thwarted theme, the Golden Age custom of permitting the guilty party to kill himself rather then face arrest and trial. As in the case of most of the after-Poe recurrent themes, the time and place of origin of this one are unknown.

I will begin with what must be the best known instance, the suicide of the narrator–confessed murderer Dr. Sheppard, in Christie's *The Murder of Roger Ackroyd* (1929). Here is the ending of Dr. Sheppard's account:

> "When I have finished writing, I shall enclose the whole manuscript in an envelope and address it to Poirot.
> "And then—What shall it be? Veronal? . . .
> "I have no pity for myself . . . " (197)

That lack of pity for the criminal becomes, as we will see, one of the constants of the justice thwarted theme.

According to Earl Bargainnier, Christie used the device eight times. In five novels (all featuring Hercule Poirot) the detective does nothing to prevent suicide, and in the other three the act takes place before anyone can intervene. It was Christie's attitude, says Bargainnier, that discovery of the murderer was sufficient, with the innocent saved and the perpetrator removed from society. Affirmation of social and moral codes is the requirement of classic detective fiction that necessitates the removal of the criminal from the community. "As long as he is removed, the form of retributive justice is, for Christie, relatively unimportant . . .".[6]

Bargainnier does not include *Curtain* (1975) in his count, apparently because it represents a variation on the theme, where Poirot accomplishes the purpose by voluntarily cutting off his own life-support. "Good-bye, *cher ami*," he says in his farewell note to the faithful Hastings. "I have removed the amyl nitrite ampoules away from beside my bed. I prefer to leave myself in the hands of the *bon Dieu*. May his punishment, or his mercy, be swift!" (237). Like Dr. Sheppard, Poirot asks only mercy, not pity.

After solving the complex locked-room problem in Van Dine's *The Canary Murder Case* (1927), Philo Vance explains his solution to District Attorney Markham, while the murderer waits in the next room. Suddenly there is a loud pistol shot and Markham shouts, "He's shot himself," to which the urbane Vance replies, "Fancy that." When Markham accuses him of purposely giving the murderer the opportunity, Vance says, "However unethical—theoretically—it may be to take another's life, a man's own life is certainly his to do with as he chooses. Suicide is his inalienable right" (255). Van Dine varies the device in *The Bishop Murder Case* (1928), in which Vance switches wine glasses, causing the accidental suicide of the real murderer, who had tried to do the same to an innocent suspect. Once again Markham accuses him of taking the law into his own hands, whereupon Vance responds, I took it in my arms. It was helpless," and tells Markham he feels no more compunction than he would in crushing a poisonous reptile (255).

Vance's cynicism and contempt for democratic institutions are not shared by Peter Wimsey, who allows the privilege to the murderer in Sayers's *The Unpleasantness at the Bellona Club* (1928). Wimsey asks the guilty party to write an explanatory note, then leaves him alone with a gun at his side (189). Lord Peter's motive is humane and even sporting, but he also wants to protect a young woman who had become involved and who might have been convicted along with the real perpetrator.

The device apparently reached the height of its popularity in the 1920s and was even used by Hammett in *The Dain Curse* in 1929. It appears in several of Rex Stout's novels featuring Nero Wolfe who, although a generation later than Vance and Wimsey, is solidly in the classic tradition. Wolfe spends chapter 16 of *Too Many Clients* (1960) explaining to Benedict Aiken his solution to the murder and the steps by which he had proved Aiken to be the killer. He leaves Aiken with an option of suicide that will expire on the following morning, at which time Wolfe will call the police. His strategy is somewhat different from that of Wimsey and Vance but is pure Wolfe: his primary motive is to protect the interests of the corporation that employed him, and, incidentally to protect his own fee.

His professional obligation as a private investigator, as usual in the Stout stories, is decidedly secondary to Wolfe's convenience (180-81). In *Gambit* (1962) he forces a confession and suicide from a man who could never have been convicted, and when Lieutenant Cramer accuses him of trickery Wolfe replies, "You have been delivered from the ignominy of convicting an innocent man, and from the embarrassment of arresting a guilty man who couldn't be convicted" (187). Like Vance, Wolfe does not hesitate to make judgments that disregard the public standard of justice, but the added ingredient in these stories is Wolfe's own mercenary interest, which is likely to assume first priority.

The Justice thwarted theme is virtually unused today, having apparently proved to be a fad that exhausted itself instead of a convention endowed with the quality of endless repeatability. Unlike some of the old repeatables like the Most likely suspect, the Dying message, and dozens of others, Justice thwarted was not adopted by the private-eye tradition, possibly because it tends to be conspicuously trendy and contrived. Hammett made use of it in *The Dain Curse*, possibly because the date of its publication (1929) placed it within the heyday of the convention's popularity, though its appearance there is a variation rather than a restatement of the theme itself. In that novel Mrs. Leggett, after a lengthy confession, bolts from the room with a gun in her hand. The Continental Op catches her and wrestles with her on the staircase: "Gunfire roared in my ear, burnt my cheek. The woman's body went limp. When [two policemen] pulled us apart she lay still. The second bullet had gone through her throat" (57). The variation is the position of the suicide, which occurs long before the end of the book, and even a considerable time before the end of the first part of the novel on page 98.

These are only a few of the instances of the theme; there must have been dozens of others. Whatever the reason for the fadeout, it was certainly not a lack of flexibility: as we have seen, it is subject to quite as many variations as the perennial death warrant. The reason must be found rather in an inherent lack of hermeneutic value resulting from the accident of its position outside the hermeneutic structure. We should add, moreover, that the justice thwarted theme does not satisfy any need in terms of game or myth: Anglo-American detective fiction rarely even mentions the punishment of the criminal. The principle can be expressed in terms of the detective story as play, since nobody takes much interest in what happens to the loser; there will be a new game tomorrow, a new book to read next week. If, with Auden, we read detective fiction as celebration of myth, then the ritual is concluded when catharsis is achieved, or when the guilty society has been cleansed (Winks, *DF* 16).

Instances of historical developments of this kind demonstrate the principle that the detection genre is tolerant toward only those innovations that meet the test of hermeneutic value. This principle, coupled with the strong conventionality of detective fiction, has endowed the genre with its own special dynamic, which responds to its unique literary inheritance.

The conservative intentionality of the detection genre is actually the inheritance of "The Murders in the Rue Morgue" and its two successors. Poe unwittingly built into the Dupin stories a genetic coding that not only determined the purpose of the genre but in several respects pointed the direction for its future development. We can cite two evidences of this coding, in the shift away from violence and toward ratiocination, and in the changing relationship between the detective protagonist and the official police. Each of these elements originated in "The Murders in the Rue Morgue" and was further developed in the other Dupin tales. Thus, by the time it left Poe's hands, the new genre had confirmed not only a set of traditions but also a genetic code.

One of the most obvious features of the history of the detective story has been its tendency to work out solutions through the exercise of intelligence rather than physical violence. The pattern is clear enough in the changing intent of the three Dupin tales: "The Murders in the Rue Morgue" is a violent story, with its highlighting of the savage murders of Madame L'Espanaye and her daughter. The murder in "The Mystery of Marie Roget" is also violent, but the violence is offstage and is the object of dispassionate analysis, and "The Purloined Letter" is almost free of violence. The avoidance of violence reached its height in the Golden Age, especially in the stories of Agatha Christie, whose fictional crimes achieved such a level of neatness that *The Gentle Art of Murder* was the title Bargainnier appropriately gave his study of Christie as a literary figure. The hard-boiled story restored much of the brutality to the genre, but even there the coding is manifest in the fact that the private detective avoids force whenever possible; most private-eye detectives in fiction do not carry guns: Paretsky's Vic Warshawski in *Indemnity Only* has not owned a gun in years and must buy one before undertaking a dangerous mission, and Dawson's Jeri Howard remarks at one point in *Take a Number* that having a gun in the house is like keeping a rattlesnake for a pet.

Another instance of genetic coding is the changing relationship between the detective protagonist and the Paris police in the Dupin stories. The police resent Dupin's successful intrusion in "The Murders in the Rue Morgue," and the Prefect offers an observation toward the end of the story about the appropriateness of people minding their own business. Things soften up a little, however, in "The Mystery of Marie Roget," when the Prefect comes around to see if Dupin has any ideas on the matter, and at the beginning of "The Purloined Letter" it is the Prefect who dumps the problem in Dupin's lap. Here is another of those stamps Poe placed upon the Dupin stories that are replicated in the structure of the genre: open hostility, followed by cautious toleration, and finally friendliness and even dependence. It is obvious in the relationships between Holmes and Scotland Yard, between Perry Mason and Lieutenant Tragg, and even in the hard-boiled novels, although he gets some rough handling from them on occasion, Chandler's Philip Marlowe discovers that the police are as a rule tolerant and even cooperative when approached in the right spirit. Today, the same spirit of cooperation has developed to the point where Calvin Morgan in Beck's *Amateur Night* envies the private detectives in books and on TV with such terrific sources in the police department, and private investigator Sydney Bryant in Wallace's *Deadly Devotion* is about to marry a policeman.

The conservatism of the genre is a consequence of the nature of the detective story as play. Play experience tends to be fixed, and the rules of games are changed only rarely and then within narrow limits. Because it is fundamentally a play experience, the detective story is inclined to control its own direction. Consequently, the evolution of the detection formula cannot be described as an orderly advance from rigidity to increased flexibility, marked by a progressive discard of the obsolete and reinforcement of the useful. The detection genre tends to be a closed system within which there exists a referential field of impressive variety, composed of a rich stock of conventions "known,

accepted, and endlessly repeatable," and possessed of considerable hermeneutic value (Hall and Whannel, *PA* 57).

Changes in the genre are the result of a continuing state of
tension between convention and creation. As we have seen, the
formula resists change, but innovative writers continue to probe
its boundaries, and the detection formula does make some
allowance for change. By definition the constitutive conventions
are not subject to alteration; there have been no real break-
throughs to date, although writers can alter the interpretation of
the convention. This is the case with the rule that the only acceptable closure in a detective story is solution of the problem, which
is considered impervious to change. The rule is generally accompanied by a regulative corollary, that the solution must be postponed until the end of the story. This one has been challenged a
number of times, most successfully by R. Austin Freeman with his
"inverted" story, which gave the reader a complete account of the
commission of the crime (including the identity of the perpetrator) at the beginning of the story but preserved its hermeneutic
structure in the efforts of the police to discover what the reader
already knew.[7]

Changes in the regulative conventions are easy, as we have
already observed in the case of the standard seven-step plot,
where the sequence of confusion–dawning light–solution, for
example, may be repeated several times, as when the initial solution proves wrong. The same flexibility exists in the case of the
efficiency principle, which is considerably relaxed in the private-
eye story.In that large stock of conventions we are calling recurrent themes, variations are really needed, in order to keep the thematic material from becoming stale. If the most likely suspect
always turned up innocent, the convention would soon lose its
hermeneutic value, and so the suspect is occasionally guilty.
Sometimes the convention needs to be updated in order to
strengthen its plausibility, as in the variations in the dying message. Here, the controlling influence is hermeneutic intent:
changes are permissible as long as they do not violate it, transforming the detective story into a different genre. Most of the
trends we have examined are illustrated in the following recent
novels, previously discussed:

K.K. Beck, *Amateur Night* (1993)
Carol Higgins Clark, *Decked* (1992)
Max Allan Collins, *Nice Weekend for a Murder* (1986)

Trella Crespi, *The Trouble with Moonlighting* (1991)
Janet Dawson, *Take a Number* (1993)
Patricia Wallace, *Deadly Devotion* (1994)
Eric Wright, *A Fine Italian Hand* (1994)

All of these are currently or recently displayed paperbacks on the shelves of a popular bookstore, chosen without special regard for distribution of amateur vs professional detective, or male vs female author. The 4:5 distribution between men and women writers probably represents the actual ratio on the current market.

"Conventions such as generic forms," says de Beaugrande, "become stabilized as integrative frames for managing the complexity of individual acts of writing or reading. In exchange, authors and readers feel impelled to innovate against these frames, at least over long periods of time" (*CD* 11).

For those stories in which the protagonist is one of the analytic masterminds of the school of Dupin or Holmes, readers have become accustomed to the telling of the tale by either an awestruck assistant or an impersonal author, because that is the only kind of narration that protects the suspense. For the reader to be admitted to the mind of a secretive eccentric like Peter Wimsey or Nero Wolfe would be a betrayal of the "sacralized closure" so prized by mystery fans. Not so, however, with a Sam Spade or a Philip Marlowe, who is often quite as baffled as the reader and with whom the reader feels a sense of comradeship that could never be shared with Sherlock Holmes. Here is one of de Beaugrande's integrative frames for the management of reading and writing, and it has, true to form, become a regulative convention of the genre.

This convention is a good one with which to begin a discussion of innovation because it has been the subject of more experiment than any other in the genre. Three of the private-eye stories in our list (*Decked, Deadly Devotion and All Things Under the Moon*), test the limits of the genre by using author narrators. The other two (*Take a Number* and *The Long-Legged Fly*) follow the Hammett-Chandler convention. The proportion of convention to invention is approximately the same in the stories featuring amateur detectives. In *The Trouble with Moonlighting* and *Nice Weekend for a Murder* the protagonist is the narrator, but the story of *Amateur Night* is told by the author. The one police novel, *A Fine Italian Hand*, follows the formula of author narrator.

It would be unwise to generalize a trend on the basis of these few instances, except to say that the first-person narrator appears to be a convention that invites innovation. The tendency seems reasonable, because the roles of the detectives themselves have become less stereotyped in recent books. There is no danger to hermeneutic structure in admitting the reader to the mind of Jane da Silva in *Amateur Night* or of "Mal" Mallory in *Nice Weekend for a Murder,* because neither of them comes close to the status of eccentric genius. At the same time, it seems quite natural for Simona Griffo (*The Trouble with Moonlighting*) to tell her own story. Although she works for an advertising agency, Simona has much in common with today's private detectives in fiction: she is divorced, she is conscious of her age she lacks self-confidence, and before the end of her story she becomes involved in considerable violence. As a matter of fact, none of these novels has created any appreciable aesthetic distance from the expectations of their audiences.

Two other innovations in the first list of novels above deserve comment. The first is the probe of the detective protagonist convention in Clark's *Decked.* Regan Reilly, the protagonist, is a private detective, but she is invited into the investigation of murder chiefly because she had been the victim's roommate. Regan does become involved in the apprehension of another criminal, but the original problem is solved by the police with minor assistance from her. This brings us to the second innovation, a modification of the original commission—expanded commission, where the private investigator is first engaged for a noncapital crime and is later involved in a murder. *Take a Number* follows the standard plot: Jeri Howard's first commission is to collect evidence to support a divorce proceeding, but when her client is accused of the murder of her estranged husband, Jeri's task is transformed into a murder investigation. The convention is tested in *Deadly Devotion,* in which the private detective is engaged in a murder investigation from the start, and in *Decked,* where the private detective is initially asked to help the police on a murder case.

As a result of such continual probings as these, there appears to be one discernible trend in recent literary detection, a weakening of the former barriers between the classical and the private-eye structures. What may be happening is a process not uncommon in popular fiction, in which two types borrow successful features from each other. Apparently the classic story is adopting more action and considerable violence, while the private-eye type is settling into the classic structure.

At any rate, the outlines are not as sharp as they once were: except for her amateur status, Simona lives the life of a private investigator, and Regan Reilly might as well be an amateur in *Decked*.

The books discussed up to this point are generally conventional, offering very few meaningful challenges to the limits of the formula. There are two, however, currently in circulation that probe the bounds of the genre with much more serious intent: Robert Morgan's *All Things Under the Moon* and James Sallis's *The Long-Legged Fly*.

Readers unfamiliar with Morgan's unusual themes would probably approach *All Things Under the Moon* in the expectation of a story that conforms to the structure of the detection genre, in the hard-boiled mode. These expectations are reinforced by the publisher's blurb, which reads as follows:

P.I. Teddy London never met a client as desperate and driven as Maxim Warhelski. The haunted European had devoted his life to one purpose, hunting down the killer who butchered his family. It happened on the first night of the new moon—a pattern repeated in similar circumstances in Russia, India, and Afghanistan. Now, after a lifelong quest, Maxim wants Teddy to help him find this human monster. There's just one problem. The tracks belong to a wolf.

The reader is led to believe that the novel follows the private-eye structure, which it does for the most part. The fact that Teddy London's detective agency specializes in the elimination of vampires, werewolves, and other such spectral creatures is no real problem for the detection genre, especially when we remember the number of successful stories that combine the theme of detection with that of the supernatural, like "The Sussex Vampire" and *The Hound of the Baskervilles*. Note, for example, how clearly the blurb's statement "The tracks belong to a wolf" echo the familiar "Mr. Holmes, they were the footprints of a gigantic hound." The difference in the Teddy London series is that the supernatural is real, not the result of faulty perception, as in the Holmes stories.

With the exception of a few tentative probes and one real challenge, *All Things Under the Moon* falls within the limits of the constitutive conventions of detection. The detective protagonist is in this case corporate, Teddy London's Monster Killers, but team detection is traditional, as in the police story, where a team of detectives or even a whole department will work on a single case. This novel does test the convention of the primacy of detection, however, in the tendency of the theme of supernatural horror to crowd out conventional detection. The Veiled Secret, how to kill the immortal werewolf, though unusual in detective fiction, conforms to the generic structure of the impossible problem. Finally, the resolution of this story does represent a real breakthrough; the problem is solved when the werewolf is eliminated, but the method of solution violates the regulative convention that forbids supernatural intervention.

Despite its gruesome content, *All Things Under the Moon* adheres to the play structure of literary detection. Stress is eliminated throughout by constant reassurances that the werewolf will be killed, as in the remark of one of London's team, "You just say the word, big man, and I'll fry our puppy's ears off" (125). The to-and-fro movement of transformed play is natural to fantasy, which by definition is not going anywhere in real-world terms; readers familiar with the *Cat Who* stories of Lillian Jackson Braun should have no difficulties sharing the scene with a werewolf.

The novel probes some of the regulative conventions of the private-eye genre, as have several other recent stories. In keeping with what appears to be a current trend, the narrator is an impersonal author instead of the traditional first person. On the other hand, the book follows the convention of the expanded commission: the original commission, to eliminate the werewolf, is intensified when several of London's people are killed by the beast. The police (in this case the FBI) are pompous and stupid, in keeping with the tradition that goes back to Poe.

Is *All Things Under the Moon* a detective story? A librarian might experience some problems placing it within the present system of classification. As an innovation it could represent the beginning of a new parallel formula or even a variant of the detection genre if it is successfully imitated by other writers and overcomes the aesthetic distance between it and the rest of the genre.

Much more experimental than anything we have discussed so far, *The Long-Legged Fly* by James Sallis is a good illustration of detective fiction as a dialectic of context (conventions, rules of the game, present horizons) and negativity (innovations, aesthetic distance). This dialectic becomes the dynamic of the novel: as the story unfolds, the play structure and the reader's expectations and horizons are increasingly dominated by the exchange between the context of convention and the negativity of invention.

The point is illustrated in the negativity created by the opening and closing scenes of the novel. Chapter 1 begins with a dialogue between two men named Harry and Carl and ends when Carl kills Harry to avenge somebody called Angie. The negativity is deepened at the beginning of chapter 2, with a switch to an entirely different scene with a new set of characters. There is no further reference to the events of chapter 1 until twenty-three pages later, when Harry and Angie are tentatively identified. Carl is not identified but is presumably the name used by Lew Griffin, the protagonist narrator. One difference between reading fiction and reading nonfiction is that there is in fiction no ready-made context; the reader must assemble one during the process of reading (Eagleton *LT* 88). In this novel, the negativity is intensified by the fact that the reader must supply two contexts, one for the initial disparity between chapter 1 and what follows, and another for the rest of the book. That the situation in chapter 1 is never developed beyond a few tentative identifications creates what Iser calls the "hollow form of the text," which must be "filled by mental images of the reader" (*AR* 225). As the story unfolds, negativity is piled upon negativity, and each in turn enters the reader's horizon.

In this way, the normal interchange between text and reader is modified, with the result that "degrees of indeterminacy relate less to the text itself than to the connections established between text and reader during the reading process" (181). Significantly, the negativity is not dispelled at the point of resolution, by which time the first-person narrator Lew Griffin has become a successful novelist. The concluding paragraph negates all that has gone before with a reminder that all this has been a fiction:

> And so, another book. But not about my Cajun this time. About someone I've named Lew Griffin, a man I know very well and not at all. And I have only to end it now by writing: I went back into the house and wrote. It is midnight. The rain beats at the windows. . . . It is not midnight. It is not raining. (184)

The plot structure of *The Long-Legged Fly* is unconventional, composed of a sequence of four stories, each an account of a case handled by Lew Griffin, a black New Orleans private investigator. At the beginning of the novel, Lew is a standard professional private detective, short of funds (10), divorced (45), who has been under treatment by a psychiatrist (41). The first story is a standard missing-person problem, in which the private detective is commissioned to find a woman scheduled to deliver a lecture in New Orleans but who never appeared. Although Lew finds her, the cause of her disappearance is left unresolved; she is confined to a nursing home, hopelessly psychotic. At this point, the reader does not experience any great aesthetic distance between this book and the rest of the genre, aside from the negativity created here by the partly solved mystery and the one still undetermined from chapter 1. Much the same is true of the second case, of a runaway teenager, which shares the conventional structure of the first plot. Lew finds the missing youngster, but not in time to save her from murder (80). Now the reader's expectation, based upon earlier experience, is that one of these stories is the subplot of the other, or that they are parallel plots, because at this juncture, only halfway through the book, neither of them has been resolved in conventional style.

Neither of these plots represents any fundamental violation of the institutionalized conventions, but the situation begins to change in the third commission, which specifically challenges the hermeneutic structure itself. Lew seeks another missing person, this time the sister of a friend, undertaken as a personal favor (115), but he does not really find her—she shows up of her own accord (150). The fourth problem is the search for his own son (165), who is never found and is presumed dead (181). By this time the private investigator has become a successful novelist and apparently the "author" of his own story (184).

In spite of the novel's apparent drift away from the detection genre as the story progresses, the author seems unwilling to abandon the standard formula. Late in the book, when the private eye has become a sensitive novelist, we come upon a sudden recurrence of conventional self-reflexivity, with a reference to Chandler's *The Big Sleep* on page 161, to Sherlock Holmes ("I remind you of the curious incident of the dog in the nighttime") on 172, to Andre Gide's remark about detective stories on 174, and a to a 1940s style black-and-white movie as late as page 182, as if to assure the reader that the formula is still in control. Moreover, the novel follows the structure of transformed play, based in this case upon the dominance of negativity. The reader, much more thoroughly puzzled than would be the case in another book, is faced with an abundance of tasks and is challenged to interpret them within the framework of the detection formula. What, for instance, are the explanations for the half-solved mysteries, as in those cases where missing persons are found but the mystery is not really cleared up?

The book is rich in the to-and-fro motion of transformed play. The absence of intention of social or cultural significance is confirmed in the reminder at the end not only that this is just a detective story but also that it is merely fiction, an affirmation that in addition eliminates the possibility of stress.

The question of whether *The Long-Legged Fly* is a successful novel will depend to a very large degree upon its ability to change readers' expectations. The early portion of the novel raises and satisfies most of the generic expectations, like those with regard to the original commission and the expanded commission in the first two plots. The hopeless psychotic Lew finds at the end of the first plot is to all intents dead, and the original commission is expanded to murder, although, as we have already noted, a negativity is created in the fact that the real reason for the woman's condition is never discovered. The expectations effective in the second plot are satisfied in somewhat more conventional fashion except for the fact that the murder is solved more by inference than by real detection.

The innovations against the integrative frame in *The Long-Legged Fly* can be summarized: First, the detective protagonist is transformed from the role of the hard-boiled private eye who kicks a couple of porn moviemakers that try to impede his investigation (68), to that of sensitive novelist. At the same time, the dominant detection plot of the early part of the story successively yields to other concerns. Third, the mysteries become more thinly veiled; the problems of the missing lecturer and the runaway teenager are mysterious enough to satisfy the requirements of hermeneutic specialization, but the missing sister returns when she is ready, and the disappearance of Lew's son really involves no mystery at all. Finally, resolution in the "detective story sense" is not achieved in either of the last two plots.

The question of whether *The Long-Legged Fly* is a detective novel is not nearly so important as that of its possible effect upon the genre it challenges. If the literary quality of a new book can be measured in terms of its aesthetic distance from the existing genre, says Jauss, then it follows that the gap between the new work and the genre can disappear if the work becomes "self-evident" and is accepted into the horizon of future readers (*TAR* 25). This is what happened in the case of the Hammett novels in the 1920s and 1930s. Hammett gained wide popular acceptance and was soon followed in the same generic frame by writers like Chandler and Macdonald, who not only imitated Hammett but improved his method, with the result that within a short time the private-eye story was accepted as a subgenre on its own. The future of a creative work like *The Long-Legged Fly* will depend, according to Jauss, upon the question of whether it presents a "pleasing or an alienating new perspective" to the reader whose expectations are pre-conditioned by the current genre. This novel is unusually well written for a popular work, and it consequently presents a "pleasing perspective" to the extent that the reader is willing to rise to the unusual demands it makes.

One point must be made in the discussion of this novel, which, because of our concentration upon structure, has necessarily neglected the artistry of its thematic development. It represents, for example, an unusually well-developed exploration of the theme of appearance vs reality; as the story progresses, plots become increasingly mimetic and correspondingly less hermeneutic, its purpose no longer "to create a mystery for the sole purpose of effecting its effortless dissipation" (Grossvogel *MIF* 15), but a participation in life the way it is, where most mysteries are not solved. We should also note once more the creative ending of the book, where novel envelops detective story, as the artist reminds the reader that he is still there: "It is not midnight. It is not raining."

The only reason for using recent books to illustrate the process of change in the genre is their immediacy: developing a scene for change necessarily involves the examination of a large number of books current at that point in the genre's history. Actually, the same kind of examination could be made at any point since the earliest days of detective fiction, and it would undoubtedly reveal much the same scene, with readers conditioned by the prevalent conventions and inventive writers undertaking to pass the limits of the generic mold. Because of the conservatism of the genre, most of their innovations are never accepted as conventions, but those writers who do successfully overleap the bounds of formula become the instruments of generic change.

We have previously discussed the "hard-boiled" or "private-eye" story in various contexts, as the one major breakthrough in the history of detective fiction and as the classic contrast to the classic genre. In chapter 5, we will consider the private-investigator story as part of a continuity "in which every earlier element extends and completes itself through the later one" (Jauss, *TAR* 88).

5

The Mean Streets and the Mall

An Agatha Christie addict might have experienced a considerable jolt in undertaking Mickey Spillane's *I, the Jury* during the 1950s, but I doubt if a reader of Emma Lathen or Amanda Cross today would sense much difference in a novel by Dick Francis, because the thematic differences between private-eye and formal-problem detection are apparently disappearing. As we saw in chapter 4, the private-eye formula shares the basic structure of mainstream detective fiction and has access to the same store of conventions, and it has, during its more than sixty-year history, generated a new structure and some conventions of its own.

Before discussing the kind of detective novel first written by Dashiell Hammett and later developed and refined by Raymond Chandler, there is need to clarify some terms, because the members of this genre are sometimes grouped according to *status* ("private eye," as opposed to the official police or the gifted amateur) or according to *ambience* ("hard-boiled," as distinguished from the "soft-boiled" or "English" mystery). Although the meaning of both terms is apparently satisfactory for advertising, neither is completely suited to our purposes. If by *private eye* we mean a professional private detective, then we must include a number of fictional private investigators outside the Hammett-Chandler tradition, like some of the best ones, Sherlock Holmes and Nero Wolfe. *Hard-boiled* is even less descriptive, largely because its view is too narrowly synchronic. It was completely appropriate to a roughneck like Spillane's Mike Hammer and even, to a more limited degree, Hammett's Continental Op, Chandler's Philip Marlowe, and Macdonald's Lew Archer. In the 1990s, although the term may be appropriate to the occasional gunplay in Robert Parker or the explicit cruelty in Dick Francis, it does not do well for the work of Marcia Muller or Jon Katz.

The critical literature dealing with the private-investigator story is considerable, much of it devoted to contrasts between the stable world of Sherlock Holmes and the tempestuous environment of the Continental Op and Philip Marlowe. I want to suggest, however, that the most reliable and also the simplest means of distinguishing between the two schools is a comparison of their methods of detection. Stout's Nero Wolfe and Carter Brown's Danny Boyd are both private investigators and they inhabit the same turbulent world; the difference between them lies in the way they solve mysteries. Boyd is an energetic detective, heavily dependent upon physical activity, following up leads and interviewing witnesses; Wolfe is the "ratiocinative" detective, drawing upon the resources of his brilliance, and accomplishing much of his work while closing his eyes and pushing his lips in and out.

The ratiocinative pattern, like so many of the other conventional forms of the classic detective story, originated with Poe's Dupin: not for him the frenetic searches and the checking out of endless data carried on by the official police. Dupin uses his intellect in order to conserve physical effort, as in his location of the missing letter in "The Purloined Letter," where the method is almost purely syllogistic. He begins with the statement of two "givens": first, "the daring, dashing, and discriminating nature of D——— ," (the minister who had hidden the stolen document), and second, the presumption that the letter was not hidden within the limits of the police search. Combining these givens with the inference that the document must always be at hand in order to pose a constant threat, Dupin reaches the astounding but logical conclusion that the letter is not hidden at all (Poe 306). The spectacular intellectuality of Dupin and his successors has two qualities that have consistently appealed to readers: it avoids physical effort and it is infallible. Not all the classic detectives could employ a method so purely rationalistic, however, and Sherlock Holmes, with his utilitarian combination of physical energy and logical accuracy has consequently replaced Dupin as the legendary classic detective.

Not intellectually equipped to match the refined thought processes of Dupin or Holmes, the private eye of the hard-boiled story resorts to a more pragmatic approach, relying upon probabilities rather than certainties. At one point in *The Maltese Falcon* Sam Spade orally summarizes what he has learned about a meeting attended by several people involved in the mystery. The passage is remarkable for what it tells us about the difference between the private investigator of fiction and his ratiocinative predecessors. Spade cites only facts that he can confirm, and the report is regularly documented with inserts like "as far as I could learn," and "I got that from the watchman." When he draws inferences, he reasons only from hard evidence and is careful not to reach any conclusion until all other possibilities have been eliminated. Speaking of Brigid O'Shaughnessy's visit to ship's captain Jacobi, he says: "She got there a little after noon yesterday. . . . That means she went straight there after leaving the cab at the ferry building. . . . It's only a few piers away. . . . She asked for him by name. He was uptown on business. That means he didn't expect her, or not at that time anyway" (138-39). The passage represents a basic change in the interaction between reader and text, because here the detective is taking his audience along with him as he reasons step by step, instead of engaging in the secretive antics of Queen and Wolfe, and he is doing so in language most readers can understand.

In Paretsky's *Indemnity Only* Vic Warshawski performs a neat piece of problem solving, when she finds herself faced with the necessity of learning whether two suspects are in collusion. Starting with the assumption that the two have been getting together in a bar somewhere in the Loop area of downtown Chicago, she defines the geographical area within which the meetings must have taken place. Vic's first step is to break this formidable job down into manageable chunks, allowing her to work a reasonable number of blocks per day. After two unsuccessful tries, she hits upon a better method and changes her approach. Vic does at last find her answer, as a result of pure serendipity, not in a bar but in a restaurant where she is having lunch. The demands of plausibility are satisfied, and so are the reader's expectations. At one point in the search she neatly summarizes the difference between her method and that of the classic detective: she makes the best possible use of what she has to work with, she says, with "no Peter Wimsey at home thinking of the perfect logical answer for me" (150).

If Dupin's method is an example of rationalism, Spade's is pragmatic and Warshawski' s an exercise in heuristic, the method of discovery. She organizes the job in terms of its purpose, modifies it to fit the resources available to her, and revises it when she hits upon a better method. Vic's method should fit comfortably into the reader's own horizon of expectations; it is not brilliant, but it gets results. Cawelti in *Adventure, Mystery and Romance* summarizes the difference as "the subordination of the drama of solution to the detective's quest for discovery and accomplishment" (142).

A recent example of the tension between stable and changing expectations in the genre is Jon Katz's *The Family Stalker*, featuring a suburban private investigator, Kit Deleeuw. Far removed from the mean streets of downtown Los Angeles and Chicago, Deleeuw has his office on the second floor of a mall in Rochambeau, Connecticut, a moderately affluent suburb of New York. Unlike most of the fictional private investigators of tradition, Kit has plenty of clients, and he is happily married with two children and a wife who loves him. A reader experienced in Sam Spade and Philip Marlowe may be puzzled by the account of Kit's interview of a busy housewife; arriving to find her just pulling into the drive and rushed to prepare dinner, he not only helps her carry the groceries into the kitchen but finds the ingredients in the refrigerator and sets about making a salad while they talk (46).

The conventionality of the genre, however, is decidedly present in *The Family Stalker*. In spite of the location in a mall, Kit keeps sloppy records and a sloppy office, to the disgust of his meticulous secretary. Like his predecessors, most of whom had experience in police work before going into private investigation, Kit received his training in the military police, and he is constantly mindful of some of the admonitions of his old army mentor. He owns a beeper but never uses it, and he is uncomfortable with a gun; he bought one when he received his investigator's license but locked it in a safe and forgot the combination (233-34). Attacked by a suspect, he does not fight back except to defend himself, and he gets out of there in a hurry (259). As with most private-eye fiction, the predisposition of *The Family Stalker* is a blend of tradition and creation, as well as a probing of the bounds of the genre.

In terms of the historical interpretation of meaning and text, where "every earlier element extends and completes itself, through a later one," a new book is most reliably judged as a product of earlier texts that preconstituted it (Jauss, *TAR* 88). In this view *The Family Stalker* must be considered as part of the present corpus defined by the works of Paretsky, Pronzini, Grafton, and other influential contemporary writers. It also falls, however, within the horizons earlier set by Chandler, Spillane, and Macdonald in the 1940s and 1950s. Ultimately, elements of the Rue Morgue formula extend and complete themselves in books like *The Family Stalker*, *The Long-Legged Fly*, and *All Things under the Moon*, as part of Jauss's "continual founding and altering of horizons" (88).

The historical concept of continuity, with its emphasis upon changing horizons of expectations, offers an especially sound base for a study of the development the private-investigator genre, because the differences and similarities between Kit Deleeuw and Sam Spade, for example, remind us that even though they belong in the same tradition, the private eye of the 1990s is not the private eye of the 1930s.

Phenomenology, which affords much of the theoretical base for the historical interpretation of literature, holds that the effect of expectations on the reading process is not only to anticipate what is to come but actually to bring it to fruition. The principle is especially important to the development of detective fiction, in which survival depends upon sales, and the expectations of the reader consequently determine the preintentions of the genre. Each set of popular works creates a horizon of expectations for its period, including rules and earlier elements, and extends itself by means of preparation for the next step. Jauss's dictum is well illustrated by the detective novels of Dashiell Hammett. *The Dain Curse, The Maltese Falcon,* and *The Thin Man* all met the expectations of classic structure: each conformed to the Rue Morgue imperatives and the seven-step structure, and each drew upon the accumulated store of thematic conventions. In addition, they contained the beginnings of a new set of expectations, especially the original commission and the expanded commission, and set a new horizon for future developments by Raymond Chandler and his successors. As a continuation of this process, experimental novels like *The Long-Legged Fly* and The *Family Stalker* will define the horizon of the 1990s, provided of course that they sell well and are widely imitated.

In view of the changing nature of the detection genre, and especially of the image of the fictional private investigator, critics and historians should be especially careful to avoid the temptation to overinterpret the personal qualities of the private eye of fiction in the direction of either nobility or brutality. The elevation of the private detective to the level of myth leads Grella to write of him as "the avatar of Natty Bumppo" and of his job as "the knight's battle against evil as well as his quest for truth" ("The Hard-Boiled Detective Novel," *DF* 106, 115), and Cawelti to state that "his personal qualities bear more than a little resemblance to the chivalrous knights of Sir Walter Scott" (*AMR* 151). Such critical statements tend to follow the lead of Chandler, especially that much-cited passage in "The Simple Art of Murder" beginning,

"Down these mean streets a man must go who is not himself mean, who is neither tarnished nor afraid" (qtd. in Haycraft *AMS* 237).

Such statements are appropriate enough in reference to Philip Marlowe and Lew Archer, but they do not hold up for Kit Deleeuw and the general run of the private investigators of popular fiction.

If, however, not all private eyes are Marlowe or Archer, neither are they Mike Hammer. The violence of the hard-boiled story unquestionably distinguishes it from the relative tranquillity of the traditional tale of detection, but the traditional image of the private eye as one who solved problems with his fists, or as Symons describes him, "put his faith in his gun" (*MC* 136) is not valid for the broad view. Most of the private detectives, as we have seen, do not carry guns and many do not even own one. For the most part, they can take care of themselves in emergencies, but they are not gunslingers.

The brilliant amateur of the school of Dupin, Queen, and Vance has all but disappeared from the scene, but the private investigator is alive and flourishing, though in considerably altered form. The fictional private eye of the early days was inevitably a man of the type envisioned by the critics we have just quoted, one who was likely to use fists and gun and even, especially in Spillane's muscular types, to resort to gross sadism. The private investigator of the last twenty years or so is more likely to be a woman, who relies upon her training and experience rather than her physical strength or her gun.

The old style, whom we will call Private Eye 1940, was possessed of an egocentric sense of justice, which led him to espouse the cause of his individual client in defiance of the conventions of society: Philip Marlowe on more than one occasion altered or suppressed damaging evidence, and it was part of the code of the 1940s type that he did not hesitate to break laws and bypass the police at his own convenience. Today's private detectives usually know better than to tamper with evidence, and their motivation is more strongly influenced by a sense of professionalism. His job for his client, says Kit Deleeuw, was a "matter of loyalty and professionalism, of trying to do my job and earn my fee" (266). We have earlier referred to their changing relations with the police, which tend to repeat a cycle within a series or even within a single book, from initial hostility to cautious acceptance, and finally to a genuine collegiality. Today's private eye tends to work out of sight of the police as much as possible, but she knows the rules. More often than not she has one or more old buddies in the department who can be called upon for favors.

One quality of the old-style private eye that distinguished him from both the gifted amateur and the police detective was his curiosity: both Marlowe and Archer persisted in investigations even after they had been discharged from a case, as did MacDonald's Travis McGee, Michael Collins's Dan Fortune, and Prather's Shell Scott. The habit apparently became dormant for a while, but it has reappeared in detectives like Vic Warshawski and Kit Deleeuw.

At least two of the conventional characteristics of the early private eyes have persisted into the present. Almost all of them had police experience before entering private practice, and they were almost always divorced and still suffering some emotional trauma from the breakup of their marriage. This second one, as we have seen, may be giving way to the image of the happily married detective. The convention of prior police experience, however, seems to have strong enough hermeneutic value to keep it alive; not only does the private eye of the 1990s find her associates in the department useful, but a knowledge of police routines may even help her avoid inconvenient contacts with the cops.

This tension or balance between stability and change in the detection genre suggests that there may be laws of change, which are somewhat more rigorous in literary detection than in other types of fiction. One of these seems to have held firm since "The Murders in the Rue Morgue": themes are always changing, but structures tend to remain fixed. Changes in the detection genre are subject to controls. The first of these is hermeneutic specialization, as we have seen in the respective histories of the death warrant and justice thwarted, and just a few lines back in the case of the private detective with police experience. The second is the reading market, where the guiding rule is the old slogan that nothing succeeds like success. Whatever sells well is likely to be imitated, and popular works set the stage for future developments. Finally, there is the law of conventionality, which not only permits but encourages the recycling of old themes, to the extent that it is hard to find an example of a traditional detective usage that has not been revived, sometimes after long periods of dormancy.

If the mean streets were the accepted symbol of the era of Raymond Chandler and Ross Macdonald, it may be that the suburban mall will become that of the present time. Kit Deleeuw has this to say about the transformation in *The Family Stalker:*

> Private investigators these days don't exactly resemble Philip Marlowe and Lew Archer. We deal much more in computers and balance sheets than in actual snooping. We must hunt for the hidden assets of deadbeat husbands, follow the computer traces and trails of insurance fraud, and pore over warehouse inventories to figure out how VCRs and microwaves disappear. (111)

He refers half-jokingly to his three-person "staff" of specialists. His psychological consultant is his wife, Jane, a graduate student to whom he refers as his "shrink in training" and who more than once puts him on the right trail (116). The second member is an expert hacker known to him only as "Willie," whom he contacts by phone; Willie can access any information needed, including material from the files of the police and various insurance companies (128). The third is Lieutenant Tagg of the New Jersey State Police, who will oblige Kit by running a name through the state computers to check for "priors" (128).

The rules of the game have obviously changed, but, says Jauss, a system of literary norms "can most readily still be constructed through the horizon of expectations of a genre-system that pre-constituted the intention of the works" (TAR 108). Thus, according to historical critical theory, before undertaking an interpretation of the world of Kit Deleeuw and *The Family Stalker*, we must know something of the private-eye tradition that preconstituted it.

One element that set the private-eye story apart from the classic tale of detection was a considerable relaxation of the efficiency principle. It was part of the reader's expectation that in the formal-problem tradition any material introduced was likely to be important. This was the case in a novel like Sayers's *The Nine Tailors*, where the reader might have been puzzled by that extended description of the new flood-control project fairly late in the story (341-46), even to the point of suspecting that the digression served no purpose other than delay. Later, of course, the flood-theme proved essential, and the confirmation of the principle played an important part in programming the blanks in the classic tale and contributed to its "differentness" from other fiction.

The early readers of the mean streets novel soon learned, however, not to expect as strict an application of the efficiency

principle as the formal-problem had demanded. John D. Mac-
Donald illustrates the new expectation in *The Lonely Silver Rain*, in
the form of a recurrent theme that is developed exactly like a standard clue. As the story proceeds, McGee repeatedly finds figures
of cats made from twisted pipe cleaners hidden about his house-
boat, and the reader is alerted to watch for their significance in the
detection of the mystery. Actually, they have no bearing on the
case in which McGee is involved, but in a separate resolution following the solution of the mystery, they prove to be important to
McGee's personal life, in a strand that has extended over several
of the novels (247 ff). Such relaxation is generally practiced in the
private-eye novel, with a resultant shift in the horizon of expectations of the genre.

We have already briefly discussed the convention of the
expanded commission as a trademark of the private-eye tradition.
The Continental Op, Sam Spade, and Nick Charles are all commissioned in noncapital crimes, and in each case a murder growing out of the original problem involves the detective's attention
for the rest of the story. The story must begin with a plausible
problem for the sake of reality but must evolve into murder for
the sake of suspense. The effect upon reading is the addition of an
added degree of negativity; each blank encountered by the reader
in the original plot is doubly programmed, first in expectation of
solution of the original problem and second by anticipation of the
introduction of murder. Ross Macdonald's *The Blue Hammer* opens
in the conventional manner: Lew Archer keeps an appointment
with a couple who want him to find a painting that has been
stolen from their home.

For a reader new to the private-eye formula the blank is
structured: Where is the painting? But the experienced reader is
also guided by an expectation generated by the genre itself, When
will the murder take place?

The private-eye novel lacks the quality that John Reilly calls
"the neat conclusiveness of the classic story that is usually absent
from real life."[1] Instead of the tidy solution expected in the classic
tale of detection, the completion of a job by a private detective
often leaves a residue of mystery, with the result that the detective
must proceed past the point at which the classic sleuth considers
his work finished. The residue-of-mystery plot was introduced by
Raymond Chandler in *The Big Sleep*, in which Marlowe completes
his original commission by solving the blackmailing of Carmen
Sternwood early in the story, but he has by that time encountered

another mystery, with which he proceeds although he has been discharged by his original employer. In so doing he established the stylistic device of the curious detective: "Nothing made it my business except curiosity," says Marlowe in *Farewell My Lovely* (15), and the image continues to manifest itself in so recent an instance as Sharon McCone's determination to go ahead with a case for which she is receiving no fee in *There's Something in a Sunday* (41). Curiosity is not the only motivation for the residual mystery structure, however. On occasion the detective will continue with a case only out of concern for the safety of a friend, as Dan Fortune does in Michael Collins's *The Silent Scream* (61). Another variant is the one in *The Lonely Silver Rain*, where McGee can not escape commitment because his involvement in the plot has made him dangerous to the criminals in the story (68).

The other standard quality of the traditional private-eye story, the protagonist narrator, will be the subject for a later discussion of William Stowe's treatment of the fictional private eye as hermeneutic interpreter in the Gadamerian sense.

The myth of the mean streets endowed the traditional detective protagonist with several special qualities that have led us to characterize him broadly as a roughneck. Cawelti aptly calls him an antihero, whose "commonness is a mask for uncommon qualities" (*AMR* 145). Hammett set the pattern especially with Sam Spade and the Continental Op, neither of whom suggests chivalrous knighthood; their efforts are marked by professional competence rather than omniscience. Most of their successors suffer some kind of physical or emotional trauma; characteristically, the private detective is divorced, after an unrewarding marriage and a painful breakup. They tend to be conscious of their advancing age, and their self-assessments are marked by contempt in place of the happy self-confidence of the classic sleuth.

One quality of the traditional private eye that came to be incorporated into the horizon of expectations of the genre was his egocentristic sense of justice. The fictional private detective, says Grella, acts according to his own apprehension of the truth (qtd. in Winks, *DF* 107); he is, according to Cawelti, "forced to define his own concept of morality and justice," which is often in conflict with the norms of society (*AMR* 143). Philip Marlowe freely exercises his personal code of justice, rearranging and suppressing evidence, as he does in *The High Window* to protect Merle Davis (172). Shayne, in *This Is It, Michael Shayne*, by Brett Halliday, hides an essential murder witness-suspect (71) and repeatedly refuses to tell the police where she is. The image of the detective who makes his own rules because he is at war with a corrupt society was part of the myth of Chandler's solitary hero of the mean streets. "The Simple Art of Murder" concludes, "If there were enough like him, I think the world would be a very safe place to live in, and yet not be too dull to be worth living in" (Haycraft, *AMS* 237). The convention of the uncommon common hero is one of the traditions that has not faded but has rather undergone transformation in later works. People like Kinsey Millhone, Kit Deleeuw, Sydney Bryant, and Lew Griffin may not strike most readers as particularly heroic characters, yet each of them seems to be trying to bring at least a moderate sense of decency into a value-free world.

The police of the mean streets unfortunately acquired a bad name as a result of a few episodes in Chandler and Macdonald that represented them as brutal, incompetent, and corrupt.

Actually, their degree of competence and concern spans just about as wide a spectrum as might be expected of policemen in nonfictional life. On the one hand, there are police like the ones in *Poor Butterfly*, who want to write the case off after a perfunctory investigation (48), or the ones whom Kinsey Millhone in *G as in Gumshoe* describes as "long on concern, short on solutions" (74), but then there are others like Captain Gazzo in Collins's *The Silent Scream*, who is competent and persistent as well as friendly and cooperative. Almost invariably, they are overworked and subject to political pressure. As a rule they are strong on routines but tend to be unimaginative; they have clout, which they do not hesitate to use, but they seldom find it necessary to resort to brutality.

Although the themes of the hard-boiled story vary considerably, the structures are remarkably constant. As has been pointed out, the genre inherited the four Rue Morgue "givens": the detective is the protagonist, and it is chiefly his or her story; the business of detection is the primary plot; the mystery is deep and complex; the problem is solved before the story ends. Because of the derivative nature of the genre, these last two deserve special comment. Hammett set the pattern for the veiled secret: before he can sort out the problem in *The Dain Curse*, the Continental Op must dig deeply into some tangled family history; Sam Spade encounters the complications of the exotic story of the mysterious falcon; and Nick Charles almost falls victim to the criminal world before he can resolve the problem of *The Thin Man*. The fourth element has developed one twist that may develop some significance with the passage of time, in the realization that, even though the game may be over within the framework of the novel, it is not necessarily so in actuality. In *The Dain Curse* the Op, who has solved the case, reminds another character that the final solution must await the decision of a jury (123), a concession that was to become a staple of the police story, as we have already seen in *A Fine Italian Hand* (242). Regardless of variation, then, it is still these four basics that establish the regulative context for the reading of the private-eye story.

The apparent difference between the world of the mall and that of the mean streets is largely superficial, because the new myth is part of the continuity that produced the old. The horizons are much the same, and so are the rules of the game inherited from the mean streets and before them from the vicar's rose garden. Thus the reader opens *The Family Stalker* with a narrowly defined set of expectations: the story will be told by the detective protagonist, the efficiency principle will be largely inoperative, and the structure of the plot will follow the standard sequence of original commission followed by murder and an expanded role for the private detective.

The expectation of a first-person narrator is established as soon as the reader turns to page 1: unlike some of the other private detectives of the 1990s, Kit Deleeuw tells his own story. Conventional structure is confirmed early in chapter 1: the story of *The Family Stalker* begins in the conventional manner, when Marianne Dow appears in the office of Kit Deleeuw in the American Way Mall to engage him to find out why and how a woman by the name of Andrea Lucca is breaking up Marianne's marriage (13). Kit's job is considerably expanded when Marianne's husband, Gil, becomes the victim of an ostensible attempted suicide (72). When Gil dies, the reader's expectations are fulfilled: the attempted suicide becomes the preprogrammed murder, and Marianne becomes the Most Likely Suspect (171).

Chapter 2 further confirms the reader's sense of formula, through the relaxation of the efficiency principle in the first of a number of Kit's commentaries on the Rochambeau milieu (16), in the manner of Pronzini's descriptions of the countryside of Southern California and Paretsky's of Chicago. The continuity is further sensed in the revelation of Kit's previous police training while serving in the army (22); the deviations begin to appear when the reader learns that Kit is a family man of conservative tastes, more like the policeman of recent fiction than the private eye of the mean streets.

His relationships with the police conform in general to the pattern inherited from Poe and reinforced by the early writers in the mean streets tradition: hostility, followed by cautious acceptance, leading finally to full collaboration and even dependence. Kit's local nemesis is Chief Leeming, who is still smarting from a former case in which Kit made him look bad, but "fortunately, he was an ex-New York City precinct commander who had seen too much of everything, including too many FBI agents, and made his own judgments" (69). They collaborate in the search for Andrea Lucca (126), but Kit knows Leeming will get his license revoked if he catches him withholding information, as Lieutenant Cramer was always ready to do with Nero Wolfe (130). Finally, when Kit solves the mystery, Leeming has him arrested for obstructing justice (303). Some FBI men enter the story briefly, and they are conventionally mean-spirited and bureaucratic (155).

In spite of the drastic change of scene, *The Family Stalker* must be classed as a traditional private-detective novel. Structurally, it never really tests the boundaries of the genre, and it reveals considerable hermeneutic strength in its handling of negation and negativity. Since these two elements are basic in detective fiction, it might be well at this point to give them some attention: negation, first, occurs when the text points out defects in a prevailing thought system (Berg, *TLT* 261). As Kit Deleeuw seeks to discover marriages besides Marianne Dow's that are being broken up by Andrea Lucca, he is completely puzzled by his interview of Gay Tannenbaum, who takes the full blame for her own marital problems. After talking to Gay, Kit wonders if "Marianne Dow had her head on straight," because Gay's story is a total negation of Marianne's (111). The indeterminacy created is not a simple blank but a contradiction: Kit's perplexity is the result of his being completely committed to Marianne's interpretation. Most of the suspense value of negation and negativity in this story is created by the shadowy Andrea Lucca, who never really makes an appearance; to Kit, Andrea's behavior does not make sense (235). The formulated text has a kind of unformulated "double," which Iser calls negativity (*AR* 226). This double begins to work when the text for a long stretch ignores the story of Donna Platt, whose marriage is unquestionably being broken up by Andrea and who also has a strong motive for violence (201). The reader's double, guided by the directions that are uniquely programmed into detective fiction, goes to work, not just asking What? or Why? but literally anticipating upcoming developments.

In a passage cited earlier, we noted how Kit illustrates the nature of his job by comparing his methods with those of Philip Marlowe and Lew Archer. In fact the self-reflexivity of the genre asserts itself shortly after the novel opens, when Kit feels a twinge of nostalgia for the mean old days before the mall era: "Thirty years ago the hard-hitting private eye could have scared the hell out of somebody, even roughed a suspect up a bit" (15). As in the case of most of the private-eye fiction of our own time, *The Family Stalker* seems intent upon asserting that it lies within the tradition of the detective story.

So it does in the conventionality of the novel, where a number of fresh themes are superimposed upon the conventional structure. Before the story is well under way, the reader catches the signal when Marianne Dow says of Andrea Lucca, "I want to kill her," (13) and when an unexpected murder occurs later, Chief Leeming predictably suspects Marianne (139). The use of Marianne as Most Likely Suspect considerably intensifies the effectiveness of the surprise ending, which is a neat turnabout in the classic style.

Another convention with strong hermeneutic value is that of Something bothering the detective: "Something about Babst [a lawyer] bugged me, although I couldn't put my finger on it," says Kit (175), and a reader with previous experience of the convention knows automatically that whatever bugs the detective is important and that it will be revealed after a suitable interval. That reader is not likely to miss the signals in the detailed description of the murder scene (82-83), another manifestation of hermeneutic strength programmed into a convention by the detection genre. The same is true of the conventional summary, as when Kit reviews the situation, ostensibly for the benefit of "Willie," but actually for that of the reader (189). Toward the conclusion, the author becomes exceptionally secretive, and the detection formula extends and completes itself in an example of classic concealment: "Where had I seen a brown Honda wagon? I thought I knew," says Kit (244), and the experienced reader resists the temptation to search the text for that Honda, knowing that it will be identified in due time.

As in mainstream detective fiction, the private-eye novel shares the deep structure of transformed play; the Chandler-Macdonald formula, with its conventional first-person narrator, combination of first commission and expanded commission, residue-of-mystery complication, and relaxation of the efficiency principle, offers as many occasions for the relief of stress, renewal of convention by constant repetition, and optional tasks as did the Poe-Doyle tradition. The first-person-narrator technique, for example, provides unusual opportunities for witty private investigators like Parker's Spenser to spice up the text to as great a degree as did Lord Peter Wimsey.

Although Kit Deleeuw is not the humorous narrator of the Spenser type, *The Family Stalker* is a satisfactory illustration of the way in which the era of the mall achieves double relief from stress: the self-reflexivity of the novel removes the reader not only from nonfictional reality but also from the strains of the mean streets: the hard-hitting private eyes of 1940s and 1950s frequently roughed up suspects, but the conventions of the mall do not permit such primitive tactics; the detectives of suburbia are likely instead to employ high-tech methods in the pursuit of white-collar criminals. The structure of play becomes apparent when a task is presented shortly after the attempt on Gil Dow, Marianne's husband. The text pulls away from the reader, creating an indeterminacy that offers two possible tasks: Where is Andrea? and What was that splash Marianne heard at the time of the attack on Gil? (92). As usual, the reader can work on either or both of these problems or can proceed with reading, confident in the expectation that both will be answered before the end of the story.

Organized play does not easily readjust its structures to fit current conditions, and the history of literary detection seems to demonstrate that the social background of the detective story, which is by nature thematic, has less influence over the development of the genre than one might suppose. As we have seen, the "differentness" of the detective story is primarily structural, and while thematic material is constantly changing in any popular genre, structure is not. A good example is the game of Monopoly, which achieved enormous popularity during the Great Depression and in which the textual signals of the contemporary scene were transformed into the deep structure of the game itself, with the result that the depressed economy of the 1930s is still the norm, despite the fact that $200.00 salaries and $12.00 rentals seem absurd for big-time speculators; Monopoly addicts apparently like those signals as they have always been. A real mystique has grown up around its financial system, to the extent that there is at least one book on the economics of Monopoly.

At the same time, the methods of fictional investigators may be susceptible to changes in method that correspond to shifts in fundamental modes of thought, as William Stowe argues. His essay, "From Semiotics to Hermeneutics: Modes of Detection in Doyle and Chandler" (*PM* 366-83), is worth examining at this point, partly because of what it says about the difference between the detectives of the classic and the private-eye traditions, and partly what it says about the reader's participation in the process of interpretation.

Stowe calls Dupin and Holmes semiotic interpreters who distance themselves from a problem in order to gain a desirable level of objectivity; Marlowe is the hermeneutic interpreter who purposely immerses himself in the case, seeks to learn more than "facts," and throughout the investigation engages in a continuing process of self-definition and self-interpretation.

The semiotic interpreter "treats facts as signs of other facts, and eventually of 'the truth.'" Stowe illustrates the principle in literary detection with Holmes's analysis of the facts in "A Case of Identity" (370), where Mary Sutherland interprets Hosmer Angel's preference for evening visits, his tinted glasses, and his weak voice as evidences of a genteel and retiring nature. Holmes, looking at the same set of facts, sees a pattern of concealed identity. Holmes's method is "a practical semiotics: his goal is to consider data of all kinds as potential signifiers and to link them, however disparate and incoherent they seem, to a coherent set of signifieds, that is, to turn them into signs of the hidden *order* behind the manifest confusion, of the *solution* to the mystery, of the *truth*" (367-68). The experienced reader should be able to see in Stowe's characterization a reasonable description of the methods of a number of classic detectives, such as Dr. Thorndyke, Hercule Poirot, and the early Ellery Queen.

Stowe bases his conception of the hermeneutic interpreter upon the teachings of Hans-Georg Gadamer, who is of special interest to us both because of his effect upon Iser and Jauss, and also because of his influence upon contemporary literary theory. For Gadamer, interpretation involves constant introspection on the part of the interpreter, who must question the value of both self and method as well as the problem under investigation. We can not discover truth by cultivating method: "Gadamerian hermeneutics is an activity of mind in which subject, object, and mental processes meet and act upon one another" (PM 374). Distinctions between "objectivity" and "subjectivity" lose their meaning. "To try to eliminate one's own concepts in interpretation," says Gadamer, "is not only impossible but manifestly absurd. To interpret means precisely to use one's own preconceptions so that the meaning of the text can really be made to speak for us" (374, quoting from *TM* 397).

Stowe assigns the hermeneutic method to Philip Marlowe in the sense that he is not simply a solver of puzzles but an investigator who considers a case closed only after he has satisfied himself regarding both the outcome of the case and the crises his own participation has provoked. He illustrates the principle with reference to *Farewell My Lovely*, where Marlowe does not so much "enter" the case as he is (literally) pulled into the tangled affairs of Moose Malloy as participant rather than unprejudiced analyst, with the result that his involvement hastens the deaths of four people. Instead of holding himself aloof and thus insuring a disinterested perspective, Marlowe takes account of his own preconceptions and finds a meaning to which his own values had predisposed him: "Like Gadamer's reader of texts, Philip Marlowe cannot avoid prejudging everything he experiences, but like that reader too he is capable of adjusting his judgments the better to fit the text, the circumstances, the facts, or the voices that he hears" (378-79). The same description will apply to the methods of Lew Archer and Travis McGee, and in possibly slightly reduced measure to those of Vic Warshawski, Pronzini's nameless detective, and most of the others, including Kit Deleeuw.

Gadamer's dictum has twofold significance here, because of its implications for both the fictional private eye and the reader of the private-eye novel. Stowe's analogy of detective-as-interpreter with Gadamer's reader-as-interpreter, as a matter of fact, involves Gadamer's description of the process as a fusion of "horizons" of text and interpreter, using the term in the same sense as we have seen in Jauss (379).

The difference between the classic tale of detection and the private-eye novel, viewed in this light, becomes a difference in the mode of reading, or in the reader's participation in the narrative. One clear indicator of the distinction between semiotic and hermeneutic methods of detection is the variation in narrative points of view. The first one employed, historically, and the one usually associated with the ratiocinative detective, was the Watson-type worshipful observer, whose function was not merely to report and applaud but to give the reader a comfortable position in relation to the characters. The typical Holmes story, says O'Toole, involves two time-sequences, one lived by Holmes and Watson, and the other by Holmes's client. As the story develops, the detective is always one step ahead of his client, "with us, the readers, perhaps, half a step between them, half conscious of the way his deductions are leading, pleasantly mystified, yet gratified by our superiority over the client and the stooge, Dr. Watson" (qtd. in Fowler, 152). The normal point of view in the classic story, however, is that of the impersonal author, not the Watson. In other genres this type of narration would lack mediation, but not so in the detective story, where the detection formula itself mediates between reader and text, preserving that dyadic relationship unique to the author and reader of the detective story.

In the context of (philosophical) hermeneutic detection, the first-person point of view assumes new significance, chiefly in the reordering of the probabilities of the story. Certainly one of the comfortable qualities of the classical formula is its predictability; the world of Dupin and his successors is dependable to the extent that the reader can trust the guidance of the efficiency principle, assured that all motifs are bound and that anything in the story may be considered contributory to the resolution. One of the more obvious effects of the subjective point of view of the private-eye story is an increasing reader involvement in the diversions to which the protagonist is susceptible, with the result that, for the reader, any motif may be considered free.

The explanation must lie in the sense of identification generated by hermeneutic interpreter-narrator. The reader, now an interpreter of an interpreter, shifts from the role of spectator who observes in expectation of a solution to that of participant, identifying with the protagonist to a degree not attainable with Dupin and Holmes. Because of their sense of involvement with McGee, the readers of MacDonald's *The Lonely Silver Rain* are not disturbed by the digression of the pipe-cleaner cats, which in the context of the classical story would be read as a standard clue but which proves in this instance to have bearing not on the mystery but on an aspect of McGee's private life.

It is their involvement with the narrative that makes experienced readers sensitive to a habit of the detection formula that is a result of its "powerful generic logic" (Lovitt, CC 76). As we will see in chapter 6, the most pronounced point of difference between detective fiction and other genres is its disposition to program negativities. Early in Patricia Wallace's *Deadly Devotion* private investigator Sydney Bryant interviews Keith Reilly, the man she has been hired to prove not guilty. "If you didn't do it," she says, "someone else did." A few lines later she is discussing the case with the lawyer who engaged her. "He is innocent, you know," says the lawyer, to which she replies, "I hope you're right," and the lawyer says, "He is. You'll see" (62). The reader can hardly miss the reiteration of textual signals to pay attention: this passage is important. The negativity of the passage creates several new blanks, and these blanks are not merely structured but programmed; they do not simply raise questions of Who? or Why? but even suggest eventual vindication of the innocence of Keith Reilly. The element that makes the difference here is the convention of the most likely suspect, the agent that alerts the reader to remember similar cases where suspects are defended by the protagonist and are proved innocent. The process is conditioned by the context of the genre, reminding the reader of the presence of the hermeneutic mode, pushing the story toward resolution.

6

Mapping Negativity

Negativity, says Iser, is the unformulated background that conditions the text, leaving the formulated part open to multiple interpretations (*AR* 226). Negativity might be compared to a blank sheet behind the printed page that offers an opportunity for the reader to write his or her own version of the story; when the negativity is filled, it becomes part of the reader's interpretation or "reading" of the text. In this sense programming is a special application of Husserl's "protensions," which lead not so much to fulfillment as to the continual modification of expectations.

In the case of detective fiction, Iser's unformulated background is programmed by the genre, so that the pattern the reader imposes on the text is the one intended by the formula. The experienced reader's sensitivity to the nature of the genre suggests that the assumed innocence of Sydney's client in *Deadly Devotion* will assume unusual significance as the novel proceeds; the stimulus for the process is the reader's awareness of the convention of the most likely suspect, which does not offer any clue to guilt or innocence but supplies the map for the negativity and consequently sharpens the reader's perceptions by offering a guidebook for interpretation of what is to come.

One of the special differences between the detective story and the simple mystery is that the problem to be solved by the fictional detective is not just a question to be answered but a deep secret, all but impossible of solution, like the complex situation in Paretsky's *Guardian Angel*. As the story opens, private detective Vic Warshawski has an apartment in an older area of Chicago that was once a good upper-middle-class residential neighborhood but has suffered from the negligence of its elderly inhabitants, who are no longer able to maintain its former style.

The first mystery is introduced in the conventional fashion, when Vic is hired by her landlord, Mr. Contreras, to find his roomer, Mitch Kruger, who has been unaccountably missing for several days; that puzzle is complicated shortly when a shadowy

145

figure materializes claiming to be Mitch's son (144). A second missing-person theme develops when Vic, in an unrelated development, calls on an elderly neighbor, Mrs. Frizell.

She finds her suffering from a serious fall that has left her unconscious, with the result that Mrs. Frizell too is figuratively "missing" for the rest of the story (93). As part of her search for Mitch Kruger, Vic undertakes an investigation of the Diamond Head plant, the place of Mitch's employment, where some obviously illegal activities are underway. During the course of her investigation, Vic begins to suspect that she is being shadowed by two men, and her suspicions are confirmed when she narrowly escapes attack and later finds her apartment has been broken into. A fifth perspective is added by the presence of the Picheas, a yuppie couple who are determined to "upgrade" the neighborhood by forcing out the older residents, and who have gained control of Mrs. Frizell's assets. Finally, there is the involvement of another elderly neighborhood woman, Mrs. Polter, whom Vic at first trusts but later suspects of watching her for some unknown reason.

Most readers will try to impose meaning on such an avalanche of signals by arranging the components of the text into some kind of structure, and a natural starting point is the question of whether all these plots are in any way related to each other. Regardless of previous experience, or lack of it, with the detective story, a reader can safely assume that there is no reason for their introduction into the text other than some kind of connection that will become apparent as the story unfolds.

Thus, the veteran in detective fiction and the novice alike will catch the signals suggesting that both Mitch Kruger's disappearance and the men who repeatedly menace Vic's work are related to the situation at the Diamond Head plant. Both readers are, as noted in chapter 5, writing their own versions of the story on the blank sheet behind the printed page. As they seek to organize things into meaningful configurations, each of these readers will begin to catch on that the Picheas are probably involved in Mrs. Frizell's fall and also somehow connected with the strange behavior of Mrs. Polter. Because the reader has no immediate way of checking whether these interpretations are correct, an "indeterminacy" appears between reader and text, and the unformulated space between the six different perspectives of the story becomes a negativity in the Iserian sense. This negativity, however, is not a simple vacancy; it supplies the organizing principle that allows the reader to construct the meaning of the story, and this is why the reader of *Guardian Angel* can project associations that are not explicitly stated in the text.

At one point Iser calls negativity the "hollow form of the text," which is filled by the mental images of the reader, but for the detection fan that hollow form is preorganized in such fashion that it may be filled more efficiently than by a reader inexperienced in the detection mode. The veteran reader, for example, can hardly overlook in *Guardian Angel* the convention of the missing person, which we discussed in chapter 3. Guided by similar cases from past reading, the reader foresees that both Mitch Kruger and Mrs. Frizell are dead: in Mitch's case the projection is literal and in Mrs. Frizell's the loss of memory produces the same effect. In addition to earlier acquaintance with the missing person theme, however, the reader knows that the author of a detective story would not take the trouble to develop both of these cases as minutely as she does without some kind of intention to tie them in with the other plot segments.

Both the experienced and the inexperienced readers perceive the "hollow form" of the negativity in *Guardian Angel*, but the signals of the text cause the veteran reader's expectations to be *programmed* in addition, with the result that he or she has access to a map or guide book that projects a general outline of upcoming developments. This guide, we want to note, is not intended to help solve the mystery, because that would spoil the fun; its effect is basically aesthetic, much like that of a manual on how to listen to music or how to watch a soccer match.

We can illustrate the process of programming in detective fiction with a quick review of a structure that has become conventional within a single series, the recurrent intrusion of the Deaf Man into the 87th Precinct stories by Ed McBain. The evil genius who calls himself the Deaf Man has made five appearances in the 87th Precinct;[1] capable of infinite cruelty and wanton destruction, he has developed a special grudge against the 87th Squad that drives him not only to beat them at the game but to make them look like idiots. Because of the comic irony that runs through the series, however, the Deaf Man is always defeated when something unexpectedly goes wrong, usually without the participation of the police, who never quite understand the situation.

The sequence begins when somebody answers a phone in the detective squadroom and hears a voice say, "You'll have to speak louder. I'm a little hard of hearing." The reader's response will depend upon one of two sets of expectations: for the reader without previous experience in the series, the request is a simple one, with no secondary meaning. The reaction of the 87th Precinct fan, however, is more likely to be something like Here he is again, followed by a reach for the Deaf Man file on the mental reference shelf and a review of the familiar structure:

1. The Deaf Man will come up with a devilishly ingenious plan to completely baffle the police, as he did with the mysterious series of pictures mailed to the squad in *Let's Hear It for the Deaf Man*.

2. One thing will go wrong, as it did on that occasion when, at the worst possible moment, a rookie cop developed a craving for an ice cream pop.

3. The Deaf Man will be defeated by his own ingenuity, as he was when, during the great bank heist, he ran headlong into the one person he did not want to meet, Steve Carella.

4. He will escape capture, with an implied promise to be back.

5. The police will never understand what really happened.

The phenomenon of the Deaf Man is useful at this point as a representative example of the way in which the detection genre programs the reader's reception. We want to note especially that the element triggering the expectations of the veteran reader is the recognition of the convention, which signals the presence of a programmed structure. We should remember, too, that in the case of detective fiction, the reader's expectations are conditioned by certain special qualities of the genre: the operation of the efficiency principle, which assures the reader that none of this would have been introduced without some purpose, and the assurance of resolution, a promise that the plan of the Deaf Man will not succeed. The most important conditioner is the mode of play: the reading proceeds without stress as a result of the reader's expectation that the Deaf Man will be thwarted; the reader is offered the opportunity to second-guess the development of this new plot; and, with each return, the convention is stronger as a result of frequent repetition.

Earlier we compared the programming of expectations to a map or what-to-watch-for guide, which heightens the enjoyment of the reading by employing a set of heuristics that are unique to the detection reader: they allow the reader to compare this one with the earlier Deaf Man stories, to estimate the probabilities that the Deaf Man will overlook the one detail that will spoil his great plan, and to try to predict the methods that will be used by the Deaf Man and by the police. Here again we must remind ourselves we are using a what-to-watch-for, not a how-to-solve-it, manual. Programming helps the reader to anticipate the strategy of the text in much the same way that a well-informed fan watches baseball: anticipating a walk or a bunt helps the viewer to interpret and appreciate the fine points of the game.

Suleiman uses the word *programming* to describe one side of the dichotomy in Iser's position: he implies that readers are free to interpret the text in their own way, but this conclusion is opposed by other statements "which suggest that the reader's activity of filling in the gaps is 'programmed' by the text itself, so that the kind of pattern the reader creates for the text is foreseen and intended by the author" (*RinT* 25). My own theory of programming conforms to the principle stated by Suleiman, except that the conditioning of expectations in a detective story is guided by the reader's individual interpretation of the genre, not the text. The distinction becomes clearer in the difference between the reactions of inexperienced and experienced readers to the Deaf Man convention; the textual signals are the same for both, but it is the individual genre that alerts the veteran reader to the presence of a programmed structure.

Programming theory seeks to explain how a strongly conventional, hermeneutically specialized genre maps the infrastructure of a narrative and in so doing prepares the reader for a broad reinterpretation of the signals of the text. At the beginning of this chapter, negativity was compared to a blank sheet beyond the text, on which the reader projects his or her own version of the story. At this point we will borrow a term from the floppy disk users' manual and say that in detective fiction the reader's blank sheet is also *initialized* by the genre, that is, made compatible with the special sense of the detective story. A part of that compatibility is the manner in which the genre programs the areas of indeterminacy in the text by giving the reader a key to later developments.

Programming maps negativity in two ways: it supplies the guide for the "nothing" between the positions of the text, as in *Guardian Angel*, and also for the "nothing" between the present (the investigation) and the past (the crime). Moreover, it patterns the unformulated background of the text by establishing parameters and priorities, as it does in a familiar section of Sayers's *The*

Nine Tailors. Near the beginning of that novel the reader runs into an unusually detailed treatment of English church architecture and change-ringing, both fascinating enough in themselves but questionable in a detective story. The experienced reader, though, knows two things: first, this digression cannot be a major plot element, because one of the constitutive conventions of the genre is that the main plot must be detection; and second, the hermeneutic drive of the genre (expressing itself in this case in the efficiency principle) mandates that the digression must eventually prove to be important, because of the amount of space it is allowed. In this way the negativity is programmed: it is endowed with a sense of probability that assures the reader that the digression will prove to be important; at the same time, the program sets parameters, which in this case preclude the digression's becoming a major plot element.

Literary initializing sets limits and states rules for the special mode of the "detective story sense." These rules recognize the formation of expectations, including the possibility that they may under certain circumstances be programmed. First, there must be an agent to alert the reader to the presence of a potentially programmed structure, which, in the case of detective fiction is a convention known to the reader. This is the point in a Deaf Man novel at which the reader recognizes the meaning of the voice on the phone and anticipates a patterned sequence that will continue through the story. As might be expected in so strongly formulaic a genre, however, the programming of expectations is closely conditioned by rules compatible with the initialized blank page, such as the efficiency principle and the assurance of resolution. In this mode, the reader knows not to be disturbed by the apparent menace of the Deaf Man, because he will at some point make a fatal mistake that will defeat him. Finally, these conditioned expectations make available a set of heuristics that intensify the aesthetic experience of the reading in the same way a viewer's guide intensifies the watching of a game, by giving the reader a set of guide questions: What method will be followed by the Deaf Man and by the police? How big is the problem? Have there been any similar cases? A reader of McBain's *Mischief*, for example, reviewing the chain of events in the other four (books in the series), can have a great deal of fun anticipating the next move of the police, or of the Deaf Man, at any point in the sequence, or can try to guess whether, this time, the Deaf Man will be killed or captured. In summary, we can consider these three elements to be the guides to a programmable structure: the presence of a convention, the guidance of those conditions compatible with detective fiction, and the availability of a set of heuristics to promote the process of discovery.

Is the tale of detection the only genre that lends itself to programming? In terms of the concept I am developing here, the degree of programming in any genre depends upon the intensity of its conventionality and its hermeneutic specialization. Only a highly conventionalized genre like detective fiction could supply both the agent to signal a programmable structure and the rules to condition its development, and only a hermeneutically specialized one would generate the anticipatory guides an experienced reader follows. Neither conventionality alone nor hermeneutic mode alone invites programming. A nondetectional mystery story, for example, may have a powerful hermeneutic drive but lack the storehouse of convention available to the detective story, and the reverse of the same principle would apply to any strongly conventional fiction not at the same time hermeneutically specialized.

Two matters may cause some problems in this discussion. The first is the question of *where* programming takes place, in the reader or in the text, a confusion that may have been intensified by our earlier references to a "programmable structure" of the text and the "programmed expectations" of the reader. Actually, in phenomenological interpretation the two perspectives are inseparable, but there is an even simpler explanation in the unique author-reader compact of detective fiction, which controls both the intention of the author and the perception of the reader; both are shaped by rules resulting from earlier experience of reading or writing. Programming takes place in the author, in the process of writing the book, and in the reader, in reading it. The other is the question of *what* is programmed, the negativity or something else. From here on I will refer to the programming of blanks and gaps as well as negativity, but without contradiction. The term as Iser uses it has enormous breadth, almost equivalent to his "indeterminacy," encompassing not only the blank and the gap but also negation, which was discussed in chapter 2 (*AR* 226).

Let us compare programming with what Iser in *The Act of Reading* calls the structuring of the blanks in the text. Structured blanks, he says, stimulate the thought processes of the reader, on terms set by the text. The normal indeterminacy between text and reader arouses the mental activity of the reader; this activity is given a specific structure by the blanks arising from the text, and this structure controls the process of ideation (169-70). Iser uses the term *structure* here in a sense somewhat different from my own use of *program*. For Iser structure may be an idea that provides direction, that implies instead of stating: he speaks of a textual pattern that structures something but "leaves it out"; it may also be thought of as imposing limits and definition, as in "structured indicator" and "structure of comprehension" (9). The difference, then, is that *structuring* gives shape, implies, defines; *programming* assigns purpose, suggests involvements yet to come, points directions. Programming is made possible solely by a traditional context available to the reader, encompassing not only familiar episodes and probabilities, but rules and parameters from former reading. A blank is structured for all readers by the negativity it suggests, but it is programmed only for the experienced reader of detective fiction by the presence of a convention recognized by the reader.The difference may become clearer in a quick review of two blanks, one structured and one programmed, in Grafton's *H Is for Homicide*. After a violent fight in that novel an unknown woman emerges from the crowd and kneels beside an injured man. "Help," she cries. "Please help this man. Can't anybody help?" (89). The blank is structured in the sense that it raises such questions as Who is this woman? and What is this all about? but it is not programmed, because no convention is present to point toward a course of development. Note the difference between that blank and the one created shortly after the story opens. Private Detective Kinsey Millhone, returning to her office and barred by a parking lot swarming with police and paramedics, soon learns that a murder investigation is underway, and the reader is alerted to a programmed blank (5-8). The agent is one of the best-established conventions of the genre: a murder-mystery early in the novel will be solved, probably by the detective protagonist. The program is also conditioned by the efficiency principle, which holds that nothing would receive this much attention without being important. In familiar terms, the structured blank asks, "What gives?" to which the programmed blank adds, "It looks as if things from here on might be developing according to a certain pattern."

Thus when Philo Vance in *The Kennel Murder Case* says, "I begin to see method in all this seeming madness" (97), the blank is immediately programmed as a result of an idiosyncrasy of the detection formula. The agent of programming here is a statement of the protagonist who, in Golden Age novels and especially in the Vance series, is virtually infallible. The code directs the reader's expectations toward the upcoming break in the pattern and the ultimate explanation of the "seeming madness." For the new reader the blank is structured in the sense that it is identified and defined as mystery, but for the veteran it is also programmed, because it orients the reader to the impending redirection.

The difference can be seen most easily in one of those cases in which the reading mode is transformed from simple mystery to detective fiction, and the structured blank becomes programmed in the process. This is the case with one of Emma Lathen's John Putnam Thatcher novels, *Green Grow the Dollars*, in which the murder does not take place until the story is well into its second half. The recurrent blank that increasingly captures the reader's attention during the first half (where the theme is the conflict between two seed companies over a newly developed tomato plant), is the mystery surrounding the behavior of Barbara Gunn, employed by one of the contending companies as a secretary and research assistant. After Barbara is murdered, that blank is transformed into the key to a possible motive. In the early chapters of the novel, the blank is clearly structured: Barbara's unexpectedly strong reaction to the value of the tomato plant is a signal to the reader of an especially meaningful textual pattern, but not a predictable course of action (96). Further developments confirm the structuring, as when Barbara discards the name tag identifying her with one of the contending companies (127), some of the characters notice that she looks ten years older (135), and several other confirmations of the mystery are added. Clearly these events are related, and the only missing element, the cause of Barbara's distress, is the one the text has, in Iser's words, "structured but left out" (*AR* 9).

When Barbara is murdered and the reading mode changes from simple mystery to detection, the structured blank (Why was Barbara worried?) emerges as a clue to the motive for her murder; the blank has been programmed by the introduction of the factor that was missing from the pre-murder phase, the element of *purpose*. The agent in this case is the convention of the veiled secret, which replaces the mystery of the earlier portion of the narrative. Shifting to the detection mode, the reader will make certain adjustments in expectation: first, Thatcher will solve Barbara's murder; second, the amount of space given to the mystery indicates that it must be taken seriously; and third, the reader must be on guard against the possibility that the cause of Barbara's worry is not the motive for her murder after all. In response to the suggested program, the reader calls upon several kinds of available heuristic devices, including reference to detective novels that follow the pattern of the murder postponed until fairly late in the story (Tey's *Miss Pym Disposes*, Crespi's *The Trouble with Moonlighting*) and a projection of the method to be followed in unveiling the secret.

In summary, the principles of programming theory can be most easily summarized in terms of the effect of programming on readers' expectations. In detective fiction especially it is the expectations of the genre, not the text, that predispose the reader to the programmed text: the presence of a convention within the reader's horizon alerts the reader to prepare for a programmed sequence, the special rules of the genre provide shape and structure for processing, and the reader's personal guide book suggests things to watch for. As a result of this special combination, the reader proceeds through a tale of detection with a predirected sense of assurance regarding certain conventional themes: the most likely suspect will be innocent, the death warrant will be fatal, the information in the dying message will eventually become available. It is also part of the formula, however, that the expectations of programming are indicative rather than infallible: the author reserves the right for the most likely suspect to turn up guilty, the maker of the death warrant appointment to survive for the meeting, or the dying message never to be deciphered. Programming controls structures, not themes.

One key to the formation of reader expectations is the special process of transformation in which the signals of the text are modified by the reader's individual genre. As we have seen in numerous illustrations, the special difference in the reading of detective fiction lies in the experienced reader's unique response to those signals. Iser refers to the process by which experience conditions the reader's expectations as "a dialectic of protension [expectation] and retention [memory], conveying a future horizon yet to be occupied, along with a past (and constantly fading) horizon already filled." Commenting on Husserl, Iser says that the reader occupies a position between the memory of what has been read and expectation for future reading. "Throughout the reading process there is a constant interplay between modified expectations and transformed memories. However, the text itself does not formulate expectations or their modification; nor does it specify how the connectability of memories is to be implemented. This is the province of the reader himself . . ." (*AR* 111-12). In detective fiction especially, the conditioning of expectations is guided by the individual genre, which is formulated in part by an author-reader relationship that is quite different from any other in popular fiction.

The effect of that relationship is clearest in the processes by which the reader interprets a blank in a typical classic detective situation, like those that occur in abundance in Philip MacDonald's *The Rasp* (1925). This novel is a model of the "cozy" English mystery, heavily dominated by the play mode and rich in stress-free tasks for the detection-minded reader to work on. It is also characterized by a strong minor plot, the detective's falling light-headedly in love with one of the characters. At one point in the story, the reader is presented an obvious blank, which is also the major problem of detective protagonist Anthony Gethryn: Was the murder in an old country home the work of an insider or an outsider? The reader's response to the question is conditioned by the self-reflexivity of the genre, manifest in the presence of a familiar tradition of the classic novel, the English country house convention.

The reader knows several things almost instinctively: first, on the basis of the efficiency principle, the amount of space given to the question is a signal of its importance; second, that the police favor the theory of the outsider makes it almost automatically wrong; and third, that Gethryn favors the insider theory virtually assures its being right.

The detection formula does not fill the blank; the insider vs outsider question is still there, but the convention is that murder in English country houses is always the work of an insider. The function of the regulative context here is to transform the questions from the state of free play to that of programmed game. The question of *whether* (insider or outsider) becomes *which* (of the insiders), and the field of probabilities is considerably narrowed. Presumably none of these responses would affect the reader unfamiliar with the detection formula; they have been conditioned solely by that unique context available to the veteran of literary detection.

The essentials of programming theory are further clarified in the examination of two detective novels, one a classic of the Golden Age and the other a recent private-eye story.

A showcase example of complex plotting and classic programming is Anthony Berkeley's *The Poisoned Chocolates Case*

(1929). The story opens with the arrival at his club of a box of chocolates addressed to Sir Eustace Pennefather; Sir Eustace, because he dislikes chocolates, gives the box to Mr. Bendix, who takes it home and shares it with his wife, who dies of poisoning. Chief Inspector Moresby, baffled by the mystery, submits the case to a group of six amateur detectives, known as the Crime Circle and headed by Roger Sheringham, the series protagonist. The complexity (as well as the self-parody) of the story arises in part from the fact that the puzzle is solved eight times, once by the police and seven times by the members of the Crime Circle (one member offers two solutions), and in part from the existence of two possible victims, Sir Eustace, to whom the chocolates were addressed, and Mrs. Bendix, who died of them.

The self-parody naturally lends itself to almost boundless self-reflexivity; hardly a chapter fails to contain at least one reminder that this is a detective story. Each of the seven solutions of the Crime Circle seems perfectly plausible, and any one of them could serve independently as a main plot. When one particularly ingenious member offers to prove that he himself committed the crime, Roger Sheringham's reply is "I couldn't disbelieve you" (168), a reminder of the practically unlimited possible variations available to the tale of detection.

The first blank we will discuss is the one at the end of chapter 1, where the members of the Crime Circle, awaiting the presentation of the police version of the case by Chief Inspector Moresby, fall into a discussion of some of the theoretical aspects of the art of detection. At this point the agent of programming is the familiar convention of the police vs the brilliant amateurs, predisposed by the generic supposition that the police version will be wrong and the problem will be solved by one of the Circle, presumably Roger Sheringham, the series detective. It is also heavily conditioned by the presence of the play element, in the straight-faced to-and-fro exchanges regarding the relative merits of inductive and deductive reasoning, even before the review of the problem (34-35).

Finally, the pattern suggested by the programming is the prospect of a mystery with broad parameters, together with the probability of a broth spoiled by too many cooks.

Even at this early point, the dyadic relationship between author and reader is firmly in place. To use Horton's phrase, there is already a context of situation understood by the reader (II 28), who knows before opening the book that this is a tale of detection and therefore likely to be strongly dominated by convention. The date of publication (1929) sets it in the pre-hard-boiled era, and the fact that the author is English provides additional assurance that this novel will be of the soft-boiled Golden Age variety. By the end of chapter 1 the elements of play and self-reflexivity have been added as conditioners of programming, with the result that there is now a well-defined regulative context available to both author and reader.

One reason *The Poisoned Chocolates Case* makes such a good subject of study is the unusually strict initialization of the negativity that underlies it, with the result that the reader's expectations are artfully directed and limited. Its nice balance of clues offers boundless opportunity for development, with the result that programming is almost impossible to avoid.

At the end of chapter 2 when the police version of the problem has been presented, a second agent of programming is in place, the convention of the insoluble problem (48). The blank is at this point conditioned by one of the earmarks of the classic formula, a series of reminders to the reader to pay attention, such as a pointed reference to the importance of the time element ("the porter glanced up at the clock") and hints of a large number of suspects ("a few husbands here and there, or a father or two"). The prospective pattern programmed into the negativity is one of maximum complexity, involving not only a large number of suspects but also an unusual number of detectives, all members of a detection club. As this element develops, the reader familiar with the Black Widower stories of Isaac Azimov may also perceive the programmed pattern of the least likely detective, wherein all the "regulars" prove to be wrong and the correct solution comes from an unexpected source.

A third example is found at the end of chapter 9, where the blank is created by a step in the hermeneutic structure, the dawning light, and reinforced shortly by a familiar convention, the concealed clue. This is where Roger Sheringham, perplexed by the difficulty of the problem, starts to put on his coat, pauses with one arm in the sleeve and murmurs *"By Jove!"* The chapter ends a few lines later with the provocative statement that "for the rest of the day Roger was very busy indeed," but the next chapter opens on a different track, leaving the reader uninformed regarding the cause of Roger's exclamation or the nature of his activity during the afternoon. The reader is mystified, but the program is clear: the pattern is that of *The Murder at the Vicarage*, where Miss

Marple murmurs, "So that was it," also signaling the dawning light and forthcoming explanation.

Finally, there is in *The Poisoned Chocolates Case* an example of counter-programming, that is, a blank programmed with contradictory expectations. One of the few near-certainties of detective fiction is that the mystery will be solved by the series protagonist, at the very end of the story. Here, the complication in programming is created by an irony: the novel is structured around the successive solutions by the six members of the Crime Circle, the order of presentation having been determined by lot, and Roger Sheringham, who by convention should have the last word, draws fourth place in order of presentation. Chapter 14, Roger's solution, is a carefully reasoned analysis that would be a credit to the formulaic hero in most tales of detection, but the chapter closes with two members yet to be heard from and fifty-six pages of text to be read. The formula seems to contradict itself; the agent of programming is the convention of the infallible detective, but the blank is heavily conditioned by the self-reflexivity of the novel exemplified in the six plausible solutions. We must not forget the influence of the compact between author and reader, which forces the reader to ask not only Where is he going with this one? but also How is he going to work himself out of this mess? The tension created by the conflict produces a secondary meaning, forcing the reader to reinterpret not only this novel but the detection formula itself.

The same general principles apply to the private-eye novel: programming occurs only in the presence of a convention, and the store of conventions available to a private-eye story is practically identical with those common in the classic. The same is true with the set of available heuristics: the reader develops a sense of what to watch for. The only real difference is in some peculiarities of the private-eye story, which condition the narrative differently. as for example the relaxation of the efficiency principle, which reduces the certainty that anything given any space is likely to be important.

Thus the programming process is not limited to the classic Golden Age novel. *There's Something in a Sunday* (1989) is one of Marcia Muller's series featuring San Francisco private investigator Sharon McCone. The novel follows the standard private-eye format: Sharon has been hired by Rudy Goldring to shadow a man by the name of Frank Wilkonson in an effort to discover what his intentions are. When Goldring is mysteriously murdered, Sharon continues her search until she identifies his killer. As usual, there are several parallel plot strands, but the major point of focus is Sharon and her investigation.

The differences in the programming of a formal classic tale of detection and a private-eye novel are largely the result of those three special methodological qualities of the private-eye formula discussed in chapter 5, the expanded commission, the relaxation of the efficiency principle, and the protagonist point of view. The reader familiar with the convention of the expanded commission proceeds through the early chapters (the shadow-job) in expectation of impending murder, and in *There's Something in a Sunday* the pattern is augmented by a residual mystery, in which the detective continues on her own without a commission. At the end of chapter 16 Sharon's client has been murdered and she is out of a job, but she goes ahead with her pursuit of Frank Wilkonson. At this point the programming of the blank is governed rather by the precedent of Philip Marlowe ("Nothing made it my business except my own curiosity") than by any attempt at realism.

The generic relaxation of the efficiency principle has a more marked effect upon programming than does the expanded commission; in the classic formula, the probability is that any element introduced is likely to be important, but the odds are narrowed a little in the private-eye story by the possibility that any newly introduced element could be a free motif. For the most part, however, the reader assumes that the efficiency principle will always hold true. Actually, there are not many of such relaxations of the principle in this novel, but the possibility of their presence naturally affects programming. Sharon, on her way to an appointment with Goldring, notices a tramp lounging outside the building (17); in a classic tale the reader, sensing the possibility of a clue, would take more than superficial note of that tramp, but here the probability is that he is another of those pitiable creatures that are part of the scenery of the mean streets.

The effect of the protagonist point of view is even more far-reaching, because it introduces the element of subjectivity into the conditioning of every blank. Instead of the doting admirer or the impersonal author, the narrator in this case is Sharon McCone, whose view of the events is prejudiced by a strong element of self-contempt and lack of self-confidence, together with a nagging consciousness of her age. Sharon is one of Stowe's hermeneutic interpreters, who becomes one with the problem in order to solve it.

Aside from these three effects, the programming of the private-eye story is much the same as that of the classic novel. The special kind of attention demanded by the classic story is just as necessary in the reading of a private eye-novel; repeated references to an unidentified personal problem of Wilkonson in the early pages of *There's Something in a Sunday* is a clear signal to the reader that here is a plot element of some importance: the influence of the efficiency principle is never completely absent, and no writer will waste this many references on something insignificant.

Although *There's Something in a Sunday* lacks the parodic tone of *The Poisoned Chocolates Case*, the "protecting wall of play" is still there, and the play mode makes itself felt at one point in this story, in the assignment of an easy task for the reader. Two women named Irene appear on the same page, an obvious easy clue to involve the reader for a while; characteristically, the coincidence is explained four pages later, when it is revealed that the two are the same person (98-102).

With a few exceptions, private-eye fiction draws upon the same stockpile of convention as does the classic. In *There's Something in a Sunday* such familiar devices as excessive detail and the summary of the situation consistently become agents of programming. Another well-known convention is the missing person: when Wilkonson fails to check into his motel (123) and Sharon can not pick up his trail later, the blank is programmed by precedent: Wilkonson is himself a murder victim, as was the case in Van Dine's *The Kennel Murder Case*, Kemmelman's *Sunday the Rabbi Stayed Home*, and a long string of other instances.

Finally, the private-eye story is bound by one near-inviolable principle of the classic formula: the mystery will be solved, but not until the end of the story. Thus when on page 146 Sharon asks, "You think he [Wilkonson] killed Rudy?" and Irene replies, "Yes," the program says *no:* it is too early for a solution.

For insight into the mechanics of programming, we will examine the blank created early in the story when Sharon is commissioned to tail Frank Wilkonson. The reader is presented two questions: What is Wilkonson up to? and What is his involvement with Rudy Goldring? The agent of programming is the expanded commission, which creates a dimension of expectation regarding the mystery, because the reader knows from experience that sooner or later this assignment will involve murder. The program is further conditioned by the efficiency principle. When Sharon first catches sight of Wilkonson early in the story (6), he is holding two pieces of paper, one pink and one yellow. The experienced reader, perceiving the conditioned blank, can be reasonably certain that something will come of this. The pattern of programming, at this early stage, involves the narrowing of parameters; at the beginning they are very broad, as Sharon is unable to determine whether Wilkonson is even involved in the problem; they are narrowed to near certainty when Wilkonson, with Sharon trailing him, begins to show his real intentions with some completely unexpected behavior, making an apparently irrational sudden turn in heavy traffic (10).

When the story reaches the point of Goldring's murder, and the blank is widened from the question, What are Wilkonson's motives? to include Who killed Rudy Goldring? the programming has assumed much the same form as in the classic novel, except for two conditions imposed by the private-eye formula. First, there is always the possibility of relaxation of the efficiency principle: some of this may have no bearing on the main plot. Second, the point of view is subjective; every detail of the account comes to the reader through the consciousness of Sharon McCone, who, because she is the narrator, is also the sole interpreter of events.

We can summarize the special reading mode of detective fiction with a review of the three elements of programming, referred to previously in times this chapter. First, there is an agent to alert the reader to the prospect of a programmed sequence; in literary detection, this agent is one of the familiar conventions of the genre. Second, because of the "differentness" of detective fiction, there may be one or more conditioners to limit programming to the special mode of the story. Finally, the product of former experience is a set of heuristics to which the reader has access and which can focus the possible paths of development of the programmed structure.

Most of the conventions of detective fiction, especially such familiar recurrent themes as the most likely suspect and the death warrant, automatically initiate the process of programming. One such example is the unidentifiable vctim, discussed briefly in chapter 3. If a murdered corpse in a detective story has been disfigured in such fashion as to be unrecognizable, the reader is reasonably assured that the first identification of that body will be wrong; it is really somebody else. The prototype is Doyle's *The Valley of Fear,* in which the first assumption regarding the identity of the murder victim misleads the investigation for a considerable part of the story and leads to one of the most effective surprises in the Sherlock Holmes canon. Imagine that the reader of that novel is also familiar with several other stories in which the identification of a murder victim is mistaken.

Now suppose such a reader turns to Troy Soos's *Murder at Fenway Park*. At the beginning of the 1912 baseball season, rookie second baseman Mickey Rawlings of the Boston Red Sox stumbles over the body of a murder victim whose face has been beaten into unrecognizability with a baseball bat. Fairly early on, the dead man is identified as Red Corriden of the Detroit Tigers; on the basis of past experience, the reader will automatically assume that the body is not that of Corriden but of some other person, and the reading expectations from here on are controlled by the conventionally programmed structure.

Because the "detective story sense" is the chief difference between the detective story and any other kind of fiction, the programming of the text is shaped by some of the special features of the detection genre that create its unique reading mode. The reader proceeds, for example, with the assurance that the mystery in a tale of detection will be solved at the end of the story. The principle conditions reading in several ways, offering for example a caution against premature solutions. Thus when a character in Sara Shankman's *First Kill All the Lawyers* confesses to a murder on page 185, the reader will have some reservations about that confession, especially with thirty-two pages yet to go. Moreover, unless there is good reason to believe otherwise, the reader can be assured that it will be the detective who solves the mystery. At one point in Patricia Wallace's *Deadly Devotion* an opposing lawyer refers to his side as the winning side; when private investigator Sydney Bryant replies, "You haven't won yet," (102) the reader is inclined to believe her, because this is the way things normally are.

Transformed play is another conditioner of the programming process; it might be said that the "double of the text" is first initialized by play, and then programmed by the genre. If Paretsky's *Guardian Angel* were a crime story instead of a tale of detection, for example, reading it would be a stressful experience indeed. In one of her raids on the Diamond Head plant Vic Warshawski is injured, but instead of complaining of the pain she remarks, "Move over, Michael Jordan. This here is Air Warshawski" (242). As if comments like this were not enough, who could be stressed out by a story with chapter headings like "Sex and the Single Girl" and "Showdown at the OK Morgue"?

The efficiency principle, which holds that any element introduced into a detective story is likely to be important, can be a conditioner of a programmed sequence, especially if the story
belongs to the classic school of detection. When a strong witchcraft motif enters John Dickson Carr's *The Crooked Hinge* (108), the
experienced reader will immediately know two things: first, the
degree of attention it receives virtually assures that it will become
an important element in the novel, and if the reader has read
much of Carr, the assurance is almost beyond question. This same
reader will also be aware of a second condition on programming,
however, this one imposed by the genre itself: witchcraft can not
become the *major* plot of this novel. The principle is modified in
the private-eye genre, but it can still assert some priority, as in the
episode cited from *H Is for Homicide.* That a murder is introduced
at the beginning of the novel substantially ensures its importance.

A reader of detective fiction running into a mysterious element (a "blank" or "area of indeterminacy" in the language of
reception theory), because he or she *is* a reader of detective fiction,
will have at hand a bag of tricks (heuristics) produced by earlier
experience. Such a reader can, for example, size up a problem to
estimate its importance in the story, cite other instances of the
same type as the present mystery, and even estimate the probabilities of its future line of development. But also, being a reader of
detective fiction, that reader will participate as interested observer
only and can be content to watch the problem being solved
instead of trying to solve it.

For most readers, the "sizing up" of the problem in *Murder at
Fenway Park* would be shaped by the successive limitations placed
on Mickey Rawlings during his investigation of the mystery of
the unidentifiable victim. Early in the story Mickey is warned by
the team management to keep his mouth shut (45), and he
squelches his desire to tell his friend Peggy about it (66). Realizing
that he will probably be turned over to the police as the prime
suspect at the end of the season, Mickey feels the pressure to solve
the mystery before the season ends, and keeps reminding himself
that he has only a few weeks, then only twenty-one days, then
fourteen, and so on. This is a familiar structure in detective fiction, in which the problem "narrows down" to a point where
solution is inevitable. Because of the conventionality of the genre,
and especially because a convention is the prime agent of a programmed sequence, a reader will inevitably recall other stories in
which the same situation has developed. The convention of the

unidentifiable victim, being one of the oldest, will afford a fairly broad choice of similar cases. The reader should remember not only *The Valley of Fear* but other instances like Ross Macdonald's *The Blue Hammer*, Ellis Peters's *The Potter's Field*, Ellery Queen's *The Tragedy of X*, Dorothy Sayers's *The Nine Tailors*, and Sharon McCrumb's *The Windsor Knot*, in each of which the victim's body has been rendered unidentifiable as a result of the purposeful destruction of its facial features, or because of exposure to the forces of nature, or, in one case, because of the victim's having been cremated. In each of those stories, the murdered person proves to be someone other than the original supposition.

Thus the reader of a detective story, meeting one of these unidentifiable victims, can be reasonably certain that the program will follow the customary pattern, and most people will normally follow that line in reading to the big surprise ending, where it is revealed that the corpse originally unidentified has also been misidentified. It must not be forgotten, however, that convention, despite its strength, is only one control; the other is invention, the right of a creative writer to innovate against the established frames of the genre. Innovation is one of the ways the genre protects itself against the danger of monotony.

In the hands of a gifted writer, a positively programmed convention becomes a useful device in the creation of suspense, allowing such a writer to work the literary equivalent of a draw play, in which the reader is systematically led to assume a certain state of affairs, only to discover that the situation is exactly the opposite. This is how Christie uses the convention of the most likely suspect in *Murder at the Vicarage*, where the author builds up a conventionally programmed pattern and then allows the suspect to turn up guilty. The result of such a turnabout is that the reader makes some adjustments in expectations and enters a note under "probabilities" in his or her personal reference shelf.

This is what happens in *Murder at Fenway Park* where, despite all the insistent generic signals to the contrary, the unidentifiable victim does indeed prove to be Red Corriden. This is another example of counter-programming: the convention is programmed in two directions. The first break in the pattern comes on page 119, when Peggy (who reads detective stories) raises the question, "What if it wasn't really Red Corriden?" thereby breaking the suspense and interrupting the hermeneutic "logic of enigma and solution" (Culler *SP* 203). Expectations become confused by two sets of signals and the reader feels the opposite pull of two sets of rules. On the one hand there are the rules for the programming of a familiar convention, which hold that a convention introduces a given pattern of development for the story to follow: the most likely suspect never turns up guilty, and the unidentifiable corpse is always misidentified. On the other hand, there is the generically programmed rule against early revelation of the solution: Peggy must be mistaken. For the reader who is a stranger to the detection formula, the suspense is not at all damaged, because such a reader's expectations are not guided by the genre anyhow.

Neither is it diminished for the experienced reader, who responds to the counter-programming with an awareness of a new tension, this time created by an apparent contradiction in the rules. We might remind ourselves here that the rules of the detection genre, as we are defining them, are not prescriptive but are rather descriptive statements of the genre as it is. They represent the accumulated experience of the past, which becomes part of the repertoire of the veteran reader. Part of that experience would be the ever-present possibility of counter-programming, as in the parallel development in *The Poisoned Chocolates Case*, in which the correct solution is offered by the last speaker, not the series detective, in keeping with the rules of the genre.

All this should remind us that the detective story is not a simple exercise in problem and solution but a play experience in which the rules are constantly tested by the innovations of creative writers and the changing tastes of an experienced reading public Change and development, however, are guided by the special "differentness" of the tale of detection, which is the expression of a kind of tension or dialectic of context and negativity. Thus the experienced reader proceeds through the story with two kinds of awareness. The first is that of a pervading mystery, Iser's "nothing" of negativity that is not simply a vacancy but a space prepared for interpretation by having been initialized in previous experience. This same reader, however, is also aware of the control of context, which includes not only such familiar recurrent themes as the most likely suspect but also the rules perceived from past reading and the accumulated history of the genre that continues to shape the current detective novel. This juxtaposition is a dialectic rather than a conflict because, as we will see in chapter 7, the forces of negativity and convention give each other meaning.

7

Are We Supposed to Take This Stuff Seriously?

I hope the student who raised that question in my class twenty-some years ago reads these pages, because her question has been a substantial guide to my study of the detection genre ever since. As I recall, my answer at the time was a suitably professorial evasion, "It depends." Now, however, I'm afraid I can't do much better: it does indeed depend. On a number of things.

What must have bothered her, as it bothers most students confronting the serious study of popular literature for the first time after having read only genres with well-established critical norms, is the problem of making valid interpretations of material in which the criteria are fluid and subject to continual revision. The whole business of interpretation is even more complicated in the detective story, which we "take" differently from other genres. How shall we take seriously a story in which we already know in a general way how it will come out, in which anybody who makes an early confession to a crime is almost never guilty, or in which the point of view may suddenly change, brazenly excluding the reader from important developments?

The key terms in my student's question are *we* and *take*. As we have already seen, one of the bases of reception theory is the crucial position of the reader in the act of interpretation, that is, in how *we* take things. Any attempt to eliminate oneself and one's own concepts from the act of interpretation, says Gadamer, is not only impossible but absurd. When we interpret something we inevitably bring our own preconceptions into play, with the result that the meaning of any text must always "speak for us" (*TM* 397). In the special reading of detective fiction, we want to remember, many of those preconceptions that accompany the act of reading are the result of our experience with a strongly formulaic genre.

Our "taking" anything in the act of reading obviously depends upon vastly more than simple response to the marks printed on a page. It depends, as we have seen, upon not only the formulations of the text but also the experience of the reader and the rules of the genre. We derive meaning from the signs on the pages, or impose meaning on them, in a complicated exchange to which Iser assigns the term *realization*, which is the result of our continuing effort to fill the gap of indeterminacy that exists between ourselves and the text; in short, meaning is born of our effort to catch up with the text.

Because of the negativity that underlies all literature, a reader can never understand a text as a whole but must experience it only as a sequence of changing perspectives, each with its own restricted meaning and consequently needing further interpretation. This added interpretation is the process by which Iser says a reader "realizes" the overall picture (*AR* 68). The process of realization is, however, much more than a simple translation of signals into meanings, and it can not take place until the reader has developed, for the text, a system of relationships and identifications (81-82). During the process the themes and allusions of the text already familiar to the reader are "recoded" and supplied with a revised context and new meanings (*AR* 74; Eagleton 78).

The point is especially important in the detection text, in which the meaning of a given set of signals can change drastically as a result of increased experience with the conventionality of detective fiction. In a sense, the signals of the text in a detective story are not only "coded" but *loaded*, with some of their associations as old as the appearance of the most likely suspect in "The Murders in the Rue Morgue." A situation can, in other words, become standardized as a result of having been reintroduced so regularly that it assumes the quality of ritual. So strong is the conventionality of the genre that the familiar structure need not even correspond to external reality, as in the case of the locked room or the expression on the face of the murder victim.

For illustration of the special effect of the genre upon the signals of the text, we will turn to Ellery Queen's *The Chinese Orange Mystery* (1934), a detective novel unquestionably dominated by the classic formula from beginning to end. Even before opening the book, the reader has access to a whole context of literary values familiar to the Golden Age and especially the early Ellery Queen, who was famous for his complicated, involuted mysteries and quite as capable of trickery as Agatha Christie.

From the first page on, the author wastes no time in arousing the "certain kind of attention" necessary for interpretation: in chapter 1 the reader is given the conventional tour of the prospective murder scene, with attention focused upon two items of obvious hermeneutic significance, the tangerine in the fruit-bowl and the valuable Chinese stamp. The experienced reader will already feel the assurance that the murder (since there is certain to be one) will be solved, probably at the very end of the novel, and undoubtedly by Ellery Queen.

What Kermode calls the "values appropriate to this kind of reading" correspond generally to the conditions of programming, and they are, in *The Chinese Orange Mystery*, the values of the classical formal-problem story, such as those implicit in the efficiency principle. At one point in the first chapter, one can hardly miss the fact that the reader is being swarmed with statements of the exact time. One person, asked for the time, answers "five forty-three"; chapter 2 opens with the words, "At precisely 5:44"; two pages later it is "twenty-five minutes past six," and shortly after, "It was exactly 6:35," and then "6:45 to the minute" (21-29). At this point the references are unfocused, but one of the values of the genre is a commitment to efficiency: this writer is not wasting words. Its very recurrence makes the time element significant. The focus is supplied shortly afterward when the doctor estimates the time of death "about six" (35), and the sorting-out of the hermeneutically relevant acquires new meaning.

A second set of values is supplied by the play element, in the person of the unknown murder victim, who is given the title of "Mr. Nobody from Nowhere," and whose anonymity relieves the reader of emotional involvement. One evidence of the play structure in traditional detective fiction is the role of the victim, who is customarily a convenient nobody rather than an object of pity. This kind of thing was undoubtedly one of the reasons why my student demanded to know how one is expected to take seriously a story in which a nobody, who in another book would be an object of pity and a reproach on an uncaring society, becomes nothing more than a corpse for the detective to work on.

In addition, the formal-problem novel is cleared of stress by those repeated reminders that it will all be solved in the end. When at the conclusion of chapter 4 the house detective confesses to Ellery that he does not know a thing, Ellery replies, "Nor do I" and adds a thunderously significant "yet." We do not want to miss the point that these instances can involve plenty of mental *strain* on the part of the reader, since they both demand considerable interpretation, but no *stress*. At any rate, the reader can exercise the usual option: enjoy the fun of trying to identify Mr.

Nobody and decide what Ellery has in mind, or sit back and watch the author work.

A whole new package of values is introduced when it becomes apparent that *The Chinese Orange Mystery* is a locked-room story; the signal is clear in the careful validation of genuine lockedness that is almost ritual in narratives of this type, with not only a tightly locked door but windows completely unreachable from outside. One of the qualities of the locked-room subgenre is its susceptibility to constant reinterpretation, as is the case here. In *textual* terms, the room is not, strictly speaking, locked (there is still access via the corridor), but the "gestures" here (especially the ritual of validation) prompt the reader to interpret it as such, illustrating Kermode's observation that when the "certain kind of attention" has been aroused, we read according to the appropriate values, in this case the rules of the locked-room tradition.

"Ideally," says Kermode, "we are always sorting out the hermeneutically relevant from all other information . . . " (*PM* 181). Shortly after the introduction of the locked-room problem, the reader learns that in the murder room, where everything has been turned backward, one singular fact appears; the victim's necktie is missing (46). No reader experienced in the detection genre can overlook the hermeneutic significance of that missing necktie, for at least two reasons. First, the blank it creates is conditioned by the efficiency principle, which mandates that its appearance here is an indicator of its importance; and second, that blank is an instance of the anomaly convention, the one thing that does not fit, which is critical in a classic story.

Sacralized closure is the term Kermode uses for the taboo that guards against premature revelation: "to give away the solution that comes at the end is to give away all" (180). The reader, meanwhile, moves ahead in the expectation that it will "work out," in contrast to the unpredictable problems one faces in nonfictional life (188). The reading of *The Chinese Orange Mystery* is rich in such expectations. When one character during the early stages of the investigation insists that Ellery must have some theory to account for the bizarre nature of the crime, his response is "Generally, yes, specifically, no" (63). The signal is likely to produce two expectations: first, the reader can proceed with the dual assurance that the problem will be solved, but not before the very end of the story; and second, the reader can enjoy the feeling of security that leaves one free to sort out which is which between Ellery's "general" and "specific." Here is another example of the way in which the play element of detective fiction relieves the reader of stress, while allowing full experience of the pleasure of strain.

One of the strongest drives of human perception is our need to fill in blank spaces, to project patterns onto vacant areas. Among the oldest patterns of detective fiction is what might be called the glittering object (or concealed clue) convention, wherein the Holmes-type detective dives into the shrubbery, plucks forth something at which he stares with great satisfaction and conceals in his pocket, leaving the reader to work out an identification of the find and its importance to the investigation. The device has enormous hermeneutic value, pushing the reader's expectation ahead to the point at which the object and its importance will be revealed. Early in *The Chinese Orange Mystery* Ellery writes a name on a slip of paper and hands it to his father, with the suggestion that he look for a person of that name. The Inspector is galvanized into action; the reader is left with the task of filling in the blank (72). The situation may strike the reader of the 1990s as a little contrived; concealment is still a hermeneutically useful device, but it is handled by writers today somewhat more plausibly, as when Mickey Rawlings in *Murder at Fenway Park* says, "One more thing to do" and then passes out, leaving the reader to wait awhile before discovering what it was that Mickey wanted to do (233).

There is another yawning blank at the end of chapter 16, when Ellery, who has worked out the solution to the entire puzzle, sits and talks for an hour to Inspector Queen, whose brows are drawn up into a concentrated frown. The chapter ends with the Inspector's reaction: "And then, all at once, he grinned all over his face and cried: 'Well, I'll be double-damned'" (172). The rest of the page is suitably blank, a spatial metaphor of emptiness (*CD* 140): "The lack of a sign can itself be a sign," says Iser, quoting Merleau-Ponty (*AR* 169). Here, though, the hermeneutic drive results not so much from the lack of a sign as from an initialized blank: the reader cannot be said to react to absence alone, because the reading is guided by a consciousness of the detection formula, which supplies the expectation that the blank will be filled.

We should not leave the discussion of this novel without examining the most dramatic example of the hermeneutics of transformed play, in the device that became a trademark of the early Ellery Queen, the challenge to the reader. On page 164 the author stops the narrative and speaks directly to the reader, in the conventional self-reflexive style of the classic formal-problem story. "It's really a simple matter," says the writer who has just spun a narrative of such hopeless complexity as to render impossible any interpretation that so much as hints at simplicity. "I maintain that at this point in your reading you have all the facts in your possession essential to a clear solution of the mystery." The challenge is to put all the clues together and through the exercise of pure logic "arrive at the one and only possible solution." The challenge must be considered a play device, because most readers could never take it literally. The reader experienced in the detection formula will recognize it as an example of the straight-faced persiflage of the genre, along with Dupin's reading of the narrator's mind and Holmes's analysis of the history of Watson's watch. Nevins's comment on the resolution is an appropriate summary of the absurdity of the proposition: "Despite the Challenge to the Reader, the solution can't be called completely fair, since it hinges on physical manipulations so outlandish that not one reader in ten thousand could even conceive of them."[1] The implied challenge to the reader is not to solve the problem but to participate in the forward movement of the narrative; instead of going back over the evidence in an effort to follow Ellery's line of reasoning (plot analysis), the reader pushes on toward the resolution. Here, as in the instances we cited earlier, the real invitation is to a play experience, in this case involving a pseudotask; the element of stress is eliminated by the fact that the reader cannot possibly take the challenge seriously.

The direct practical effect of the play element upon the reading of detective fiction can be stated in just those terms: it prevents our taking the tale of detection with the same kind of seriousness we would exercise in reading *Brideshead Revisited* or *The Good Earth*. The successful experiencing of detective stories demands that the reader adapt to the play-detection mode by tolerating situations that would be rejected in other reading. As we have noted earlier, for example, the detective story does not hesitate to modify the nature of reality to suit its own purposes, as in the case of the revealing expression on the face of the murder victim. Nor does the story hesitate to modify the reader's normal aesthetic values, with the result that we not only tolerate but enjoy such outrages to the fitness of things as we encounter in the explanation of the reason why the corpse had those two African spears shoved inside his clothing in *The Chinese Orange Mystery*: Ellery's explanation is so absurd that even if the reader considers it plausible, most people with any sense of appropriateness would be affronted by its artificiality.

In addition to those produced by the play experience, one other special effect upon the reading of detective fiction is created by the hermeneutic specialization of the genre: to a greater degree than in most other kinds of fiction, the reader is guided to the perception of secondary meanings in the narrative. Most readers, even after a limited experience with the formula, will develop some skill in inferential reading, with the result that when Ellery abruptly rises from the dinner table and awkwardly splashes wine all over his neighbor, we know he has something special in mind, and of course our expectation is confirmed a few pages later when we learn that his real purpose was to steal a note from the man's jacket pocket (65, 71). The blank is programmed, the agent being a convention at least as old as "The Golden Pince-Nez," in which Holmes, furiously smoking one cigarette after another, scatters ash all over the bedroom carpet with feigned carelessness, for the real purpose of seeing whether someone leaves tracks in it later. The hermeneutic advantage is twofold: the reader enjoys the short-term expectation of the reason for the trick and the longer one of confirmation of the detective's superior ability.

One aspect of the perception of secondary meaning is the reader's ability not only to recognize the blanks of the text but to anticipate the development of blanks forthcoming. The signal at the end of chapter 1 of *The Chinese Orange Mystery* is clear to the experienced reader, when the author stops the action and carefully locates each of several of the people in the story: Miss Diversey and Mr. Osborne are in the office; Donald Kirk is "off somewhere"; Dr. Kirk's nose is buried in a book; and so on through an accounting of the nine persons who will figure in the story (21-22). The reader can hardly miss the mapping of the negativity: each of these people will become a suspect in the upcoming murder, and the glaring signal of Donald Kirk's being merely "off somewhere" already identifies him as someone to watch, probably in the role of the most likely suspect.

Under the influence of the detection mode, the reader's perception of secondary meanings also generates a heightened awareness of structure and a tendency to anticipate structural change. The classic formal-problem novel is noted especially for its tendency to tap the reader on the shoulder periodically, calling attention to the progress of development of the plot. Near the end of chapter 15 of *The Chinese Orange Mystery*, for example, we come upon this sentence: "He [Ellery] fell silent, sucking his thumb and staring at the littered desk" (159). For the reader experienced in the classic Ellery Queen, the signal of approaching transition from period of confusion to dawning light is quite clear. Ellery tends to wander about with his hands in his pockets and even (as here) to engage in such extraordinary habits as thumb sucking immediately before some tremendous insight. The signal is intensified when, one page later, Ellery's "deep frown" becomes a "rapt expression," followed shortly by "Eureka! That's the answer!" (160-63).

One other such signal deserves mention. At the beginning of chapter 27, after the challenge has been delivered to the reader and after Ellery has given his father a complete explanation (from which, as we noted a little earlier, the reader was excluded), we find that all the main characters in the story (the same ones whose whereabouts had been carefully catalogued just before the murder) are assembling for a meeting called by Ellery Queen. This, of course, is the traditional assembly of suspects, which immediately precedes the final phase of solution and explanation.

The grand style of a Golden Age novel like *The Chinese Orange Mystery* is especially useful in illustrating how the detection genre modifies the signals of the text into the special receptions of the reader, because in the classic mystery the bones of structure stick out so obtrusively as to be almost impossible to miss. When we turn to *The Lady in the Lake*, one of Chandler's novels that served as a model for a number of the writers of the private-eye school of detection, it should become evident that the influence of the formula may not be so obvious, but the secret is just as deeply veiled and the suggestions and hints just as effective as in the traditional novel. Among writers of recent years some of the lines of distinction between the gifted amateur and the professional investigator have been softened and some of the former rules revised in stories like *The Long-Legged Fly*, but the mode of reading is still guided by standards of hermeneutic specialization and the aesthetics of conventionality.

How we "take" a novel like *The Chinese Orange Mystery* depends partly upon the printed page before us, partly upon ourselves and our previous experience with such books, and partly upon the context in which the reading takes place. These three influences combine to make up the reading mode. When the appropriate mode has been established, the signals that my student called "this stuff" are transformed into art. Obviously, a reader's reception of a signal is much more than a translation of signs on the printed page, with the result that a word like *murder* reads differently in *The Chinese Orange Mystery* and in *Macbeth*. The shock of an inexperienced reader upon learning that murder in a detective story is not an act of infinite cruelty but a problem for the detective to work on must be something like the shock of a mother unfamiliar with Sesame Street upon learning that her four-year-old loves a monster. The signal received by the mother in terms of Caliban and Quasimodo is obviously quite a different being from the one received by the child in terms of the Cookie Monster.

A good reverse illustration of how the principle works is James Thurber's story "The Macbeth Murder Mystery," in which an avid detection fan, picking up a paperback reprint of *Macbeth*, mistakes it for a tale of detection and proceeds to read it as such. Applying sound detectional hermeneutics, she identifies Macduff as the murderer after rejecting Macbeth and Lady Macbeth as the conventional most likely suspects. The awestruck narrator tries his hand at literary detection and, in an even more ingenious analysis, names Lady Macbeth's father as the guilty party.[2]

Thurber's detection fan, having developed a certain mind-set, continued to read within that same context, without consideration of appropriateness. Everybody tends to do that, according to Kermode (*PM* 181), but most readers know how to press the proper mode button in terms of the material of the text. This establishment of a reading mode is what Iser describes as a process of feedback or reciprocal transformation, in which the reader's viewpoint is constantly conditioned and modified during the process of reading. It takes place below the level of awareness, and it becomes a self-regulating structure that exercises a strong influence upon the interaction between text and reader (*AR* 201).

One of the best tests of the special mode for reading detective fiction is to examine some of the ways it modifies the signals of the text. The same signal can convey opposite meanings to people reading in different modes, as it does in Queen's *The Tragedy of X*. About two-thirds of the way through that novel, the police go after a suspect, who barricades himself in his apartment, screams "You'll never take me alive, damn you!" and shoots himself (229). In a crime story this episode would mark the solution of the case, but here the detection mode takes precedence as a result of the way in which the generic context modifies the reader's viewpoint. For somebody to yell "You'll never take me alive" in a crime story would be a clear admission of guilt, but the detection fan reads the signal as an equally clear indication of innocence, for two reasons. In the first place gratuitous confessions are frowned upon by the detection formula, and if that is not enough, the reader must reject this one as premature; the story has seventy pages yet to go.

The generic context also guides the reading of the private eye novel. In *Jackpot* Bill Pronzini's nameless detective has identified a likely suspect, whom he has decided to follow up to Fallen Leaf Lake, three and a half hours distant. Before departure, he tries to pry some information out of his friend Inspector Craddock of the L.A. Police, but Craddock, who suspects Nameless of knowing more than he admits, is curious about the private detective's special interest in Fallen Leaf Lake. "Sometimes," says Nameless, "people run to familiar places. If they're not running too hard." "Uh-huh," Craddock answers, "You plan to drive that far on a maybe?" (79). At this point the reader anticipates something more than a "maybe"; the signal is interpreted in accord with the special compact between reader and author that governs both the writing and the reading of detective fiction.

After some experience, most detection readers develop a habit of not only interpreting a signal in terms of its position in the story but of actually being able to anticipate coming changes in structure. Early in Fedderson's *Dead in the Melon Patch* the detective protagonist discovers the body of a young woman who has apparently been killed in a fall from a ladder (20). The reader knows the death is not likely to be accidental because its location in the novel places it where the stage is set for murder.

These three examples illustrate the special reading mode of literary detection, though we could cite a considerable number of others, including several we have already discussed. There are, for example, those instances in which the text seems to be saying one certain thing but must be read otherwise, with the result that the reader perceives secondary meanings, or those instances in which normal literary values must be modified in order for a detection fan to tolerate situations that would be considered absurd or offensive in other genres. At any rate, we want to remember that the differentness of detective fiction does not consist in any one or more of these as unique to detective fiction but in their persistence and relative influence upon the reading mode.

Before the end of this chapter we will spend some time with two novels, Chandler's *The Lady in the Lake* and Eco's *The Name of the Rose,* each of which is best realized when read in the special sense we have been discussing, and each of which illustrates the importance of negativity as the underlying influence that shapes the tale of detection. Negativity in Iser is not mere absence or vacancy but a basic force in literary communication. Discussing the means by which indeterminacy conditions the reader's formulation of the text, he says that "the unwritten text shapes the written" (182). Holub casts some helpful light on Iser's concept when he explains that negativity is "like a deep structure of the text, an organizational principle whose 'abstract manifestations' are the blanks and negations the reader perceives" (*RT* 95). Because of that initilization of the blank page beyond the text we discussed in the last chapter, negativity assumes an especially vital organizational function in the special case of detective fiction.

The Lady in the Lake is one of the series of Chandler novels that established much of the pattern for the writing of private-eye fiction. In chapter 2 Marlowe is engaged by Derace Kingsley to find his wife, Crystal, who has been missing for a month. Early in the investigation Marlowe makes a visit to the Kingsley cabin, located on a lake some distance from Los Angeles; there he meets Bill Chess, whose wife Muriel is also missing. Almost by accident Marlowe and Chess discover a body that has been submerged in the lake for about a month, and it is identified as the remains of the missing Crystal Kingsley. At about this point a number of complications develop, and Kingsley keeps Marlowe on the case for several reasons, some of them involving the missing Muriel Chess.

Marlowe in this novel fills the standard role of the private investigator of fiction with his own code of ethics: he does not hesitate to remove evidence from a murder scene (94) or to mislead the police (184), but he refuses to suppress evidence that in his opinion the police may need (100). Like many of the private detectives of recent fiction he is conscious of his advancing age (125), but unlike most of them he carries a gun (137).

This novel is a good example of the limited influence of the social-cultural scene upon the tale of detection. Chandler apparently intended his historical setting to be contemporaneous with the date of publication (1943), at a time when shortages of civilian goods and general restrictions on people's lives were felt everywhere. Here, however, World War II is only incidentally sensed in those references to USO and Red Cross cards in the window of police headquarters (41), in the fact that the dam is guarded (26), and in the way people cluster around a radio for war news. Otherwise people's lives seem to go on much as they would in peacetime, in confirmation of the influence of mediated play: readers read detective fiction in order to transform the stresses of everyday life, not to participate in them.

The underlying negativity of *The Lady in the Lake* provides the organizing principle for one of the most complex mysteries of the genre, making full use of the potential of such conventions as the missing person and the unidentifiable victim, and the opportunities afforded by the parallel-plot structure. A reader whose expectations have developed within the horizon of the detection genre should begin to read signals early in the book pointing to a connection between the stories of the two missing women, Crystal Kingsley and Muriel Chess. In this novel Chandler employs a technique he was to repeat in *The Long Goodbye*, of a series of hints and suggestions that the two plots may be more closely related than the text seems to be saying. On page 56 the reader learns that the two women disappeared at about the same time, and two pages later Marlowe asks Kingsley if the women knew each other very well; on that same page this signal is supplemented with a reminder that the supposed body of Muriel Chess is unidentifiable, a hint that this may not be Muriel's body after all.

The signals continue to insist upon a relationship between the Kingsley and Chess plots until the point at which the reader begins to grasp the real truth of the situation, and they program the reader's expectations to such a degree that they organize the story on the blank page of negativity. The effect is apparent in the passage in which Marlowe tells Kingsley about the murder of his wife and the reader occupies the happy position one half-step behind Marlowe and one half ahead of Kingsley. Marlowe must be careful because of the presence of a police detective, but the reader is able to use those expectations that have been organized by the hints and suggestions of the text, to read the secondary meaning of Marlowe's account. Marlowe says Kingsley "didn't seem to get the implications of it very quickly," but the reader, of course, does, and an aesthetic element is added to the realization of the text (204).

Earlier we referred to the difference between general negativity, which underlies the overall "feel" of the story, and specific, which applies only to the problem at hand, like the ambiguity of the Crystal Kingsley and Muriel Chess plots. When we discuss *The Name of the Rose* we will see a considerably more vivid application, but Chandler also creates a general negativity that underlies the mystification in *The Lady in the Lake*. The effect begins very early, when Marlowe asks Kingsley's secretary Miss Fromsett about a man named Lavery and gets the impression that Lavery's name is not very pleasant to her; no reason is stated or even suggested, but the reader's consciousness of generic negativity supplies the assurance that there must be one (13). The reader will have the same experience a few pages later when Marlowe interviews Kingsley: it is obvious that he suspects Kingsley is lying (16). Again, no reason is given because none is needed.

Part of the negativity of this novel arises from Chandler's skillful use of the convention of the unidentifiable victim, which is repeatedly suggested until the point at which the experienced reader becomes aware of the subject the text seems to be avoiding. Soon after the supposed body of Muriel Chess is discovered, for example, the constable asks whether it is possible to determine the time and cause of death, and the medical examiner's shocked response is, "By looking at that? Good God!" (46) A little later the body is referred to as "what was left of Muriel Chess . . . . Pretty badly decomposed and all that" (53), and "The body's pretty far gone" (81). On the surface, the victim's identity is assumed by all the people in the story, but the reader accustomed to the detection mode is more likely to reserve judgment.

A workable definition of one aspect of the detection reading mode is developed by Carr's series detective Dr. Gideon Fell in *The Crooked Hinge*. Early in that novel there appears upon the scene a man who claims to be the real Sir John Farnleigh: as a result of a bizarre accident during the sinking of the *Titanic*, he says, he exchanged identities with another man, the present holder of the title and fortune. The claimant is accompanied by a man named Murray, who had been the tutor of the young John Farnleigh and who has brought with him a fingerprint test that will settle the problem beyond question. Before matters can proceed very far, however, the present and putative Sir John is murdered. This development worries Dr. Fell, because it breaks all the rules: Murray is the one who should have been the murder victim. "In any well-constructed plot," says the Doctor, "he would have been murdered. His presence cries out for it" (76). Instead Murray remains untouched, and the problem of identities is rendered more inexplicable than ever. Later, when Murray is suggested as a suspect, Inspector Elliot observes that he is the last person who should be suspected, "both in the real sense and in what [Dr.

Fell] calls the detective story sense" (189). Murray was the one person everyone was watching, thinking of him as victim.

What Dr. Fell is calling "the detective story sense" is the element which, according to Iser, is present in the normal dyadic interaction between social partners (as in conversation) but missing from fiction, a regulative context or "tertium comparationis" a frame of reference between author and reader (166). The "detective story sense" is a set of rules against which creative writers are free to rebel, so long as they do not undertake to make a tale of detection something other than a detective story. Dr. Fell's view is typically conservative: this is the way things are supposed to be within the conventional framework. Murray is the logical death warrant victim, because his removal from the scene would indefinitely postpone a solution to the problem of the two claimants. His murder is demanded by both the conventionality of the genre ("in any well-constructed plot he would have been murdered"), and by its hermeneutic specialization ("his presence cries out for it"). When Inspector Elliot implies a difference between "the real sense" and "the detective story sense," we should understand that he is distinguishing between two sets of expectations: those of the people in the story (the real sense) and those of the reader (the detective story sense). The difference is a subtle one that is part of the individual genre: *real* here means logical-real, which is not the same as detective-story real. Carolyn Wells evidently had something of the same idea in mind when she said that "detective stories must *seem* real in the same sense that fairy tales *seem* real to children."[3] Incidentally, Dr. Fell, one of the most persistently self-reflexive characters in detective fiction, is one person eminently qualified to make the distinction. Most readers will remember that he is quite capable of reminding the other people that they are all characters in a detective story, as he does in the locked-room lecture in *The Three Coffins*.

The reading of detective fiction is guided in part by hermeneutic specialization, or what Dr. Fell calls the "detective story sense," but that mode alone would produce only the drive to know how things "fit in" or "work out" that marks the traditional whodunit, a pretty tasteless business without the added dimension of the aesthetics of conventionality described by Parker's Spenser in a scene from *The Judas Goat*, in which Spenser and Susan are watching a videotaped movie. When Susan asks how many times he has seen it, Spenser tells her six or seven times. When she asks, "How can you bear to watch it again?" he replies, "It's like watching a dance, or listening to music. It's not plot, it's pattern" (167). What Spenser is describing is a reminder that the reader's individual genre is something more than a store-house of plots, characters, situations, and themes.

The guidance of the pattern in the reading of detective fiction is especially evident in those passages, some of considerable length, in which the reader receives no manifest signals from the text but moves ahead within the framework of convention, as in a novel where the murder is delayed until fairly late in the story; the reader does not analyze clues, because literally there are none. This is the case in Tey's *Miss Pym Disposes*, in which the murder is not discovered until almost three-fourths of the way through, but by that time the experienced reader will have identified a most likely victim, a most likely suspect, and in all probability a plausible motive.

The principle is illustrated in Dana Stabenow's recent novel, *A Cold-Blooded Business (1994)*, in which the scene is northern Alaska and the detective is an Aleut private investigator named Kate Shugak, who is employed by a large petroleum company to track down the source of drugs being introduced into the Alaskan oil fields. Guided by the conventions of the private-eye formula, the reader moves through the first portion of the story, with its lengthy descriptions of the Alaskan scene and the details of oil production, in the expectation of upcoming murder. Thus when, on page 66, dinner in the company mess hall is interrupted by a public-address announcement, "Medical emergency. Call the operator immediately," the experienced reader will anticipate a crime, probably murder. Here, as in *Miss Pym*, the reading is directed by the aesthetics of conventionality inherent in the genre rather than the promptings of the text.

Umberto Eco's *The Name of the Rose* is a remarkable book, in that it can be read profitably as a study of fourteenth-century monastic life, or of medieval theology, or of Christian mysticism. It can also be read as a classic tale of detection in the Poe-Doyle tradition. The historical setting is the year 1323, when the protagonist, William of Baskerville, a Franciscan monk, and his apprentice, a young Benedictine named Adso, arrive at an unidentified monastery in northern Italy. According to Adso, William is on a secret mission for the Emperor Frederick, the exact nature of which is not revealed. Hardly have they set foot within the abbey's walls, however, when they (and of course the reader) become aware of the presence of an evil that has already produced a death that may have been murder. Subsequent developments involve a series of deaths and a growing awareness of unnamed horror within the sacred precincts, all predictably worked out and explained by William in the final resolution.

William, a cleric who has already established a reputation for scholarship throughout the western world, is treated as an honored guest and is given the run of the monastery, except for the library, which becomes a symbol of negativity throughout the novel, and except for a perceptible reticence on the part of the abbot and his associates, who seem to be concealing something. As a detective, however, William is strictly in the mold of Sherlock Holmes. He is described as tall, thin, with a sharp eyes and a beaky nose, a person of inexhaustible energy interspersed with moments of inertia (15-16). Even before arrival at the monastery he is able to describe with perfect accuracy a runaway horse and even to guess its name after observing nothing more than some hoofprints and the evidence of broken branches and a few hairs (23). He also reminds us more than a little of Poe's Dupin. He and Adso stay up all night and collapse during the day (16), and he shares Dupin's ability to put himself in the murderer's position for deductive purposes (106). Like most of the classic detectives he is capable of thinking far ahead without revealing the state of his thoughts, as when he says, "Now everything is clear," without any hint of explanation (181).

The worshipful and slightly naive Adso fits nicely into the role of the narrator Watson, whose position is one full step behind William, leaving open the space between them as the domain of the perceptive reader. Just after one of the murders William calls out some confidential information in a crowded room, leading Adso to observe that "William acted unwisely" (350). Guided by convention, the reader feels otherwise: William knows exactly what he is doing, just as Ellery Queen did when he spilled the wine on his dinner companion in *The Chinese Orange Mystery*.

Partly as a result of the exotic physical and historical setting, the general negativity in *The Name of the Rose* is considerably more pervasive than in most detective novels. Several authors have intensified their mysteries by gradually unfolding an air of malevolence in the history of a family (as Macdonald does in *The Chill* and Grafton in *G Is for Gumshoe*), but Eco leaves his sense of evil unfocused and hence more broadly suggestive. Almost from the moment they arrive at the monastery, William and Adso experience a feel of dread, as when a wise and elderly monk tells them, "Be on your guard here. I do not like this place" (63), and when it is later suggested that improper things take place in the abbey at night (125). Superimposed on this atmospheric background is the specific negativity that shapes the series of murders at the abbey, developed in this case by successive hints and suggestions: it is hinted that the first victim lived in a topsy-turvy universe (76). This is supplemented a short time later by a suggestion of perverted sexuality (81-82), and much further along by a hint of the involvement of the abbot himself in the wickedness (417).

The reader of *The Name of the Rose* will inevitably develop a sense of the remarkable temporality of the novel and its effect upon the depth of mystery. The story unfolds at five distinct chronological levels: the buried past of the abbey, some of it legendary; the immediate past, those events leading up to the death of the first victim before the arrival of William and Adso; the present, consisting of the series of murders and William's investigations; the future, when William will solve the problem; and the future perfect, what must have happened before resolution is achieved.

The result is a palimpsest effect, where present evidence conceals the puzzles of the past. The pattern of the visible-invisible emerges in a passage late in the story, where some of the history of the abbey is related by a knowledgeable monk named Nicholas:

> The predecessor of the present abbot was Paul of Rimini, "a curious man about whom they tell strange stories." Paul had been librarian, but when he became abbot the man who took his place in the library "wasted away as an illness consumed him," and when Paul of Rimini disappeared—
> "He died?" William asks. "No, he disappeared," Nicholas answers. "I do not know how. One day he went off on a journey and never came back . . . ." (422)

Nicholas's account contains some information but implies a great deal more. Statements like "he wasted away" or "he disappeared" create blanks that invite those special expectations that distinguish the detection reading mode. Readers of detective stories, says Kermode, are "always sorting out the hermeneutically relevant from all other information and doing so more persistently than we have to in other kinds of novels" (181). Against the background of negativity that has been created by the strange events in the abbey and the even more ominous ones in the reader's imagination, a high-ranking character who wastes away must be the victim of something sinister. Once that certain kind of attention of which Kermode speaks has been aroused, a reader should have little trouble filling the blank sheet beyond the text with some of those strange stories they tell about Paul of Rimini.

The experienced reader will perceive at least two instances of programming in *The Name of the Rose*, one the programming of a single blank by two conventions and the other the imposition of some narrow parameters upon the investigation. When one of the monks proves to be missing, the programmed signal is that he must be dead, but another prompting has already labeled him as most likely suspect, with the expectation that he is not only dead but innocent (255). The parameters imposed on William's work are unusually effective, since they are not only temporal but political and spatial. William knows that he is working under the pressure of time because an inquisitorial papal legation is on its way to the monastery, more concerned with burning the accused than with discovering the guilty (148). The political limits are forced by the factionalism of the fourteenth- century church, with the result that the abbot reminds William that nothing must be done to arouse the suspicions of a rival sect (154). The spatial limitation is the most perplexing of all, the fact that William must not touch the obvious center of the mystery, the library (155).

Reading modes are not mutually exclusive, and there is no reason why the reading of *The Name of the Rose* as a detective story should preclude any appreciation of the richness of medieval detail. The additional guidance of hermeneutic specialization and the aesthetics of conventionality can, however, generate a whole new set of meanings, as it does in Adso's detailed description of the interior of the monastery church (40-45). His catalogue of its adornments is so long that the reader must be mindful of the efficiency principle. At the same time, however, the text is signaling the existence of a precedent, because this description of church architecture is so much like the one in *The Nine Tailors* that the reader is cautioned to be on the lookout for clues concealed in all this detail. Here is evidence of the dialectical relationship peculiar to the tale of detection: the negativity of the detective story sense and the contextual pattern of conventionality are constantly engaged in a process of interpreting and responding to each other.

The context of any reading of a detective story is limited only by the reader's individual perception of the genre, including a store of conventional themes from earlier reading, and a sense of the unique structure of detective fiction. This perception would, in the case of a long-time detection fan, be implemented by a sense of programming, including special controls exercised by the efficiency principle and self-reflexivity.

It is the context a reader brings to detective fiction that permits the interpretation of the distinctive negativity of the detective story. We have already made partial acquaintance with this unique context in our discussion of the way in which an experienced reader will, upon encountering any fresh element of mystery, call upon an assortment of earlier examples to support the interpretation of the text. Thus a character who in the early chapters seems to be a threat to several people in the story will be recognized by the experienced reader not as a potential villain but rather as a candidate for murder victim. In addition to the thematic material, the context of literary detection is composed of a sense of the special structure of the story, which places limitations on both the plotting and the narrative progress of the tale of detection.

The mutual relationship of negativity and context is visible in the opening chapter of *The Chinese Orange Mystery*, especially in that early passage in which the reader is guided through a detailed tour of the scene of much of the impending action in the story (16). The reader's skill in interpreting the special effect of the "gestures" and "promptings" of the text goes to work at once sorting out details. A well-honed sense of genre is not likely to miss certain details that signal their hermeneutic importance: the tangerine in the bowl of fruit on which the text briefly focuses, the valuable stamp, and especially the reference to the Chinese collection. Everything seems to "fit in" and "add up," in the detective story sense.

We are not likely to miss the influence of generic context here. The traditional floor plan is offered for the reader's later use as a guide to the unraveling of the mystery, but the experienced reader will know that these plans, elaborate and detailed as they are in the classic mystery, usually contribute little to the actual solution of the crime. A reader versed in Ellery Queen should catch the signal of the word *Chinese* in relation to the stamp collection, knowing that references to nationality in titles of these early Queen books often have two-edged meanings.

At the same time, the specialized negativity of detection gives point to the context of the genre. We might illustrate the effect by lifting an occurrence of the dying message, the unidentifiable victim, or almost any of the other familiar conventions and placing it in another genre, where it would assume a drastically different meaning. As we have seen earlier, the negativity of the detective story is a special case of Iser's conception, in the sense that the reader's "blank sheet" has already been initialized by the genre. Or, it is, as noted previously, a specialized case of reading in the sense that the negativity of the detective story is *mapped*. Iser's "nothing" between the perspectives of the text, where there are no "data" to connect these perspectives, is structured by the convention of the veiled secret.

Before we move into a discussion of the dialectic of context and negativity, a word of explanation may be overdue. During this chapter and the one on programming especially the reader may have wondered about a tendency of this book to repeat material already covered, such as the "differentness" or the self-reflexivity of detective fiction. Actually, what may look like a rehash is an outgrowth of the theoretical basis of this study, which draws upon the Gadamerian theory of transformed play, the reception theory of Iser and Jauss, and detectional hermeneutics as defined by Kermode: any one of the phenomena of the genre may be explained in terms of two or even all three perspectives.

An example of this overlap can be seen in the way I have treated the relatively tight bounds of the genre, which Lovitt calls the "powerful generic logic governing the text" and the "generic orthodoxy" of literary detection (CC 77, 82). This feature can be explained in terms of the discipline imposed by detectional hermeneutics, telling a story in such a manner that the reader's principal object is to find the answer to a problem. "All other considerations," says Kermode, "are subordinated to this interpretative or . . . hermeneutic activity" (PM 177). It can also be accounted for in reception theory as a manifestation of the tendency of a genre to replicate the mode of its predecessors: a new novel, says Jauss, evokes for the reader a new set of expectations and "rules familiar from earlier texts" (TAR 23). Or, the generic orthodoxy of detective fiction is explainable in terms of Gadamer's theory of play transformed into art, in reference to those conventions that renew themselves in constant repetition (TM 103). Almost any of the repeatable themes of detective fiction can be treated within several theoretical frames, such as the death warrant and the missing person. Both of these familiar conventions fit neatly into the hermeneutic structure of anticipation-disappointment-fulfillment, and as we discussed in chapter 3, each of them is itself hermeneutically structured. They also fit the mode of transformed play, each being offered to the reader as a task to be performed in order to solve the mystery, or they may be regarded as devices for the relief of stress, allowing the reader to proceed without concern over outcomes.

What we are calling the dialectic or interface of context and negativity is the real source of the special mode of detective fiction; one of its effects is to give distinct meaning to a recurrent theme that might otherwise lack special significance. Early in *A Cold-Blooded Business* Kate Shugak becomes aware of the unusually intense sex life of the tour guide, Toni Hartzler, and the reader may simultaneously catch a series of rather obvious signals from the text: Toni tells Kate, "There's a lot of me to go around"(87), and a little later another character observes that Toni goes through men like a guitar player goes through guitar strings (97). Then, on the plane back to Anchorage, Kate reflects, "not without a trace of envy, on Toni Hartzler's comprehensive love life" (99). For the experienced reader, the signal is clear: the author is setting Toni up as most likely victim. On the basis of a number of other detective stories in which a character is placed in a position of obvious vulnerability (for example, *Nice Weekend for a Murder, Take a Number*), the reader proceeds in the expectation that Toni will, sooner or later, turn up dead.

Notice how the interaction of context and negativity affects the reading of the story, with respect to both the hermeneutic mode and the frame of transformed play. In hermeneutic expectation, the repeated focus on Toni becomes a specialized statement of negativity in the sense that there must be some reason, some kind of mystery associated with her. In addition, a part of the context of the hermeneutic mode is the convention of the most likely victim, which follows the pattern of this situation. Brought into interaction with each other, the negativity of the repeated signal and the context of the convention create a set of special expectations regarding Toni's role. A similar effect is produced by the deep structure of transformed play. First of all, an obvious task is being handed to the reader, Who will murder Toni? It is also part of the conventionality of the genre that the author may be deliberately misleading the reader in order to deepen the effect of negativity.[4] The underlying structure of play, however, continues to create the expectation that, whatever else, the stress-free problem will be solved before the last page.

This study opened with a question, What is a detective story? I have undertaken one answer in the past several paragraphs, that the detective story can be described as a dialectic of context and negativity. Another definition might state that the tale of detection is a mystery story that has developed a special set of rules and conventions that determine its distinctive reading mode. We began the approach to definition with a review of the question that apparently intrigued the early commentators in the field, What is the real "differentness" that sets detective fiction apart from the general body of popular fiction? As we have seen, this differentness can be expressed in terms of the unique purpose of the detective story. The realization of that purpose embodies a strong element of ritual or game, with the result that the solution of a detectional mystery must be attained only in a certain way. The principle is nowhere more evident than in the achievement of the specialized denouement of the detective story. If the only purpose of reading a tale of detection is to find out who committed the murder (or stole the jewels or is pushing the drugs), the whole business could be easily cleared up by turning to the final chapter and finding out. The difference lies in the special quality of detective fiction, that the reader, proceeding in the hermeneutic mode, may reach the resolution only after observing certain conventions.

What I have just said about the nature of the detective story may also help to answer the question of my exasperated student, Are we supposed to take this stuff seriously? The answer is yes, in the same way that one would take any organized play seriously. One principle in the interpretation of detective fiction is that, in the detective story, literary values become simpler than in other genres, with the result that the tale of detection may strike a serious reader like my student as naive and critically unproblematical. As this study has tried to show, the real seriousness of the tale of detection is best understood in terms of its special reading mode, which can be explained most simply as transformed play.

In "The Simple Art of Murder," Chandler proposes that a detective story displays an effect of movement, intrigue, cross-purposes, and the gradual elucidation of character. "The rest," he says, "is spillikins in the parlor" (in Haycraft, AMS 236). We can only agree with Chandler that the detective story is indeed movement, intrigue, cross-purposes, and elucidation of character, but it has another quality, a mystique, that makes it different from the other types of popular fiction. This is what Chandler, probably with a different purpose, called "spillikins in the parlor." Spillikins, better known to us as jackstraws or pick-up-sticks, is a game in which the purpose is to use a small instrument with a hook at the end to lift tiny slivers of wood off a pile one at a time, without disturbing any other sliver. The game involves terrific effort and a steady hand, but it is completely free of stress: ordinarily, it is not played for any purpose other than relaxation. It has picked up a number of conventions during its history, one of which is that a player must not touch the pile with fingers or anything other than the hook provided. Finally, the game offers optional tasks, which the player may accept or reject: players can, if they wish, add various kinds of jobs on the side just to make the game more interesting.

The mode of transformed play determines the expectations of a reader of detective fiction in several respects. Because we read a detective story with the assurance that the mystery will be solved, presumably by the detective, before the end of the book, our reading is relieved of the anxieties we can experience in a novel like *Jurassic Park* or *The Pelican Brief*. Patricia Wallace's *Deadly Devotion* is as tense as either of these, but the element of stress is canceled by the assurance that things will turn out all right.

The spillikins effect makes possible the constant renewal of a generic convention through repetition, with the result that a writer at any point in the history of detective fiction can recover an old convention, renovate it as desired, and use it with as much hermeneutic effect as if this were its first appearance. At a critical point in *The Name of the Rose*, Eco relies upon one of the hoariest of the conventions of the detection genre, the dying message. William discovers Malachi, the latest victim of the series of murders just in time to catch the monk's last words:

[Malachi] raised a trembling hand, grasped William by the chest, drawing his face down until they almost touched, then faintly and hoarsely uttered some words:
"He told me . . . truly. . . . It had the power of a thousand scorpions. . . . "
"Who told you?" William asked him. "Who?"

But to no avail. Malachi is dead (414). Malachi's words are limited by circumstance instead of being deliberately cryptic, but the suspense effect is unimpaired. The other characteristic of play transformed into art is the voluntary acceptance by the participant of tasks that are tied only to make-believe goals. These tasks, says Gadamer, are playful ones, because they do not determine the outcome of the game but rather give meaning to the experience of the play itself. Spillikins, for example can be spiced up by occasionally playing a game left-handed. Detective fiction abounds in such offerings, which really serve the purpose of allowing the reader to "play himself out" without actually affecting the outcome of the story, as in those cases in which the reader is offered the option of working out the meaning of a dying message or of trying to figure out the location of a missing person.

There can be no question, then, that Chandler was right. A detective story that lacks movement, intrigue, cross-purposes, and the elucidation of character in not worth reading. At the same time, however, it must never be forgotten that the underlying structure of transformed play, or what we have called the mystique of the tale of detection, is the real source of its differentness among popular genres. It is more than possible, then, that spillikins in the parlor is the biggest game around.

Abbreviations

Secondary sources frequently cited in the text have been indicated by the following abbreviations.

AMR	*Adventure, Mystery and Romance* (Cawelti)
AMS	*The Art of the Mystery Story* (ed. Haycraft)
AR	*The Act of Reading* (Iser)
CC	*The Cunning Craft* (ed. Walker and Frazer)
CD	*Critical Discourse* (de Beaugrande)
DF	*Detective Fiction* (ed. Winks)
II	*Interpreting Interpreting* (Horton)
MC	*Mortal Consequences* (Symons)
MIF	*Mystery and Its Fictions* (Grossvogel)
MP	*Murder for Pleasure* (Haycraft)
MWA	*The Mystery Writer's Art* (ed. Nevins)
PA	*The Popular Arts* (Hall and Whannel)
PM	*The Poetics of Murder* (ed. Most and Stowe)
R inT	*The Reader in the Text* (ed. Suleiman)
R-RC	*Reader-Response Criticism* (ed. Tompkins)
RR	*Reading the Romance* (Radway)
RT	*Reception Theory* (Holub)
SP	*Structuralist Poetics* (Culler)
TAR	*Toward an Aesthetic of Reception* (Jauss)
TIRT	*A Teacher's Introduction to Reader-Response Theories* (Beach)
TLT	*Tracing Literary Theory* (ed. Natoli)
TM	*Truth and Method* (Gadamer)
VI	*Validity in Interpretation* (Hirsch)
WWHH	*What Will Have Happened* (Champigny)

Notes

1. The Different Story
After the first reference, most of these titles will be cited in the text.

1. Howard Haycraft, *Murder for Pleasure* (New York: Biblo and Tannen, 1974) 38.

2. Julian Symons, *Mortal Consequences* (New York: Harper, 1972) 44.

3. Symons accepts "The Gold Bug" as a "forerunner" of the detective story only (*MC* 30-1). I reject both "The Gold Bug" and *The Woman in White* .

4. W.H. Auden, "The Guilty Vicarage," *Detective Fiction*, ed. Robin Winks (Englewood Cliffs: Prentice-Hall, 1980) 15.

5. David Grossvogel, *Mystery and Its Fictions* (Baltimore: Johns Hopkins UP, 1978) 15.

6. R. Austin Freeman, "The Art of the Detective Story," *The Art of the Mystery Story*, ed. Howard Haycraft (New York: Bilbo and Tannen, 1976) 9, 12-13.

7. John Cawelti, *Adventure, Mystery and Romance* (Chicago: U Chicago Press, 1976) 99.

8. Roger Caillois, "The Detective Novel as Game," *The Poetics of Murder*, ed. Glenn W. Most and William W. Stowe (New York: Harcourt, 1983) 4.

9. John Dickson Carr, "The Grandest Game in the World," *The Mystery Writer's Art*, ed. Francis M. Nevins, Jr. (Bowling Green OH: Bowling Green State University Popular Press, 1970) 230.

10. Stuart Hall and Paddy Whannel, *The Popular Arts* (New York: Pantheon, 1965) 57.

11. Novels will be cited in the text by page number only. For publication information, see the list of primary sources in the bibliography.

12. Frank Lentricchia, *After the New Criticism* (Chicago: U of Chicago P, 1980) 150; William Stowe, "From Semiotics to Hermeneutics: Methods of Detection in Doyle and Chandler," *PM*, 347.

13. Robert Holub, *Reception Theory: A Critical Introduction* (New York: Methuen, 1984) 36, 40, 48.

14. Temma Berg, "Psychologies of Reading," *Tracing Literary Theory*, ed. Joseph Natoli (Urbana: U of Illinois P, 1987) 262-63.

15. Richard Beach, *A Teacher's Introduction to Reader-Response Theories* (Urbana: National Council of Teachers of English, 1993) 20; Terry Eagleton, *Literary Theory* (Minneapolis: U of Minnesota P, 1983) 76-77; Holub *RT* 93; Wolfgang Iser, *The Act of Reading* (Baltimore: Johns Hopkins UP, 1978) 181.

16. Beach *TIRT* 22-23; Berg *TLT* 262-63; Holub *RT* 59; Hans Robert Jauss, *Toward an Aesthetic of Reception* (Minneapolis: U of Minnesota P, 1982) 23.

17. L.M. O'Toole, "Analytic and Synthetic Approaches to Narrative Structure," Style and Structure in Literature, ed. Roger Fowler (Ithaca: Cornell UP, 1975).

18. Janice Radway, *Reading the Romance* (Chapel Hill: U of North Carolina P, 1984) 11.

19. The idea is from speech-act theory. Barrie Straus, "Influencing Theory: Speech Acts," *TLT* 215 ; Beach *TIRT* 17.

20. Hans-Georg Gadamer, *Truth and Method* (New York: Crossroad, 1987) 101-03, 112.

21. Robert Champigny, *What Will Have Happened* (Bloomington: U of Indiana P, 1977) 4.

22. Northrop Frye, *Anatomy of Criticism* (Princeton: Princeton UP, 1957) 47.

23. Cf. Albert Divver, "Tracing Hermeneutics," *TLT* 54-79; Susan Horton, *Interpreting Interpreting* (Baltimore: Johns Hopkins UP, 1979) 16.

24. Jonathan Culler, *Structuralist Poetics* (Ithaca: Cornell UP, 1975) 203.

25. With regard to transformation into structure, Gadamer offers this special caution: "When we speak of play in reference to the experience of art, this means neither the orientation nor the state of mind of the creator or of those enjoying the work of art, nor the freedom of a subjectivity engaged in play, but the mode of being of the work itself" (*TM* 101-02).

26. Robert de Beaugrande, *Critical Discourse* (Norwood NJ: Ablex, 1988) 11.

27. I should explain at this point why I have not used Panek's valuable discussion of the play element in British detective novels between the two World Wars in *Watteau's Shepherds*. Relying on the definition and criteria in Huizinga's classic study *Homo Ludens*, Panek treats play as play and game as game, not as mode of being. The method of *Watteau's Shepherds* concentrates almost exclusively upon theme, whereas the primary concern here is structure.

28. The most notorious example is Edmund Wilson's reaction to the Nero Wolfe stories: "What I found rather surprised me and discouraged

my curiosity. Here was simply the old Sherlock Holmes formula. . . . " *A Literary Chronicle: 1920-1950*. (Garden City: Doubleday, 1952) 324.

2. Reception Theory and the Hermeneutics of Detection
1. I.A. Richards, *Practical Criticism* (New York: Harcourt, 1929) 175-81.

2. E.D. Hirsch, Jr., *Validity in Interpretation* (New Haven: Yale UP, 1967) 164.

3. Art Berman, *From the New Criticism to Deconstruction* (Urbana: U of Illinois P, 1988) 149.

4. Stanley Fish, *Is There a Text in This Class?* (Cambridge: Harvard UP, 1980) 171.

5. Susan Suleiman, ed., Introduction, *The Reader in the Text* (Princeton: Princeton UP, 1980) 23.

6. In discussing phenomenology, as with any philosophical position, we must make clear whose version we are talking about. When I use the term here, I refer to the phenomenology of Edmund Husserl, particularly as it affects the works of Gadamer, Iser, and Jauss.

7. Jauss estimates that Iser "has rehabilitated the aesthetic character of fiction texts under the dominant category of 'indeterminacy' (and 'redeterminacy')" (*TAR* 145).

3. The Detection Genre
1. See Todorov, for example, who says that "the whodunit par excellence is not the one which transgresses the rules of the genre, but the one which confirms them." Tzvetan Todorov. *The Poetics of Prose* (Ithaca: Cornell UP, 1977) 43.

2. John Cawelti, "The Concept of Formula in the Study of Popular Literature," *Popular Culture and the Expanding Consciousness*, ed. Ray B. Browne (New York: Wiley, 1973) 109-19.

3. See Champigny, "The mystery in a mystery story is a narrative secret, not a conceptual mystery; it is physical, not transcendental" (*WWHH* 13).

4. The seven-step division is to a degree arbitrary: Barthes lists ten (Culler *SP* 211-18).

5. This occurrence also illustrates the aesthetics of conventionality, another product of the negativity of the genre, to be considered in chapter 7.

4. Conventions, Inventions, and the Bounds of Genre
1. Robin Woods, "'His Appearance Is Against Him': The Emergence of the Detective," *The Cunning Craft*, ed. Ronald G. Walker and June M. Frazer (Macomb: Western Illinois U, 1990) 15.

2. Wolfgang Iser, "The Reading Process: A Phenomenological Approach," *Reader-Response Criticism*, ed. Jane P. Tompkins (Baltimore: Johns Hopkins UP, 1980) 53.

3. Ed McBain, "The 87th Precinct," *The Great Detectives*, ed. Otto Penzler (Boston: Little, Brown, 1978) 90-91.

4. Various attempts have been made, some of them quite ingenious, to demonstrate a subtle connection between the Flitcraft story and the main plot, but most of them would never occur to the representative reader.

5. See for example *The Locked Room Reader* (1968), ed. Santesson, and *Tantalizing Locked Room Mysteries* (1982), ed. Azimov, Waugh, and Greenberg.

6. Earl Bargainnier, *The Gentle Art of Murder* (Bowling Green OH: Bowling Green State University Popular Press, 1980) 130.

7. Norman Donaldson, *In Search of Dr. Thorndyke* (Bowling Green OH: Bowling Green State University Popular Press, 1971) 98-99.

5. The Mean Streets and the Mall

1. John Reilly, Preface, *Twentieth Century Crime and Mystery Writers* (2nd Edition) (New York: St. Martin's, 1950) ix.

6. Mapping Negativity

1. In *The Heckler, Fuzz, Let's Hear It for the Deaf Man, Eight Black Horses,* and *Mischief.*

7. Are We Supposed to Take This Stuff Seriously?

1. Francis Nevins, Jr., *Royal Bloodline* (Bowling Green OH: Bowling Green State University Popular Press, 1974) 43.

2. The fan's identification of Macduff is based upon his launching into an obviously rehearsed speech on finding Duncan's body. The narrator's clue to the guilt of Lady Macbeth's father is her remark, "Had he not resembled my father as he slept, I had done it": the murderer, hearing somebody coming, hid the king's body and took his place upon the bed. James Thurber, *My World—And Welcome to It* (New York: Harcourt, 1942) 33-39.

3. Cited by Haycraft, *Murder for Pleasure,* 242.

4. That is what happens in this instance: Toni is finally revealed as perpetrator, not victim. Stabenow, like several other creative writers I have mentioned, is testing the bounds of the genre.

Bibliography

Primary Sources

Beck, K.K. *Amateur Night.* New York: Mysterious Press, 1993.

Berkeley, Anthony. *The Poisoned Chocolates Case.* 1929. San Diego: U of California-San Diego, 1979.

Carr, John Dickson. *The Crooked Hinge.* 1938. San Diego: U of California-San Diego, 1976.

Chandler, Raymond. *The Big Sleep.* 1939. New York: Ballantine, 1971.

——. *Farewell, My Lovely.* 1940. New York: Ballantine, 1971.

——. *The High Window.* 1942. New York: Ballantine, 1971.

——. *The Lady in the Lake.* 1943. New York: Ballantine, 1971.

——. *The Little Sister.* 1949. New York: Ballantine, 1971.

Christie, Agatha. *Cards on the Table.* 1936. New York: Dell, 1970.

——. *Curtain.* New York: Dodd, Mead, 1975.

——. *The Murder at the Vicarage.* 1930. New York: Dodd, Mead, 1976.

——. *The Murder of Roger Ackroyd.* 1926. New York: Dodd, Mead, 1971.

Clark, Carol Higgins. *Decked.* 1992. New York: Warner, 1993.

Collins, Max. *Nice Weekend for a Murder.* 1986. New York: Tor, 1994.

Collins, Michael. *The Silent Scream.* 1973. New York: Playboy, 1979.

Crespi, Trella. *The Trouble With Moonlighting.* New York: Kensington, 1991.

Cross, Amanda. *No Word from Winifred.* 1986. New York: Ballantine, 1987.

——. *The Players Come Again.* New York: Ballantine, 1990.

Cutler, Stan. *The Face on the Cutting-Room Floor.* 1991. New York: Signet, 1993.

Dawson, Janet. *Take a Number.* 1993. New York: Fawcett, 1994.

Eco, Umberto. *The Name of the Rose.* New York: Harcourt, 1980.

Feddersen, Connie. *Dead in the Melon Patch.* New York: Zebra, 1995.

Freeman, R. Austin. *The Red Thumb-Mark.* 1907. New York: Burt, 1924.

Grafton, Sue. *G Is for Gumshoe.* 1990. New York: Ballantine, 1991.

——. *H Is for Homicide.* 1991. New York: Ballantine, 1992.

Grimes, Martha. *The Man with a Load of Mischief.* 1981. New York: Dell, 1984.

Halliday, Brett. *This Is It, Michael Shayne.* New York: Dodd, 1950.

Hammett, Dashiell. *The Dain Curse.* 1929. New York: Dell, 1968.

——. *The Maltese Falcon and The Thin Man.* 1930 and 1934. New York: Vintage, 1964.

197

Hillerman, Tony. *The Ghostway*. 1984. New York: Harper, 1992.

Kaminsky, Stuart. *Poor Butterfly*. New York: Mysterious Press, 1990.

Katz, Jon. *The Family Stalker*. 1994. New York: Bantam, 1995.

Kemmelman, Harry. *Sunday the Rabbi Slept Late*. New York: Putnam, 1969.

Lathen, Emma. *Green Grow the Dollars*. 1982. New York: Pocket Books, 1983.

MacDonald, John D. *The Lonely Silver Rain*. 1985. New York: Ballantine, 1986.

MacDonald, Philip. *The Rasp*. New York: Mason, 1936.

Macdonald, Ross. *The Blue Hammer*. New York: Knopf, 1976.

——. *The Drowning-Pool*. 1950. New York: Bantam, 1970.

McCrumb, Sharon. *The Windsor Knot*. 1990. New York: Ballantine, 1992.

Morgan, Robert. *All Things under the Moon*. New York: Berkley, 1994.

Muller, Marcia. *There's Something in a Sunday*. 1989. New York: Mysterious Press, 1990.

Paretsky, Sara. *Guardian Angel*. 1992. New York: Dell, 1993.

——. *Indemnity Only*. 1982. New York: Dell, 1991.

Parker, Robert. *The Judas Goat*. 1978. New York: Dell, 1983.

Peters, Ellis. *The Potter's Field*. 1990. New York: Mysterious Press, 1991.

Poe, Edgar Allan. *The Selected Poetry and Prose of Edgar Allan Poe*. Ed. T.O. Mabbott. New York: Modern Library, 1951.

Prather, Richard. *The Trojan Hearse*. 1964. New York, Bantam, 1972.

Pronzini, Bill. *Jackpot*. New York: Delacorte, 1990.

Queen, Ellery. *The Chinese Orange Mystery*. 1934. New York: Signet, 1983.

——. *The Tragedy of X*. 1932. San Diego: U of California-San Diego, 1978.

Rinehart, Mary Roberts. *The Circular Staircase*. 1908. San Diego: U of California-San Diego, 1977.

Sallis, James. *The Long-Legged Fly*. 1992. New York: Avon, 1994.

Sayers, Dorothy. *The Nine Tailors*. 1934. New York: Harcourt, n.d.

——. *The Unpleasantness at the Bellona Club*. 1928. New York: Avon, 1971.

Shankman, Sarah. *First Kill All the Lawyers*. New York: Pocket Books, 1988.

Soos, Troy. *Murder at Fenway Park*. 1994. New York: Zebra, 1995.

Stabenow, Dana. *A Cold-Blooded Business*. 1994. New York: Berkley, 1995.

Stout, Rex. *Gambit*. 1962. New York: Bantam, 1967.

——. *Too Many Clients*. 1960. New York: Bantam, 1971.

Tey, Josephine. *Three by Tey: Miss Pym Disposes, The Franchise Affair, Brat Farrar*. New York: Macmillan, 1954.

Thurber, James. "The Macbeth Murder Mystery." *My World—And Welcome to It*. New York: Harcourt, 1942. 33-39.

Trevanian. *The Main*. 1976. New York: Harcourt, 1977.

Upfield, Arthur. *The New Shoe*. 1951. San Diego: U of California-San Diego, 1976.

Van Dine, S.S. *The Bishop Murder Case*. 1928. New York: Fawcett, 1957.

——. *The Canary Murder Case*. 1927. New York: Fawcett, 1955.

——. *The Kennel Murder Case*. 1933. New York: Scribner, 1984.

Wallace, Patricia. *Deadly Devotion*. New York: Zebra, 1994.

Wright, Erich. *A Fine Italian Hand*. 1992. Toronto: Worldwide, 1994.

Secondary Sources

Anderson, David. Afterword. *The Cunning Craft*. Ed. Ronald Walker and June Frazer. Macomb: Western Illinois U, 1990. 188-90.

Auden, W.H. "The Guilty Vicarage." *Detective Fiction*. Ed. Robin Winks. Englewood Cliffs: Prentice-Hall, 1980. 15-24.

Bargainnier, Earl. *The Gentle Art of Murder*. Bowling Green OH: Bowling Green State University Popular Press, 1980.

Barzun, Jacques. "Detection and the Literary Art." *The Mystery Writer's Art*. Ed. Francis Nevins, Jr. Bowling Green OH: Bowling Green State University Popular Press, 1970. 248-62.

Beach, Richard. *A Teacher's Introduction to Reader-Response Theories*. Urbana: National Council of Teachers of English, 1993.

Berg, Temma. "Psychologies of Reading." *Tracing Literary Theory*. Ed. Joseph Natoli. Urbana: U of Illinois P, 1987. 248-77.

Berman, Art. *From the New Criticism to Deconstruction*. Urbana: U of Illinois Press, 1988.

Caillois, Roger. "The Detective Novel as Game." *The Poetics of Murder*. Ed. Glenn W. Most and William W. Stowe. New York: Harcourt, 1983. 1-12.

Carr, John Dickson. "The Greatest Game in the World." *The Mystery Writer's Art*. Ed. Francis M. Nevins, Jr. Bowling Green OH: Bowling Green State University Popular Press, 1970. 227-47.

Cawelti, John. *Adventure, Mystery and Romance*. Chicago: U of Chicago P, 1976.

——. "The Concept of Formula in the Study of Popular Literature." *Popular Culture and the Expanding Consciousness*. Ed. Ray B. Browne. New York: Wiley, 1973. 100-19.

Champigny, Robert. *What Will Have Happened*. Bloomington: U of Indiana P, 1977.

Chandler, Raymond. "The Simple Art of Murder." *The Art of the Mystery Story*. Ed. Howard Haycraft. New York: Biblo and Tannen, 1976. 222-37.

Culler, Jonathan. *Structuralist Poetics*. Ithaca: Cornell UP, 1975.

De Beaugrande, Robert. *Critical Discourse*. Norwood NJ: Ablex, 1988.

Divver, Albert. "Tracing Hermeneutics." *Tracing Literary Theory*. Ed. Joseph Natoli. Urbana: U of Illinois P, 1987.

Donaldson, Norman. *In Search of Dr. Thorndyke*. Bowling Green OH: Bowling Green State University Popular Press, 1971.

Eagleton, Terry. *Literary Theory*. Minneapolis: U of Minnesota P, 1983.

Farrell, Thomas. "Deconstructing Moriarity: False Armageddon at the Reichenbach." *The Cunning Craft*. Ed. Ronald Walker and June Frazer. Macomb: Western Illinois U, 1990. 38-54.

Fish, Stanley. *Is There a Text in This Class?* Cambridge: Harvard UP, 1980.

Fowler, Roger, ed. *Style and Structure in Literature*. Ithaca: Cornell UP, 1975.

Freeman, R. Austin. "The Art of the Detective Story." *The Art of the Mystery Story*. Ed. Howard Haycraft. New York: Biblo and Tannen, 1976. 7-17.

Frye, Northrup. *Anatomy of Criticism*. Princeton: Princeton UP, 1957.

Gadamer, Hans-Georg. *Truth and Method*. 2nd Edition. New York: Crossroad, 1987.

Grossvogel, David. *Mystery and Its Fictions*. Baltimore: Johns Hopkins UP, 1976.

Hall, Stuart, and Paddy Whannel. *The Popular Arts*. New York: Pantheon, 1965.

Haycraft, Howard. *Murder for Pleasure*. New York: Biblo and Tannen, 1974.

——, ed. *The Art of the Mystery Story*. New York: Biblo and Tannen, 1976.

Hirsch, E.D., Jr. *Validity in Interpretation*. New Haven: Yale UP, 1967.

Holub, Robert C. *Reception Theory: A Critical Introduction*. New York: Methuen, 1984.

Horton, Susan. *Interpreting Interpreting*. Baltimore: Johns Hopkins UP, 1979.

Iser, Wolfgang. *The Act of Reading*. Baltimore: Johns Hopkins.

"Interaction Between Text and Reader." *The Reader in the Text*. Ed. Susan Suleiman. Princeton: Princeton UP, 1980. 106-19.

——. "The Reading Process: A Phenomenological Approach." *Reader-Response Criticism*. Ed. Jane Tompkins. Baltimore: Johns Hopkins UP, 1980. 50-69.

Jauss, Hans Robert. *Toward an Aesthetic of Reception*. Minneapolis: U of Minnesota P, 1982.

Kermode, Frank. "Novel and Narrative." *The Poetics of Murder*. Ed. Glenn W. Most and William W. Stowe. New York: Harcourt, 1983. 175-95.

Knox, Ronald. "Detective Story Decalogue." *The Art of the Mystery Story.* Ed. Howard Haycraft. New York: Biblo and Tannen, 1976. 194-96.

Lentricchia, Frank. *After the New Criticism.* Chicago: U of Chicago P, 1980.

Lovitt, Carl. "Controlling Discourse in Detective Fiction, or Caring Very Much Who Killed Roger Ackroyd." *The Cunning Craft.* Ed. Ronald Walker and June Frazer. Macomb: Western Illinois U, 1990. 68-85.

McBain, Ed. "The 87th Precinct." *The Great Detectives.* Ed. Otto Penzler. Boston: Little, Brown, 1978. 87-99.

Nevins, Francis, Jr. *Royal Bloodline.* Bowling Green OH: Bowling Green State University Popular Press, 1974.

O'Toole, L.M. "Analytic and Synthetic Approaches to Narrative Structure." *Style and Structure in Literature.* Ed. Roger Fowler. Ithaca: Cornell UP, 1975. 143-76.

Panek, LeRoy. *Watteau's Shepherds.* Bowling Green OH: Bowling Green State University Popular Press, 1979.

Porter, Dennis. "Backward Construction and the Art of Suspense." *The Poetics of Murder,* Ed. Glenn W. Most and William W. Stowe. New York: Harcourt, 1983. 327-40.

Radway, Janice. *Reading the Romance.* Chapel Hill: U of North Carolina P, 1984.

Rappaport, Herman. "Phenomenology and Contemporary Theory." *Tracing Literary Theory.* Ed. Joseph Natoli. Urbana: U of Illinois P, 1987. 148-76.

Reilly, John. Preface. *Twentieth Century Crime and Mystery Writers.* 2nd Edition. Ed. John Reilly. New York: St. Martin's, 1980. vii-xi.

Richards, I.A. *Practical Criticism.* New York: Harcourt, 1929.

Steeves, Harrison R. "A Sober Word on the Detective Story." *The Art of the Mystery Story.* Ed. Howard Haycraft. New York: Biblo and Tannen, 1976. 513-26.

Stowe, William. "From Semiotics to Hermeneutics: Mehods of Detection in Doyle and Chandler." *The Poetics of Murder.* Ed. Glenn W. Most and William W. Stowe. New York: Harcourt, 1983. 366-83.

Straus, Barrie. "Influencing Theory: Speech Acts." *Tracinq Literary Theory.* Ed. Joseph Natoli. Urbana: U of Illinois P, 1987. 213-47.

Suleiman, Susan. "Introduction: Varieties of Audience-Oriented Criticism." *The Reader in the Text.* Ed. Susan Suleiman. Princeton: Princeton UP, 1980. 3-45.

Symons, Julian. *Mortal Consequences.* New York: Harper, 1972.

Todorov, Tzvetan. *The Poetics of Prose.* Ithaca: Cornell UP, 1977.

Tompkins, Jane. "The Reader in History: The Changing Shape of Literary Response." *Reader-Response Criticism* Ed. Jane Tompkins. Baltimore: Johns Hopkins UP, 1980. 201-32.

Van Dine, S.S., "Twenty Rules for Writing Detective Stories." *The Art of the Mystery Story*. Ed. Howard Haycraft. New York: Biblo and Tannen, 1976. 189-93.

Wald, Gayle. "Strong Poison: Love and the Novelistic in Dorothy Sayers." *The Cunning Craft*. Ed. Ronald Walker and June Frazer. Macomb: Western Illinois U, 1990. 98-108.

Wilson, Edmund. *A Literary Chronicle: 1920-1950*. Garden City: Doubleday, 1952.

Winks, Robin, ed. *Detective Fiction*. Englewood Cliffs: Prentice-Hall, 1980.

Woods, Robin. "'His Appearance Is Against Him': The Emergence of the Detective." *The Cunning Craft*. Ed. Ronald Walker and June Frazer. Macomb: Western Illinois U, 1990. 15-24.

Wright, Willard Huntington. "The Great Detective Stories." *The Art of the Mystery Story*. Ed. Howard Haycraft. New York: Biblo and Tannen, 1976. 33-70.

Index